How to Talk Dirty
and influence people

HOW TO TALK DIRTY
and influence people

an autobiography by
LENNY BRUCE

hachette
BOOKS

New York

Cataloging-in-Publication data for this book is available from the Library of Congress.
ISBN: 9780306825293 (paperback)
ISBN: 9780306825309 (ebook)

Hachette Books
Hachette Book Group
1290 Avenue of the Americas
New York, NY 10104
HachetteBooks.com
Twitter.com/HachetteBooks
Instagram.com/HachetteBooks

Printed in the United States of America

Previously published by Da Capo Press 2016
First Hachette Books edition 2021

Published by Hachette Books, an imprint of Perseus Books, LLC, a subsidiary of Hachette Book Group, Inc. The Hachette Books name and logo is a trademark of the Hachette Book Group.

The Hachette Speakers Bureau provides a wide range of authors for speaking events. To find out more, go to www.hachettespeakersbureau.com or call (866) 376-6591.

The publisher is not responsible for websites (or their content) that are not owned by the publisher.

LSC-C

Printing 10, 2023

I dedicate this book to all the followers of Christ and his teachings; in particular to a true Christian— Jimmy Hoffa—because he hired ex-convicts as, I assume, Christ would have.

PREFACE
BY LEWIS BLACK

I wish I could remember when I first heard of Lenny Bruce. It may have been from The Realist, a magazine he wrote for. I do remember asking my dad about him. He had seen him perform. He thought he was very funny. So I read his book in my teens, and I would never be the same. Like Vonnegut, Joseph Heller, Dick Gregory, and later George Carlin and Richard Pryor, it fed a growing rebellious streak in me. He was funny, irreverent, and his scathing attacks on organized religion, politics, the death penalty, race, and the ways in which we have chosen to live made me laugh and made me think. It changed the way I looked at life. And it planted the seed in my angry brain that would eventually lead me to a career expressing my own dissatisfaction with the world. He took me to places I hadn't imagined possible. I'm asked occasionally if I'm trying to change people's minds with my comedy and I always say I don't think about changing minds; I think about getting laughs. Changing a mind is collateral damage if you will. I'm sure that's the way Lenny saw it. But Lenny wasn't just getting laughs; he was getting arrested for his jokes.

He was considered a dirty comic because he used dirty words (many of the ones Carlin made famous). I didn't consider them dirty words; I thought they were adult words. As I've discovered, lots of people still consider them dirty, and back when Lenny was tossing them about they were considered even dirtier. The bad words, as some folks still stupidly believe, didn't get him the laughs, his jokes did. It was the words that got him locked up. They were an excuse to punish him. The real reason he was deemed a threat was because his comedy went too far for the times, way too far. Even now, in many parts of this country, fifty some odd years later, in the twenty-first century no less, some of his routines would be seen as going too far. He didn't just push the boundaries; he obliterated them. His comedy was beyond edgy; it was shocking. It's one thing to say what people are thinking but afraid to say. It's another to say things that up until that time had been unthinkable, let alone speak them aloud.

This book gives us a solid context of what Lenny lived through and what he had to face. (And to think today we complain about the politically correct environment that makes comedy difficult? Are you kidding me?) We are talking about not even being able to tell your jokes without the threat of imprisonment.

Lenny's comedy is important because he is one of those who transitioned us from the family friendly comedy of the time to the comedy of improvisation, honesty, and the deeply personal. He put it all on the line. Lenny confronted and challenged his audience with hard dark truths wrapped in twisted scenarios of his own invention. It took insanity, courage, and genius—and not necessarily in that order—to look for laughs in corners where no one had looked before.

There isn't a comic who has worked since Lenny who doesn't owe him a debt of gratitude. Every time someone swears on a stage or runs counter to the prevailing thoughts of the time, it is because Lenny kicked the door down. (And Mr. Carlin made sure it stayed open.)

Enough of my bullshit, read the fucking book. You'll be glad you did.

—LEWIS BLACK
New York City, April 2016

Lewis Black is a *New York Times*-bestselling author, stand-up comedian, actor, and playwright. Besides appearing regularly on *The Daily Show* (in his own segment, "Back in Black"), he has written and starred in a string of successful HBO and Comedy Central specials and one-man Broadway shows. He has won two Grammys, an Emmy and the American Comedy Award for Funniest Male Stand-up Comedian. He lives in New York City.

ORIGINAL FOREWORD
BY KENNETH TYNAN

Constant, abrasive irritation produces the pearl: it is a disease of the oyster. Similarly—according to Gustave Flaubert—the artist is a disease of society. By the same token, Lenny Bruce is a disease of America. The very existence of comedy like his is evidence of unease in the body politic. Class chafes against class, ignorance against intelligence, puritanism against pleasure, majority against minority, easy hypocrisy against hard sincerity, white against black, jingoism against internationalism, price against value, sale against service, suspicion against trust, death against life—and out of all these collisions and contradictions there emerges the troubled voice of Lenny Bruce, a night-club Cassandra bringing news of impending chaos, a tightrope walker between morality and nihilism, a pearl miscast before swine. The message he bears is simple and basic: whatever releases people and brings them together is good, and whatever confines and separates them is bad. The worst drag of all is war; in didactic moments Bruce likes to remind his audience that "'Thou shalt not kill' *means just that*." Although he occasionally invokes Christ as source material, I think he would applaud a statement recently made by Wayland Young, an English writer and agnostic, in a book called *Eros Denied*:

"Christian and post-Christian and Communist culture is a eunuch; pornography is his severed balls; thermonuclear weapons are his staff of office. If there is anything sadder than a eunuch it is his balls; if there is anything more deadly than impotence it is murder."

If it is sick to agree with that, then God preserve us from health.

This may be the time to point out the primary fact about Bruce, which is that he is extremely funny. It is easy to leave that out when writing about him— to pass over the skill with which he plays his audience as an angler plays a big-game fish, and the magical timing, born of burlesque origins and jazz upbringing, that triggers off the sudden, startled yell of laughter. But he is seldom funny without an ulterior motive. You squirm as you smile. With Bruce a smile is not an end in itself, it is invariably a means. What begins as pure hilarity may end in self-accusation. When, for example, he tells the story of the unhappily married couple who achieve togetherness in the evening of their lives by discovering that they both have gonorrhea, your first reaction is laughter; but when you go on to consider your own far-from-perfect marriage, held together (it may be) by loveless habit or financial necessity or fear of social disapproval—all of which are motives less concrete and intimate than venereal disease—your laughter may cool off into a puzzled frown of self-scrutiny. You begin to reflect that there are worse fates than the clap; that a curable physical sickness may even be preferable, as a source of togetherness, to a social or spiritual sickness for which no cure is available. And thus another taboo is dented.

Bruce is the sharpest denter of taboos at present active in show business. Alone among those who work the clubs, he is a true iconoclast. Others josh, snipe and rib; only Bruce demolishes. He breaks through the barrier of laughter to the horizon beyond, where the truth has its sanctuary. People say he is shocking and they are quite correct. Part of his purpose is to force us to redefine what we mean by "being shocked." We all feel impersonally outraged by racialism; but when Bruce mimics a white liberal who meets a Negro at a party and instantly assumes that he must know a lot of people in show business, we feel a twinge of recognition and personal implication. Poverty and starvation, which afflict more than half of the human race, enrage us—if at all—only in a distant, generalized way; yet we are roused to a state of vengeful fury when Bruce makes public use of harmless, fruitful syllables like "come" (in the sense of orgasm) and "fuck." Where righteous indignation is concerned, we have clearly got our priorities mixed up. The point about Bruce is that he wants us to be shocked, *but by the right things*; not by four-letter words, which violate only convention, but by want and deprivation, which violate human dignity. This is not to deny that he has a disenchanted view of mankind as a whole. Even his least Swiftian bit, the monolog about a brash and incompetent American comic who tries to conquer the London Palladium, ends with the hero winning the cheers of the audience by urging them, in a burst of sadistic inspiration, to "screw the Irish." But the cynicism is just a façade. Bruce has the heart of an unfrocked evangelist.

I first saw him six years ago in a cellar room under the Duane Hotel in New York. Lean and pallid, with close-cropped black hair, he talked about Religions, Inc., a soft-selling ecumenical group on Madison Avenue whose main purpose was to render the image of Billy Graham indistinguishable from that of Pope John. ("Listen, Johnny, when you come out to the Coast, *wear the big ring*.") Clutching a hand mike, he slouched around a tiny dais, free-associating like mad; grinning as he improvised, caring as he grinned, seldom repeating in the second show what he said in the first, and often conducting what amounted to a rush job of psychoanalysis on the audience he was addressing. He used words as a jazz musician uses notes, going off into fantastic private cadenzas and digressions, and returning to his theme just when you thought he had lost track of it forever. I saw him at the Duane four times, with four separate groups of friends. Some found him offensive—a reaction they smartly concealed by calling him boring. Others thought him self-indulgent, because he felt his way into the audience's confidence by means of exploratory improvisation, instead of plunging straight into rehearsed routines. Among my guests, he was not universally liked. "Where's Lenny Bruce?" "Down the Duane," so ran a popular riposte. During the Duane engagement I met him for the first time—an archetypal night person, hypersensitive, laconic and withdrawn. Terry Southern once said that a hipster was someone who had deliberately decided to kill a part of himself in order to make life bearable. He knows that by doing this he is cutting himself off from many positive emotions as well as the negative, destructive ones he seeks to avoid; but on balance he feels that the sacrifice is worth while. By this definition Bruce was (and is) authentically, indelibly hip.

In the years that followed, it was not Bruce but my friends who improved. One by one they began to discover that they had always admired him. I recalled a saying of Gertrude Stein's: "A creator is not in advance of his generation but he is the first of his contemporaries to be conscious of what is happening to his generation." Bruce was fully, quiveringly conscious, and audiences in Chicago and San Francisco started to respond to his manner and his message. So did the police of these and other great cities, rightly detecting in this uncompromising outsider a threat to conventional mores. Arrests began, on narcotics and obscenity charges, but Bruce pressed on, a long-distance runner whose loneliness was now applauded by liberals everywhere, including those tardy converts, my chums in Manhattan. Mort Sahl, brilliant but essentially nonsubversive, had long been their pet satirist; but the election of John F. Kennedy robbed Sahl of most of his animus, which had been directed toward Eisenhower from the lame left wing of the Democratic Party. It became clear that Bruce was tapping a vein of satire that went much deeper than the puppet warfare of the two-party system. Whichever group was in power, his criticisms remained valid. Myself, I wished he had broadened his viewpoint by a little selective reading of Marx as well as Freud; but that, I suppose, is too much to expect of any comic operating west of Eastport, Maine.

In the spring of 1962, he paid his first and (thus far) only visit to London, where he appeared for a few explosive weeks at The Establishment, a Soho night club devoted to satire and run by Peter Cook of *Beyond the Fringe*. Clad in a black tunic sans lapels, as worn by the late Pandit Nehru, he roamed out on stage in his usual mood of tormented derision; 90 minutes later there was little room for doubt that he was the most original, free-speaking, wild-thinking gymnast of language our inhibited island had ever hired to beguile its citizens.

I made notes of the ideas he toyed with on opening night, and herewith reproduce them:

"The smoking of marijuana should be encouraged because it does not induce lung cancer. Children ought to watch pornographic movies: it's healthier than learning about sex from Hollywood. Venereal disease is news only when poor people catch it. Publicity is stronger than sanity: given the right PR, armpit hair on female singers could become a national fetish. Fascism in America is kept solvent by the left-wing hunger for persecution: 'Liberals will buy anything any bigot writes.' If Norman Thomas, the senior American Socialist, were to be elected President, he would have to find a minority to hate. It might conceivably be midgets—in which case his campaign slogan would run: 'Smack a midget for Norm.'"

He went on to talk about the nuances of race relations, with special emphasis on whites who cherish the Negro cause but somehow never have Negroes to dinner: about a prison movie to end them all (starring Ann Dvorak, Charles Bickford and Nat Pendleton) in which the riot is quelled by a chaplin named Father Flotsky; about the difficulties of guiltless masturbation, and the psychological duplicity ("It's a horny hoax") involved in sleeping enjoyably with a prostitute; about pain of many kinds, and laughter, and dying. At times he drawled and mumbled too privately, lapsing into a lexicon of Yiddish phrases borrowed from the showbiz world that reared him. But by the end of the evening he had crashed through frontiers of language and feeling that I had hitherto thought impregnable. The British comedian Jonathan Miller, who watched the performance in something like awe, agreed with me afterward that Bruce was a bloodbath where *Beyond the Fringe* had been a pinprick. We were dealing with something formerly unknown in Britain: an impromptu prose poet who trusted his audience so completely that he could talk in public no less outspokenly than he would talk in private.

His trust was misplaced. Scarcely a night passed during his brief sojourn at The Establishment without vocal protests from offended customers, sometimes backed up by clenched fists; and this, at a members-only club, is rare in London. The actress Siobhan McKenna came with a party and noisily rose to leave in the middle of Bruce's act; it seems she was outraged by his attitude toward the Roman Church. On her way out Peter Cook sought to remonstrate with her, whereupon she seized his tie while one of her escorts belted him squarely on the nose. "These are Irish hands," cried Miss McKenna dramatically, "and they're clean!" "This is an English face," replied Mr. Cook crisply, "and it's bleeding." A few days later a brisk, pink-faced sextet of young affluents from London's stockbroker belt booked a ringside table. They sat, half-heartedly sniggering, through jokes about money-making, sexual contact with Negroes, onanism as an alternative to V.D., and genetic hazards proceeding from fall-out. Suddenly Bruce ventured on to the subject of cigarettes and lung cancer. At once, as if in obedience to some tribal summons, the brisk, pink, stockbroker host sprang to his feet. "All right," he said tersely, "Susan, Charles, Sonia! Cancer! Come on! *Cancer!* All out!" And meekly, in single file, they marched out through the door. Bruce kept tape recordings of both the McKenna and the cancer demonstrations, and made unsparing use of them on subsequent evenings.

At the end of his engagement he was rushed out of the country with the conservative press baying at his heels. The following year, Peter Cook applied for permission to bring him back to London. The Home Secretary brusquely turned down the application; Bruce, it seemed, was classified as an undesirable alien. (Off stage, he appears to have behaved quite desirably, apart from a rumored occasion when the manager of a London hotel, awakened by complaining guests, strode into Bruce's room at four A.M. to find him conducting a trio of blondes whom he had taught to sing "Please love me, Lenny" in three-part harmony.) In 1963 the Earl of Harewood invited him to take part in an International Drama Conference at the Edinburgh Festival. Despite the august source of the invitation, the Home Office once again said no; and as I write, the edict still holds. Lenny Bruce is too wild an import for British officialdom to stomach.

We miss him, and the nerve-fraying, jazz-digging, pain-hating, sex-loving, lie-shunning, bomb-loathing life he represents. There are times when I wish he would settle in Europe, for long enough at least to realize that capitalism—from which so many of his targets derive—is not necessarily a permanent and unchangeable fact of human existence. But even if he died tomorrow, he would deserve more than a footnote in any history of modern Western culture. I have heard him described, somewhat portentously, as "the man on America's conscience." Hyperbole like that would not appeal to Lenny Bruce. "No," I can hear him dissenting, "let's say the man who went down on America's conscience . . ."

FOREWORD TO THE 2016 EDITION
BY HOWARD REICH

Time magazine called Lenny Bruce "the sickest of them all."

As if his riffs on the hypocrisies of religion, war, government, law, sex, race, money, and more proved he was the one with the problem. As if the social injustices and cruelties he railed against meant that something must be wrong with him, not with the world he dared to confront—at a rather high personal cost.

The society he chastised so fearlessly, and with such piercing humor, did not take kindly to his assaults, which he launched from the stage and, of course, in this devastating memoir. Bruce's punishments came famously in the form of obscenity trials and drug busts, trumped-up charges and stacked juries, humiliations in the press and wherever holier-than-thou authorities sought to make an example of a comedian who was so much more than that.

And yet Bruce continued to unleash his eyes-wide-open social commentary, a torrent of words that terrified some and thrilled many. The man was hell-bent on proclaiming the absurdities he saw but others didn't or wouldn't. Nothing could silence Bruce except, of course, his tragic demise in 1966 at age forty, the comic genius found dead of an overdose of either morphine or persecution, depending on your point of view.

What he left us in the pages of this book and in uncounted monologues and court proceedings, some quoted here at length, is one man's searing testimony about the world he lived in and where it went wrong—so far as he was concerned. Bruce was no preacher, telling others how to live. He was simply saying what he believed: not to win converts but only to make his case to those who bothered to encounter it.

Watching the presidential debate between Richard Nixon and John Kennedy in 1960, for instance, "convinced me more than ever that my 'ear of the beholder' philosophy is correct; that the listener hears only what he wants to hear," he writes in these pages. "I would be with a bunch of Kennedy fans watching the debate and their comment would be, 'He's really slaughtering Nixon.' Then we would all go to another apartment, and the Nixon fans would say, 'How do you like the shellacking he gave Kennedy?'"

Unlike the priests, rabbis, politicians, journalists, cops, and others Bruce skewered for their pieties, Bruce acknowledged that he wasn't necessarily going to convince anyone of anything. He just wanted to be heard. But the social and legal system that came down on him—costing him jobs, money, opportunities, and reputation—didn't want to hear it.

The loss was theirs, and ours, because most of Bruce's soliloquies, whether on the stage or the page, have proven way ahead of the society he targeted. Has anyone, after all, exposed the absurdities of our drug laws more succinctly than Bruce did in this passage: "And yet at this very moment there are American citizens in jail for smoking flowers. (Marijuana is the dried flowering top of the hemp plant.)"

Bruce wrote that more than half a century ago, and it remains as current as the latest marijuana bust.

Or consider his eloquence on war, a subject he knew better than most of the politicians who sent young men into it, Bruce having watched bodies pile up during his service in the US Navy during World War II.

"I was at Anzio," he writes. "I lived in a continual state of ambivalence: guilty but glad. Glad I wasn't the GI going to that final 'no-wake-up-call' sleep on his blood-padded mud mattress. It would be interesting to hear his comment if we could grab a handful of his hair, drag his head out of the dirt and ask his opinion on the questions that are posed every decade, the contemporary shouts of: 'How long are we going to put up with Cuba's nonsense?' 'Just how many insults can we take from Russia?'

"I was at Salerno. I can take a lot of insults."

But of everything that Bruce said and wrote, what seemed to irk those in power the most was the subject at the root of all human existence, the one issue that makes all else possible yet drove Bruce's enemies crazy: sex. Bruce was unflinching in discussing the subject in clubs and in his writings, the opening salvo of his memoirs erupting in a full-frontal discussion not only of sex but of racial stereotypes surrounding it. Even as the topic has become passé in rap songs and on cable TV—showing once again how far ahead of the curve Bruce was—you still could be fired for saying these words at work. In Bruce's era, even at the dawning of the sexual revolution, they were very nearly blasphemous.

Still, he revels in the topic, rhapsodizing on masturbation, analyzing the meaning of orgasms (and how we discuss them), contemplating how each gender perceives what drives one into the other's arms. To those who raged at these routines and charged him with obscenity, Bruce offers an utterly disarming response: "Obscenity has only one meaning: to appeal to the prurient interest. Well, I want to know what's wrong with appealing to prurient interest."

What makes his observations all the more potent, of course, is Bruce's dexterous way with a phrase. Yes, he's funny—hilarious, even, in much of his

Swiftian commentary—but the rhythms and cadences of his words reflect the soul of a jazz musician. Syllables and consonants flow with seeming effortlessness when Bruce is on a tear, his love of jazz evident not only in his references to celebrated musicians such as Miles Davis and Kenny Drew but also in the relentless forward motion and swing-beat feel of his solos. Bruce was keenly self-aware of his deep connection to the music, and not only because he played so many smoky jazz rooms on the way up.

"The reports on me were now: 'All Lenny Bruce seems concerned with is making the band laugh,'" he writes, quoting early criticism of his nascent art. "That should have been my first hint of the direction in which I was going: abstraction. Musicians, jazz musicians especially, appreciate art forms that are extensions of realism, as opposed to realism in a representational form."

Like saxophonist Sonny Rollins playing endless choruses on a classic tune, veering further and further from the original, Bruce was creating a self-styled world of sound and thought of his own, far from the one-liners and stale jokes of an earlier generation of comics. Instead of notes, he had words; instead of melodies, he had themes. But the result was the same as a master jazzman's solo, a burst of rhythm and thought—a stream-of-consciousness rush of ideas—that may seem dizzying while it's unfolding but becomes lucid by its final, climactic moments. No wonder Ralph Gleason, the great San Francisco jazz critic, stepped forward as Bruce's earliest champion, "the first one who really went out on a limb for me, to help my career," as Bruce puts it. Perhaps only a jazz connoisseur could have detected the emerging wizardry in Bruce's early work.

Equally important, though, is the heady range of ideas Bruce dares to take on in this volume: How movies have ruined our lives. How everyone has to sell out to live. How every hipster—including Bruce himself—eventually goes out of date. How pain precipitates art. Bruce's divorce, for instance, gave him "about an hour's worth of material," he writes. "That's not bad for an eight-year investment."

And Leonard Alfred Schneider—Bruce's birth name—soars when exploring the meaning of being a Jew. He does it with a laugh: "To me, if you live in New York or any other big city, you are Jewish. . . . If you live in Butte, Montana, you're going to be goyish even if you're Jewish." And he does it with a cry, addressing the most sacred and looming subject of Jewish modernity, the Holocaust.

Like all genuine sages, Bruce directs as much criticism toward himself as anyone else, which lends credibility to his skepticism of others. He confesses to the skeletons in his closet, considering himself no better than any of the rest of us, though he's surely a lot more self-revealing.

In addition to illuminating key forces in his life, such as his passion for his wife Honey Harlow and his emptiness at losing her, Bruce digs deeply into the multiple arrests and courtroom dramas he faced. Pages and pages of transcripts unfold here, Bruce either dissecting the lies of those who accused him or relishing his attorneys' skill at doing so. Bruce clearly wants the reader right there with him on the front lines, witnessing what he is enduring, as he takes the blows for what many people thought but most were afraid to say aloud. That he did so in the glare of publicity, at enormous legal peril and considerable financial and emotional cost, says a great deal about the nature of his character.

With the return of this book to print, Bruce in effect is still arguing his case, courageously pointing out what his accusers have done to him, even while they held great legal power over him. The bravery of that act should inspire us all.

If there's a central lesson running through all of this, perhaps it's Bruce's apparently boundless respect for everyone else's rights, even as his own were being so grievously violated.

"Let me tell you the truth," he writes. "The truth is 'what is.' If 'what is' is, you have to sleep eight, ten hours a day, that is the truth. A lie will be: People need no sleep at all. Truth is 'what is.'"

That's different for each one of us, Bruce is saying, and he lived his life championing that apparently dangerous principle. He did that for us, and for that we owe him an enormous and lasting debt.

—HOWARD REICH
Chicago, March 2016

Howard Reich has covered the arts for the *Chicago Tribune* since 1978 and joined the staff in 1983. He has written five books: *Portraits in Jazz, Let Freedom Swing, Jelly's Blues* (with William Gaines), *Van Cliburn,* and *Prisoner of Her Past* (originally published as *The First and Final Nightmare of Sonia Reich*). Reich has won an Emmy Award; two Deems Taylor Awards from ASCAP; an Alumni Merit Award from Northwestern University's Alumni Association; eight Peter Lisagor Awards from the Society of Professional Journalists; and an Excellence in Journalism Award from the Chicago Association of Black Journalists. The Chicago Journalists Association named him Chicago Journalist of the Year in 2011 and has given him three Sarah Brown Boyden Awards. He lives in Chicago.

How to Talk Dirty
and influence people

Chapter One

Filipinos come quick; colored men are built abnormally large ("Their wangs look like a baby's arm with an apple in its fist"); ladies with short hair are Lesbians; if you want to keep your man, rub alum on your pussy.

Such bits of erotic folklore were related daily to my mother by Mrs. Janesky, a middle-aged widow who lived across the alley, despite the fact that she had volumes of books delivered by the postman every month—*A Sane Sex Life, Ovid the God of Love, How to Make Your Marriage Partner More Compatible*—in plain brown wrappers marked "Personal."

She would begin in a pedantic fashion, using academic medical terminology, but within ten minutes she would be spouting her hoary hornyisms. Their conversation drifted to me as I sat under the sink, picking at the ripped linoleum, daydreaming and staring at my Aunt Mema's Private Business, guarded by its sinkmate, the vigilant C-N bottle, vanguard of Lysol, Zonite and Massengill.

At this tender age, I knew nothing of douches. The only difference between men and women was that women always had headaches and didn't like whistling or cap guns; and men didn't like women—that is, women they were married to.

Aunt Mema's Private Business, the portable bidet, was a large red-rubber bulb with a long black nozzle. I could never figure out what the hell it was for. I thought maybe it was an enema bag for people who lived in buildings with a super who wouldn't allow anyone to put up nails to hang things on; I wondered if it was the horn that Harpo Marx squeezed to punctuate his silent sentences. All I knew was that it definitely was *not* to be used for water-gun battles, and that what it *was* for was none of my business.

When you're eight years old, nothing is any of your business.

All my inquiries about Aunt Mema's large red-rubber bulb, or why hair grew from the mole on her face and nowhere else, or how come the talcum powder stuck between her nay-nays, would get the same answer: "You know too much already, go outside and play."

Her fear of my becoming a preteen Leopold or Loeb was responsible for my getting more fresh air than any other kid in the neighborhood.

In 1932 you really heard that word a lot—"business." But it wasn't, "I wonder what happened to the business." Everyone knew what happened to the business. There wasn't any. "That dumb bastard President Hoover" was blamed for driving us into the Depression by people who didn't necessarily have any interest in politics, but just liked saying "That dumb bastard President Hoover."

I would sit all alone through endless hours and days, scratching out my homework on the red Big Boy Tablet, in our kitchen with the shiny, flowered oilcloth, the icebox squatting over the pan that constantly overflowed, and the overhead light, bare save for a long brown string with a knot on the end, where flies fell in love.

I sort of felt sorry for the damn flies. They never hurt anybody. Even though they were supposed to carry disease, I never heard anybody say he caught anything from a fly. My cousin gave two guys the clap, and nobody ever whacked *her* with a newspaper.

The desperate tension of the Depression was lessened for me by my Philco radio with the little yellow-orange dial and the black numbers in the center. What a dear, sweet friend, my wooden radio, with the sensual cloth webbing that separated its cathedrallike architecture from the mass air-wave propaganda I was absorbing—it was the beginning of an awareness of a whole new fantasy culture . . .

"Jump on the Manhattan Merry-Go-Round—the Highway, the Byway, to New York Town . . ."

"And here comes Captain Andy now . . ."

The biggest swinger was Mr. First-Nighter. He always had a car waiting for him. "Take me to the little theater off Times Square." Barbara Luddy and Les Tremayne.

And Joe Penner said: "Hyuk, hyuk, hyuk."

"With a cloud of dust, the speed of light and a hearty *Hi-Yo Silver Away!*"

Procter & Gamble provided many Fulbright and Guggenheim fellowship winners with the same formative exposure.

Long Island had loads of screen doors and porches. Screen doors to push your nose against, porches to hide under. It always smelled funny under the porch. I had a continuing vision of one day crawling under there and finding a large cache of money, which I would spend nobly on my mother and aunt—but not until they explained the under-the-sink apparatus; and, if there was enough money, perhaps Mema would even demonstrate it for me.

I would usually hide under the porch until it came time to "get it."

"You just wait till your father comes, then you're really gonna get it." I always thought what a pain in the ass it would be to be a father. You have to work hard all day and then, instead of resting when you come home, you have to "give it" to someone. I didn't "get it" as much as other kids, though, because my mother and father were divorced.

I had to wait until visiting days to "get it."

I look back in tender relished anger, and I can smell the damp newspapers that waited on the porch for the Goodwill—they never picked up anything we gave them because we never had it packed right—and I can hear the muffled voices through the kerosene stove.

"Mickey, I don't know what we're going to do with Lenny. He was so fresh to Mema. You know what he asked?"

Then they would all laugh hysterically. And then my father would *schlep* me from under the porch and whack the crap out of me.

For being fresh to Mema. For forgetting to change my good clothes after school and catching my corduroy knickers on a nail. And for whistling. I would even "get it" for whistling.

I used to love to whistle. The first tune I learned to whistle was *Amapola*. "Amapola, my pretty little poppy . . ." I received most of my musical education from the sounds that wafted from the alley of Angelo's Bar and Grille, Ladies Invited, Free Lunch. I was enthralled with the discovery of the jukebox: a machine that didn't sew, drill, boil or kill; a machine solely for fun.

Angelo, the tavernkeeper, was a classic illustration of onomatopoeia. He laughed "Har! Har! Har!" He talked exactly like the balloons in comic strips. When he was disturbed, he would say "Tch! Tch! Tch!" To express contempt, he would "Harrumph!"

I kept waiting to hear Angelo's dog say "Arf! Arf!" He never made a sound. I told this to Russell Swan, the oil painter, sometime house painter and town drunk. He replied that the dog had been interbred with a giraffe—a reference I didn't understand, but which cracked up the erudite Mr. Swan. It must be lonesome, being bright and witty and aware, but living in a town where you can't relate to people in all areas.

Mr. Swan gave me the first book I ever read, Richard Halliburton's *Royal Road to Romance,* the tale of a world traveler who continually searches for beauty and inner peace. I loved to read.

"Don't read at the table," I would be told.

"Why do they put stuff on the cereal box if they don't want you to read?"

"Not at the table."

When I get big, I thought, I'll read anywhere I want . . . standing on the subway:

"What's that you're reading, sir?"
"A cereal box."

I almost always made a good score in back of Angelo's Bar and Grille; the loot consisted of deposit bottles. But there was a hang-up—you could never find anyone willing to cash them. The most sought-after prize was the large Hoffman bottle, which brought a five-cent bounty.

Mr. Geraldo, our neighborhood grocer, cashed my mother's relief check and so he knew we had barely enough money for staples. Therefore, the luxury of soda pop in deposit bottles was obviously far beyond our economic sphere. Besides, he couldn't relate to children. He disliked them because they made him nervous.

"Could I have a glass of water, please?"

"No, the water's broken."

When I brought the bottles to him, he would interrogate me without an ounce of mercy. "Did you buy these here? When did you buy them?" I would always fall prey to his Olga-of-Interpol tactics. "Yes, I think we bought them here." Then he would finger-thump me on the back of the head, as if he were testing a watermelon. "Get the hell outta here, you never bought any soda here. I'm going to report your mother to the Welfare man and have him take her check away."

I could hear the Welfare man saying to Mema: "Your nephew—you know, the one who knows too much already—he's been arrested on a Deposit Bottle Charge. We have to take your check away."

Then where would Mema go? We would all have to live under the porch, with the funny smell.

That was the big threat of the day—taking the check away. Generalities spewed forth: The goyim were always being threatened with the loss of their checks because of their presence in bars, and the Yidden for their presence in banks.

Another sure way for a family to lose its check was for any member to be caught going to the movies. But I didn't worry about that. My friend and I would sneak in, hide under the seats while the porter was vacuuming, and then, after the newsreel was over, we would pop up in the midst of Lou Lehr's "Mongees is da chrrazziest beeple . . ."

Anyway, my next stop with the deposit bottles would be the King Kullen Market. The manager stared at me. I returned his stare with no apparent guile. I tried to look as innocent and Anglo-Saxon as Jackie Cooper, pouting, pooched-out lip and all, but I'm sure I looked more like a dwarfed Maurice Chevalier.

"I bought them yesterday—I don't know how the dirt and cobwebs got inside . . ."

He cashed the bottles and I got my 20 cents.

I bought a *Liberty* magazine for my mother. She liked to read them because the reading time was quoted: "four minutes, three seconds." She used to clock herself, and her chief aim was to beat the quoted time. She always succeeded, but probably never knew what the hell she had read.

I bought Aunt Mema a 12-cent jar of Vaseline. She ate it by the ton. She was a Vaseline addict. She would rub it on and stick it in anything and everything. To Mema, carbolated Vaseline was Jewish penicillin.

Perhaps at this point I ought to say a little something about my vocabulary. My conversation, spoken and written, is usually flavored with the jargon of the hipster, the argot of the underworld, and Yiddish.

In the literate sense—as literate as Yiddish can be since it is not a formal language—"goyish" means "gentile." But that's not the way I mean to use it.

To me, if you live in New York or any other big city, you are Jewish. It doesn't matter even if you're Catholic; if you live in New York you're Jewish. If you live in Butte, Montana, you're going to be goyish even if you're Jewish.

Evaporated milk is goyish even if the Jews invented it. Chocolate is Jewish and fudge is goyish. Spam is goyish and rye bread is Jewish.

Negroes are all Jews. Italians are all Jews. Irishmen who have rejected their religion are Jews. Mouths are very Jewish. And bosoms. Baton-twirling is very goyish. Georgie Jessel and Danny Thomas are Christians, because if you look closely on their bodies you'll find a boil somewhere.

To trap an old Jewish woman—they're crafty and they will lie—just seize one and you will find a handkerchief balled-up in one of her hands.

I can understand why we can't have a Jewish President. It would be embarrassing to hear the President's mother screaming love at the grandchildren: "Who's Grandma's baby! Who's Grandma's baby!"

". . . And this is Chet Huntley in New York. The First Lady's mother opened the Macy's Day Parade screaming, *'Oy zeishint mine lieber'* and furiously pinching young Stanley's cheeks . . ."

Actually, she bit his ass, going "Oom, yum yum, is this a tush, whose tushy is that?" The Jews are notorious children's-ass-kissers. Gentiles neither bite their children's asses nor do they *hahhh* their soup.

Gentiles love their children as much as Jews love theirs; they just don't wear their hearts on their sleeves. On the other hand, Jewish mothers don't hang gold stars in their windows. They're not proud of their boys' going into the service. They're always worried about their being killed.

Celebrate is a goyish word. Observe is a Jewish word. Mr. and Mrs. Walsh are *celebrating* Christmas with Major Thomas Moreland, USAF (Ret.), while Mr. and Mrs. Bromberg *observed* Hanukkah with Goldie and Arthur Schindler from Kiamesha, New York.

The difference between Jewish and goyish girls is that a gentile girl won't "touch it once," whereas a Jewish girl will kiss you and let you touch it—your own, that is.

The only Jewish thing about balling is Vaseline.

One eventful day, I discovered self-gratification. An older kid conducted a school, and five of us graduated about the same time.

A few days later, I was all set for an afternoon of whacking it. I had a copy of *National Geographic,* with pictures of naked chicks in Africa.

I'm sure that when these spade ladies with the taco tits posed for Osa and Martin Johnson, they never dreamed that they would be part of an 11-year-old satyr's sexual fantasy, or they certainly wouldn't have signed a model's release.

I was propped up in bed, taking care of business. I was so involved, I didn't hear the door open. "Leonard, what are you doing?" It was my father! My heart stopped. I froze. He repeated: "I said, what are you doing?"

To say it was a traumatic moment would be euphemistic. I had to restrain myself from asking: "Would you wait outside for just a minute?" He snarled, "It's not only disgusting, what you're doing—but, goddamnit, in my bed!"

He sat down and proceeded to tell me a story, that story we have all heard, with embellishments. Its grim conclusion left three of our relatives in state insane asylums—poor souls who had never been instructed in the wisdom of sleeping with their hands above the covers. The story line implied that this sort of thing was a nighttime practice and was associated with werewolves and vampires. Their punishment was that their hands withered away into wings, and they couldn't pull it anymore, just fan it a little.

I had all sorts of horrendous visions of my future: my spine would collapse; my toes would fall off. Even though I resolved never to do it again, I felt I had done some irreparable damage.

Oh, what a cursed thing! I could see myself on a street corner giving testimony for the C.B.W.A.—Crooked Back Whackers Anonymous:

"Yea, brothers, I was of mortal flesh. Fortunately for me, my father walked in that day while I was having my struggle with Satan. Suppose he had not been an observant person, and merely thought I was doing a charade—committing hari-kari triple time—what then? But no, brothers, he knew he had a pervert living under his roof; the most dangerous of them all—a whacker! I would have to stop. No tapering off. I would have to stop *now!* In the language of the addict's world, I would have to kick the habit—cold jerky . . ."

Chapter Two

I credit the motion picture industry as the strongest environmental factor in molding the children of my day.

Andy Hardy: whistling; a brown pompadour; a green lawn; a father whose severest punishment was taking your car away for the weekend.

Warner Baxter was a doctor. All priests looked like Pat O'Brien.

The superintendent of my school looked like Spencer Tracy, and the principal looked like Vincent Price. I was surprised years later to discover they *were* Spencer Tracy and Vincent Price. I went to Hollywood High, folks. Lana Turner sat at the next desk, Roland Young was the English teacher and Joan Crawford taught general science. "She's got a fabulous body, but she never takes that shop apron off."

Actually, I went to public school in North Bellmore, Long Island, for eight years, up until the fifth grade. I remember the routine of milk at 10:15 and napping on the desk—I hated the smell of that desk—I always used to dribble on the initials. And how enigmatic those well-preserved carvings were to me: BOOK YOU.

My friend Carmelo, the barber's son, and I would "buy" our lunch at the little green store. That's what we called the student lockers from which we stole hot cold lunches. "Let's see what we've got at the little green store today."

We would usually go shopping around 11:30 on the eighth-grade floor, when everybody was in homeroom. Carmelo would bust open a locker. A white paper bag! Who used white paper bags? People who could afford to buy baked goods and make their children exotic sandwiches. Tuna on date-nut bread, four creme-filled Hydrox cookies, a banana which was unreal—the color wasn't solid brown, it was yellow tipped with green, and the end wasn't rotten—and the last goody: a nickel, wrapped in wax paper.

Some people are wrapping freaks—a little pinch of salt in wax paper, pepper in wax paper, two radishes that were individually wrapped in wax paper. The thing that really made it erotic was that it was real wax paper, not bread-wrapping wax paper.

Carmelo's father had a barbershop with one chair and a poster in the window showing four different styles of haircuts, and guaranteeing you sure-fire results in securing employment if you would follow the tips on grooming: "The First Things an Employer Looks at Are Hair, Nails and Shoes." An atomic-energy department head who looks at these qualifications in a job applicant would probably be a faggot.

Carmelo's mother was the manicurist and town whore. Those symbols of my childhood are gone—what a shame!—the country doctor, the town whore, the village idiot, and the drunken family from the other side of the tracks have been replaced by the Communist, the junkie, the faggot, and the beatnik.

Prostitution wasn't respected and accepted, but I figured that if she was the town whore, then all the people in the town had fucked her and had paid her and they were all a part of what she was. I staunchly defended Carmelo's mother.

Carmelo and I were sitting in the barbershop one lunch hour, drawing mustaches on the people in the *Literary Digest,* when Mr. Krank, the assistant principal, walked in, looked at us and almost shit. Maybe he had dropped by to pay a visit to the town whore.

He quickly asked Carmelo's father: "Got time to give me a trim?" This really confused me, because Mr. Krank was almost bald; he didn't have a goddamn hair on top of his head. We left just as Carmelo's father did away with the sideburns that Mr. Krank treasured so dearly.

My mother worked as a waitress and doubled as a maid in fashionable Long Beach, Long Island. My father was working during the day and going to college at night. His motive was to better himself and, in turn, better us all. If he had graduated, I might not be where I am now. I'm the head of a big firm today, thanks to my dad's foresight in placing handy knowledge at my fingertips.

"You're going to have that set of encyclopedias for your birthday," he had pledged. "You're going to have everything I never had as a child, even if I have to do without cigarettes." And then, to demonstrate his self-sacrifice, he would roll his own in those rubber roller things that Bugler used to sell.

Today I give my daughter what I *really* didn't have as a kid. All the silly, dumb, extravagant, frilly, nonfunctional toys I can force on her. She probably wants an encyclopedia. That's how it goes—one generation saves to buy rubbers for the kids on a rainy day, and when it comes they sit out under a tree getting soaking wet and digging the lightning.

My father instilled in me a few important behavior patterns, one of which was a fantastic dread of being in debt. He explained to me such details as how much we owed on the rent, what the coal and light bills were, how much money we had and how long it would last.

Taking me into his confidence like that made me very sensitive about my responsibilities to help out. When he'd say, "Whatever you want, just ask your father," it was like the cliché picture of the father and son standing on a high building and the father says: "Some day, son, all this will be yours!" Only, when my father made the offer, it was as if he were telling me I could have it as long as I was willing to push him off the roof to get it.

He would constantly remind me that we were living on the brink of poverty. He would go miles out of his way to look for bargains. He would wear clothes that friends gave him. I became so guilty about asking for anything that I concluded it was much more ethical to steal.

When I was in seventh grade and, for physical education, each boy had to buy sneakers that cost about $1.98, I couldn't bring myself to ask my father for the money. The previous night he had confided to me that he didn't know where he was going to get the money for the rent. I decided to steal the money for my sneakers from the Red Cross.

The class kept all the money they had collected for the annual Red Cross drive in a big mayonnaise jar in the supply closet. I volunteered to stay after school to wash the blackboard and slap out the erasers. I knew that the teacher, Miss Bostaug, was picked up at 3:30 sharp by her boyfriend.

She was the kind of woman who was old when she was 23. She wore those "sensible" corrective shoes and lisle stockings; and crinkly dresses, the kind that you can see through and don't want to. The only color she ever wore was a different handkerchief that she pinned on her blouse every day. Her short sleeves revealed a vaccination mark as big as a basketball.

As soon as Miss Bostaug left that afternoon, I picked up the radiator wrench and jimmied open the closet door. I really botched up the door, but I made the heist. My heart was beating six-eight time as I split with the mayonnaise jar.

I hid under the porch and counted the loot. Over $13 in change.

I spent some of the money on the sneakers and a carton of Twenty Grand cigarettes for my father. I figured I would take what was left and return it. Maybe no one would miss what I spent. Maybe no one would notice the door had been torn off its hinges.

But as I neared the classroom, I could hear the storm of protest, so I changed my mind and joined in the denunciation of the culprit. "Boy, how could anyone be so low? Stealing from the Red Cross! Don't worry, God will punish him." I felt pretty self-righteous condemning myself, and quite secure that no one suspected me.

But I had underestimated Miss Bostaug.

"Boys and girls," she announced, "this morning I called my brother, Edward Bostaug, in Washington. He works for the Federal Bureau of Investigation. He told me that if the criminal doesn't confess today, he is going to come up here on Monday with a lie detector." And then, in minute detail, she described the technical perfection of the polygraph in spotting the slightest irregularity in blood pressure, pulse and temperature. As she spoke, my heart was pounding and I was sweating.

After everyone left, I marched boldly up to her desk. She was creaming her face with Noxema. "Miss Bostaug, I know who stole the money. I told him the jig was up, and he told me to tell you that he only spent three dollars and is willing to give me the rest to bring back and he will make up what he spent, little by little, if you promise not to call your brother from the FBI."

A week later the Long Island Welfare Board paid a visit to my father, attempting to ascertain what sort of family atmosphere produced a criminal of my proportions.

Miss Bostaug hadn't "squealed" on me, but she had done her duty, not only to the authorities, but also to me. She was aware that my environment was as much to blame for my behavior as I was. She was trying to help.

My father didn't see it that way, however. He was simply amazed. "How could a son of mine steal, when all he has to do is ask me for anything and I'll give it to him, even if I have to give up cigarettes?"

He sat down and talked to me. It was difficult for me to answer because he was sitting on my chest.

My mother's boyfriends were a unique breed. They were buddies rather than beaux. I can't remember seeing anyone ever kiss my mother—not on the mouth, anyway—and for sure, I never saw her in bed with any man, not even that once-in-a-while "mistake" in the one-bedroom apartment when "Ssh, you'll wake the kid up!" makes going to the bathroom during the night a combination of horror and fascination.

I can remember only one "walk-in" in my life. As an eight-year-old child, I stumbled through the living room on the way to the bathroom at four o'clock in the morning. My cousin Hannah and her husband were pushing, kissing, tearing and breathing in asthmatic meter. I watched and listened in wonderful curiosity.

I had no concept of what was going on. They were maintaining a consistent rhythm that kept building in strength and force. Then the rhythm became overpoweringly intense and heavy, and his voice changed pitch—that crazy soprano sound that the funnymen in the movies affect when they imitate ladies.

I saw the sweet dizzy quality on the face of my 23-year-old cousin, as her paint and powder dissolved and mixed with her lover's sweat. She was looking over his shoulder, as if right at me, but her eyes looked funny—like my cousin Herman's when he was drunk. Her legs—lovely, smooth legs with just a suggestion of fine, soft hair, like the guard hairs on the willow-limb flowers—seemed to float heavenward, her toes twisting in a tortured fashion, praying for release.

Now her eyes started to roll as if they were completely disengaged. My cousin Harry must have broken that thing that makes the doll's eyes go up and down.

Her lips parted slowly and she joined him in a chant of submission—a chant with the vocabulary of theology, although I have never heard it again in synagogue, church or Buddhist temple—a chant that was perhaps pagan: "Oh God, oh God, oh goddamnit God! Oh it's so good, Harry—oh God it's good—don't come yet, wait for me, you better pull out, oh don't stop—oh I love you sweetheart, God I love, oh you're so good—ohhhh . . ."

Suddenly Hannah's eyes focused on me. She screamed as if I were some horrible monster, "How long have you been standing there?"

I watched as Harry grabbed at a flurry of white sheet.

She reiterated: "I said, how long have you been standing there?"

I reacted subjectively, assuming they wanted me to show off since her question related to an area of learning that I was involved with at the time. I looked up at the clock, thought for a moment, and repeated her question. "How long have I been standing here? Well, the big hand is on the five, and the little hand is on the three, that means it's—umm—3:25."

They told me that was very nice and I was a very clever boy, and that I should go to bed.

Without someone telling me what they had been doing, I could never tell you whether that was a clean act, a dirty act, a self-indulgent act, or an ecstatic act of pure religious procreation. With all the exposure I've had, I still can't tell you. You must interpret what went on in your own way—and, of course, you will.

My childhood seemed like an endless exodus from aunts and uncles and grandmothers. Their dialog still rings in my ears: "I had enough *tsooris* with my own kids. . . . How many times have I told you not to slam the door? . . . Don't *run* up the stairs. . . . Don't tell me 'Danny did it'—if Danny told you to jump off the Brooklyn Bridge, you'd jump off the Brooklyn Bridge, right? . . . Children have children's portions and big people have big people's portions—if you're hungry you'll eat more bread—and there's plenty of cabbage left . . ."

The plan was I would stay with relatives till my parents "could get straightened out."

I learned there is no Judge Hardy, there is no Andrew, nobody has a mom like Fay Bainter.

Oh God, the movies really did screw us up.

Chapter
Three

As an imaginative young sensualist, I dreamed about living over a barn, seeing the stars through a cracked-board room, smelling the cows and horses as they snuggle and nuzzle in a shed below, seeing the steam come up from the hay in the stables on a frosty winter morning, sitting at a table rich with home-canned goods with seven other farm hands, eating home fries, pickled beets, fresh bacon, drinking raw milk, laughing, having company in the morning, having a family, eating and working and hanging out with the big guys, learning to use Bull Durham.

At 16 I ran away from home and found it. Two rich, productive, sweet years with the Dengler family on their Long Island farm.

The Denglers were a combination of Swedish and German stock. Although they were still young—she in her 30s and he in his 40s—I never saw them kiss each other. I was shocked when I learned that they slept in separate bedrooms. I knew they were tired after working a long day, but I couldn't understand why anyone who could, wouldn't want to sleep in another person's arms.

I would wait for an opportunity when Mr. Dengler was enjoying a good laugh, and then I would catch him unawares and give him a big hug. Mrs. Dengler called me a "kissing bug," but she never rejected me. They said I would probably end up being a politician.

The Dengler farm faced the highway. As I carried the pails of slop to the hogs, I watched the cars whizzing by on their way to Grumman and Sikorsky and Sperry. Neither the drivers nor I realized that their day's work would some day put an end to someone somewhere also carrying slop to hogs. A couple of times when the cars overheated, they would stop for water, and I would ask them what they were making out at Sperry's.

They didn't know. "Some fittings . . ." Some fittings—the Norden bombsight to fit into the B-17. "I just do piecework." (My approach to humor today is in distinguishing between the *moral* differences of words and their connotations; then it was simply in the homonym: "Oh, you do piecework? How about bringing me home some?")

Directly opposite the highway that ran by the farm was a long dusty dirt road with crops on each side—potatoes, carrots, lettuce—everything you buy in your grocery store. They were cultivated, irrigated, weeded and fertilized by the farm hands. Some of the fertilization was direct from producer to consumer: There were no lavatories in the fields, but the itinerant dayworkers—six Polish women—had a very relaxed attitude toward the performing of their natural functions.

To this day, I insist that all my vegetables be washed thoroughly.

I was entrusted with the unromantic job of weeding, although I did get to drive the old truck with the broken manifold, back and forth across the field, which really gassed me. I imagined myself to be Henry Fonda. The only thing that bugged me was that it was so lonesome out there all day. I tried to talk to the Polish ladies, but they didn't understand me. I even brought them candy—Guess Whats, Mary Janes, Hootens—but all they did was grunt. I could watch their most intimate functions, but it was as if I didn't exist.

Mrs. Dengler would get up about 3:30 in the morning to cook breakfast for eight men; she would work in the fields herself till about eight o'clock that night, and then she would do her housework.

During the winter, the Denglers ran a roadside stand selling canned goods and eggs to the workers on their way to and from a nearby defense plant.

The canned goods would actually be sold out the first day, and we only had enough chickens to supply eggs for about two or three cars. So we bought eggs wholesale from as far away as Texas, and Mason-jar canned goods from an outfit in Georgia.

My job was to immerse the jars in hot water, wash off their labels and put ours on. I would also open the egg crates—which were packed by the gross—and repackage the eggs in our cartons, by the dozen. With my philanthropic sense of humor, I would add a little mud and straw and chicken droppings to give them an authentic pastoral touch.

People were always coming back and telling us: "How fresh the eggs are!" Sales increased rapidly and I soon had a big problem. Although I had enough straw and mud, there were only 22 chickens—and I was too embarrassed to ask if there were any wholesale chickenshit houses in Texas.

I decided to cut the pure stuff with cow manure. There was never a complaint.

Once a week a big LaSalle would drive all the way out from the city to get farm-fresh eggs. The chauffeur was a little wizened old Englishman who never, ever spoke. The owner was a woman who looked like Mary Astor. She was a very grand-type lady, about 35, which seemed quite old to me.

She said the farm was "quaint" and remarked how fortunate I was not to be "cursed by city pressures." She began to bring me things—sweaters, shoes, even a tennis racket. I fed her charitable id and exclaimed: "Oh, gosh, a real sweater! I always wanted one with no patches on it!" All I needed was "Gloriosky, Zero!" to complete the picture.

Once I sensed she was feeling a little low, so I told her that my mother and father had been killed. I fabricated a very pathetic story for her, and it really picked her up. It was a sort of Fantasy CARE Package—a little something extra added to the product, like with the eggs.

One day she forgot all about buying the eggs, and insisted on taking me to town to buy a new jacket. I had an old suede jacket with a broken zipper that had to be pinned shut. I told her I couldn't leave the stand. She told the chauffeur to get out and take over for me, and she would do the driving.

On the way back from the city, she pulled over into a shaded area and stopped. We talked for a long time, and she told me about her son who was drowned, and also about her husband who manufactured and rented candy machines. She intimated that she would like to adopt me.

She asked about my religious beliefs. She asked if I had ever been naughty with girls. I had never even kissed a girl—I hadn't gone to high school and I was very shy—I had often thought about being "naughty" with girls, but I could never seem to arrange to be in the right place at the right time.

We talked about some other things, and she told me to look in the glove compartment for a surprise. Inside I found a sheath knife and a flashlight. There was also a packet of pictures, and she asked me if I would like her to show them to me.

I had never seen any pictures like those before. They were of men and women in various attitudes of lovemaking. The nudity and the absurdity of the contortions amused me, and I started to laugh. She was quite disturbed by my reactions, but I couldn't help it. I had a genuine giggling fit.

She asked me if I thought the pictures were dirty, and when I couldn't stop laughing long enough to answer, she said that it was a cover-up for a filthy mind. Not wanting to lose the jacket, I apologized.

She forgave me and then delivered a lecture on how some women can give you a terrible disease. She explained how you can get some diseases from using towels or from sitting on toilet seats. She asked me if I knew what the symptoms of these diseases were. I confessed my ignorance, and she grew alarmed.

"Why, you can have one of those diseases right this minute and not even know it!"

And, with a very clinical attitude, she unbuttoned my pants.

A few years later in boot camp, when we got our first illustrated lecture on venereal disease, I was disappointed. It lacked the same personal touch.

The Denglers were quite upset with my impatience to volunteer for the Navy. I pestered Mrs. Dengler daily, waiting for that official letter. I had some literature about the Navy and the training courses they offered, and I reviewed it at every opportunity in my "reading room"—a four-holer (one hole was entirely sewn up by a cobweb) with a wasp hive the color of gray cardboard up in the right-hand corner of the ceiling. I always read uneasily, in dread of an attack.

The outhouse is to the farm hand what the water cooler is to the white-collar worker.

But, working for the Denglers, this wasn't necessary for me. They were easy bosses to work for. Although I put in about 60 hours a week and received $40 a month plus room and board, I felt no resentment, because they worked longer and harder.

Then, too, they were my mother and father—the mother and father I had always dreamed about—and I always had good company, which made me think about all the lonesome people who lived in furnished rooms with their container of milk or can of beer on the window ledge. Wouldn't it be nice if all the people who are lonesome could live in one big dormitory, sleep in beds next to each other, talk, laugh, and keep the lights on as long as they want to?

Lonesome people are a vast neglected segment of that mythical American Public the advertising men are always talking about. One mustn't assume that all lonesome people are pensioners, old maids and physically handicapped shut-ins. There are lonesome young men who sit in the Greyhound Bus Station and there are secretaries who live in immaculate apartments that they wouldn't mind having messed up by some guy who doesn't hang up his clothes.

Sometimes when I'm on the road in a huge hotel, I wish there were a closed-circuit television camera in each room, and at two o'clock in the morning the announcer would come on: "In Room 24-B there is a ripe, blue-eyed, pink-nippled French and Irish court stenographer lying in bed tossing and turning, fighting the bonds of her nightgown. All the ashtrays in her room are clean, her stockings and panty-girdle have just been washed and are hanging on the shower-curtain bar. This is a late model, absolutely clean, used only a few times by a sailor on leave."

Or: "In Apartment 407 there is a 55-year-old Jewish widower who is listening to Barry Gray on the radio, sitting in his underwear and looking at the picture of his daughter and son-in-law who live in Lawrence, Long Island, and haven't called since Yom Kippur. This a bargain for an aggressive young woman who can say to him, 'I like you because you're sensible and sensitive—all right, it's true young men are a "good time," but after *that,* what?—I like a man I can have a serious discussion with, a man who can co-sign . . .'"

Mrs. Dengler drove me to the station of the Long Island Railroad to catch the train that would take me away to war. I kissed her and said, "Goodbye, Ma." She smiled at me and left. She never had any kids of her own.

15

Chapter Four

I volunteered for the Navy in 1942. I was 5'2", weighed 120 pounds, and had a heavy beard that needed removing about once every six months.

One day I was standing at 90 Church Street in Downtown New York City, literally in the hands of a doctor who was telling me to cough—that universal experience which every male who gets caught in a draft undergoes.

The Navy taught me a sterile sense of cleanliness, punctuality, and gave me the security of belonging. For the first time I was able to relate to my fellow man.

My first "relative" was Artie Shaw. We took boot training together in Newport, Rhode Island. During that 21-day incubation period, the excitement of war was dwarfed by "Artie Shaw is here!" Artie Shaw: *Begin the Beguine, Night and Day,* Dave Tough, Max Kaminsky, Lana Turner, Kathleen Winsor. Artie Shaw—Orpheus, music and love—and me; we were brothers in blue. Of course, I never saw him, but it was enough for me that he was there.

(Eighteen years later I got the same gratification from those magic words, "Artie Shaw is here!"—when the owner of the Blue Angel Café whispered it to me before I went onstage. "Artie Shaw is here!" How just, how natural—we were in the War together.)

He had enlisted as an apprentice seaman. He could have gone in a dozen other ways—like Glenn Miller, for example, with a commission in clarinet—but he made it as an apprentice seaman, which was a silly-ass thing to do.

As it turned out, he had a much rougher time in service than I did. He either got an oversolicitous: "This is Artie Shaw, Captain Alden, he has agreed to give you that autographed picture of himself for Admiral Nimitz!"—or, more often: "Look, pretty boy, you're not in Hollywood now, there ain't no butlers around here!" Artie Shaw would have been glad to have been as anonymous as I was then, an ordinary seaman with a serial number, wanting to fight for his country.

Even as a kid, I was hip that 80 percent of the guys that go for Civil Service pension security have no balls for the scuffle outside. I am not knocking the desire for security; we're all kind of scared and would like to be sitting under the kitchen sink, picking at the linoleum. But it really bugged Shaw. He put in an urgent request for a transfer to the Mediterranean. We were all anxious to go and be blessed by priests and rabbis, thereby giving us the OK to kill the enemy.

Those dirty pregnant Japanese women who stood in the silent army, like Italian mothers standing over the boiling pots of spaghetti, the Jewish mothers slaving over pots of chicken soup—women unconcerned with politics; all they know is that 49 cents a pound for chopped meat is ridiculous. Those dirty Jap babies crawling on the floor, amused by the magic of a cat, his purr, his switching tail. Those dirty Japs we hated, who now fill the windows of American stores with cameras. Those dirty Japs that knocked up the portable-radio industry.

Where the hell was that syndicated Nostradamus and his *Criswell Predicts* then?

Now there are no more dirty Japs; there are dirty Commies! And when we run out of them there'll just be dirty dirt. And dirty mud. Then we'll eat the mud and Pearl Buck will write a book about it. By that time, the few hippies who discovered that it's the *earth* which is dirty will have made it to the moon for the Miss Missile contest.

On a cruel triple-brrr snow-cold gray winter morning at Coddington Point, Rhode Island, Artie Shaw and 20-odd other sailors sat in the fetal position with their red eyes and chapped thighs, waiting for chow to blow. A chief petty officer came in and told Artie that a lieutenant commander was outside the barracks and wanted to see him immediately. Shaw was sure that this was his transfer.

He marched out with his Don Winslow snap, the sailors nervously peeking through the barracks window. When you're in boot camp, a lieutenant commander might as well be the President. Shaw was understandably nervous as the lieutenant commander reached out his hand, saying, "Put 'er there, Artie," and then said 14 words that had more impact than Roosevelt's "December 7th, a day that will live in infamy" speech.

The lieutenant commander looked Shaw in the eye and said: "I just wanted to shake the hand that patted the ass of Lana Turner."

It was in the Navy that I had my first love affair—a one-night stand with Louise—the kind of chick that makes an elevator operator feel possessed of great control because he went up 18 floors and didn't rip off her dress.

Louise was 28 when I met her. Her father and mother had just died, and she and her brother inherited the business: a 13 × 13-foot combination Italian-American grocery and soda fountain, with living quarters in the back. Her brother took care of the store during the day, and she worked there at night so he could go to CCNY.

Her husband was a private in the U.S. Infantry, stationed in Iceland for the duration.

I walked into the store in white hat, dress-blue uniform and my Endicott-Johnson shoes, so new they slipped on cement. I was announced by the little tin bell—the candy-store burglar alarm. Behind the counter stood Louise.

Doctors who have probed, cut, sewn and rubber-gloved so many women that it has become a task would get shaken by a Louise.

"Hmm, your adenoids seem quite normal; perhaps the trouble is respiratory. Unbutton your blouse a moment and we'll give a listen to the old ticker. There's quite a bit of flu going around and I . . . there, uh . . . actually . . . uh, uh . . . here, uh. . . . Oh God, oh merciful Mother of God, what a body! You're so tan and yet so white. Please may I touch you? Not as a doctor. . . . Let me unbutton my shirt and feel you close to me. Please don't push me away. Here, let me . . . please . . . oh God! I'm losing my mind, let me latch the door. . . . *Let me just kiss it,* that's all I want to . . . oh, please please please please. *Please just touch it.* Just . . . *look at it.* . . . I do respect you. I just can't catch my goddamn breath!"

With eight dollars hidden in my shoe and a dollar in my hand, I walked up to the counter and spoke out with a jaded-enough tone so that Louise would know that I'd been around. "Pepsi, please, and a bag of potato chips."

She ripped the stapled chips away from the cardboard. When she spoke, her words stunned me. I never expected a woman who looked like that to talk that way to a *bon vivant* such as I.

"How the hell did you get gum in your hair?" she asked.

"The guy who sleeps in the bunk above me stuck it on the edge of my rack. I thought I got it out."

"C'mere, I've got some benzene, it'll take it out."

I followed her through the blue-rayon portals that separated the store from her home. I sat on a soda box and watched her rumble through the medicine cabinet, which was a cardboard carton under her bed.

She soaked the rag and stood over me, gently kneading the chewing gum from my hair. Her thighs, with the good-life scent of the white dove, pressed weightlessly against my cheek. The gum was long gone, and my first love was nurtured in a setting of Medaglia D'Oro coffee, Ace combs, and Progresso tomato purée.

I wonder if any Chilean chicle worker ever dreamt of the delicious fruit that I received from the by-product of his labor.

I was assigned to a light cruiser, the U.S.S. Brooklyn.

Me—Leonard Alfred Schneider—on the deck of a warship bound for North Africa, along with 1300 other men and enough munitions to bring a man-made earthquake to Ain el Turk, Bizerte, and Algiers, which was to be followed after the War by a sociopolitical earthquake—for we were blasting more than enemy breastworks; we were shaking loose the veils from shadowed Moslem faces and the gold from their front teeth.

I had two battle stations—one on a 1.1 gun and my watch was on a five-inch deck gun. A cannon in the Navy is always called a gun.

Five in the morning, reveille. Five-ten, topside: wash down the decks and do paint work. Seven o'clock, secure. Seven-thirty to eight, chow: prunes, beans, cornbread, cold cuts, Waldorf salad, coffee. Eight o'clock, turn to: painting, chipping, scraping, ammunition working party. Twelve o'clock, chow: braised beef, dehydrated potatoes, spinach, coffee, cake with icing. One o'clock, work. Two-forty-five, attack by enemy planes: man your battle stations, fight with planes.

(I could use Navy time, 0600, etc., but I had elevated to the idiomatic group: "Look out the window and see who is on the left side of the boat.")

The secure from battle may be at eight P.M. Secure at sea, ammunition working party, replace expended ammunition. Quick scrubdown, twelve-thirty, hit the sack. I never got more than four and a half hours sleep a night in three years.

Blood and salt water mixed together looks blue. Eight men followed by twelve, then by about forty more, floated gracefully by the bow of the U.S.S. Brooklyn. These dead Air Force men that just a few months ago were saying . . .

"What do you want, Hi-Test or Regular?"

"Did you get my pants out of the cleaner's, sweetheart?"

"They'll never get me—my uncle is an alderman."

"Now listen, Vera, I'm going to put all my stuff in these cardboard boxes, and I'm going to lock them in that closet back of the den. Please don't let anyone touch them—and don't just say 'Yes' to me—I don't want anyone, do you understand, *anyone,* fooling around with my stuff . . ."

His stuff. My stuff. Everyone was worrying about their stuff . . . their papers . . . their possessions.

The bodies continued to float by, their heads bumping the starboard side.

Seeing those pitiful, fresh-dead bodies, I knew then what a mockery of life the materialistic concept is. After they got the telegram, someone would go through his "stuff" and try to figure out why in the world he wanted "all that stuff." The stuff that he kept so nice would eventually be thrown out of the basement, for the stuff would now be crap.

"Hey, throw this crap outta here!"

Chapter Five

Standing on the deck of a warship in battle, you get a good look at the competitive aspect of life, carried to its extreme.

Our society is based on competition. If it isn't impressed upon you at home with the scramble for love between brothers and sisters, they really lay it down to you in school—in numbers any child can understand—that's what grading is.

You bring home 100 percent, and your mother hugs you and your father pats you on the back. The teachers beam at you. But not your schoolmates; they know they're in competition with you, and if you get a high percentage they must get a lower one. Everybody wants love and acceptance and he soon learns that one way to get it is by getting higher marks than the other fellow.

In essence, you are gratified by your schoolmates' failures. We take this with us into adulthood. Just look at the business world.

So, my first instinct in this structure of economic and critical success is to want Mort Sahl, Jonathan Winters, Shelley Berman, etc., (my "schoolmates") to bomb. If I bring in a bigger gross at a café or a concert than Mort does at the same place, I've brought home a good report card.

I struggle with this part of me which is inhumane, and now—perhaps this can be explained by the fact that I am making enough money to *afford* to be magnanimous about it—I genuinely rejoice in another's success. I would like to believe that if I were still scuffling and Mort was doing well I would still be happy for him. But I wonder. I am happy he's doing well. But not better than me.

The U.S.S. Brooklyn was a big ship, and she was considered quite a danger and a nuisance by the enemy. At night the enemy planes, unless they had inside information, could only tell what they were bombing by the firepower that was thrown at them. If they received nothing but 20 millimeter and 40s, they would assume that the largest craft below was a DE or some other small craft that carried only small arms.

We were trapped in a strange bind. We were the only heavy power in the area, but if we threw up our big stuff—our five-inch guns—they would know immediately that we were a cruiser, and then they would send for assistance, and do us in.

When General Quarters sounded at sea, it was usually an E-boat or a submarine. I loved this because I wasn't as afraid of being killed in battle as I was of being bored. Lucky for me that the guys in power at the time knew the real danger and kept me occupied. I was grateful, but it was still pretty exhausting, fighting 60 hours without securing from battle stations.

Through three years and four major invasions—Anzio, Salerno, Sicily, Southern France—I was a shell passer with a heavy helmet that was lined with smelly foam rubber. Two years of sleeping in a hammock, then graduating to a lower bunk. Three years of hearing "Now hear this!" till I didn't want to hear it ever again. Three years of being awakened by a buzzer that made the sound that a gigantic goose would, laying an egg the size of a Goodyear Blimp.

Gonk! Gonk! Gonk! Gonk!—that was the base line. The boatswain's whistle and the trumpet just lacked a rhythm section to keep them from being real hard swingers.

The impersonal voice would boom over the speaker: "All men man your battle stations, secure all hatches, the smoking lamp is out."

I'd scramble up the ladder just in time to get my helmet knocked off and my nose bloodied from the concussion vacuum created in the hatch cove.

We would be bottled up in Naples harbor, the Germans bombing and strafing every ship in the bay. It was blindman's buff.

As a child I loved confusion: a freezing blizzard that would stop all traffic and mail; toilets that would get stopped up and overflow and run down the halls; electrical failures—anything that would stop the flow and make it back up and find a new direction. Confusion was entertainment for me.

While the War was on, the alternation of routine and confusion sustained my interest, but then it was over and I wanted out.

I had been a good sailor with a sterling record of consistent performance, but I wasn't a *mensch*. However, I didn't put the Navy through any red tape coming in, so I felt they should permit me to exit with the same courtesy. A lot of guys tried to get out during the War and I considered that cowardly, but I rationalized *my* schemes with: "Why not?—the War is over."

But how does one go about shooting his toes off with an oar?

We lay at anchor in the Bay of Naples and the night closed in around me. I had to get out, and get out fast. Other guys had gone wacky—some on purpose—and the only ones that got out were those who could just sit and say "No" to everything. They got out, but with a dishonorable discharge. And by the time they were processed, it was six months in the brig, a trial, and such a hard time that it wasn't worth it. I had to think.

You spend your whole life thinking and worrying. Worrying about the deposit bottles, and where to cash them. That night it seemed that getting out of the Navy, or even getting out of the Mediterranean, was years away. I wondered who was buying Mema her Vaseline.

I closed my eyes in the pitch-black night and then, all of a sudden, the heavens seemed to light up like Times Square. For a moment, I thought: "Oh-oh, I don't have to worry anymore; my problem has solved itself; I won't have to pretend." I recalled previous flashes on my optic nerves . . .

I am sitting at the Silver Dollar Bar in Boston, next to a girl with chipped, bitten-off, painted fingernails, and lipstick on her teeth. We are having our picture taken by the night-club photographer. *Flash!*

The first time I ever saw a flashlight, my cousin Stanley was sticking it in his mouth, making his cheeks all red.

Magic lights—the flash of lightning on choppy Long Island Sound as my Uncle Bill pulls in a flounder.

Fireflies through the window screens.

The lights in the Bay of Naples kept getting brighter and brighter. I wondered for an instant—is this the spiritual illumination I've read about? Will I see the Virgin of Fatima appear next?

My vision cleared and simultaneously I felt a smothering wave of factory heat—hotter than all the asphalt roads in Arizona put together. Mt. Vesuvius had erupted for the first time in centuries. Mt. Vesuvius, the earth that bore the tree, that bore the fruit, that fed man. The carbon process—each of us one molecule in the vast universe.

The earth that saw man destroy his competitor.

The earth that saw Italians killed. Italians—the Venetians, the brilliant colorists. The Italians that would soon clothe Miles Davis.

The earth saw this and vomited that night in Naples.

In the Army you can get out if you're a wack. Why couldn't you get out of the Navy if you were a WAVE?

Down in my bunk I had a copy of *Psychopathia Sexualis* by Krafft-Ebing. There it was.

A transvestite is a nut who likes to get dressed up in women's clothing. He may never engage in homosexual practice or do anything else antisocial. He's completely harmless. But obviously he would be an inconvenience to the Navy, where they like to keep everything organized by having everyone dress alike.

I figured that if I could demonstrate to the Navy that I still had a great deal of patriotism and loyalty to the uniform, the old *esprit de corps*—rather than indulging myself with the obvious sort of feather-boa negligee and gold-lamé mules drag outfit—then maybe instead of booting me out, they'd open the door politely and escort me out like an officer and a lady.

Swanson, one of my shipmates, could sew as well as a girl. He was also a beer addict. He'd do anything for a bottle of beer.

In North Africa, Gibraltar, Malta, Corsica, Sicily—wherever we made port—they had given us chits that entitled us to so much beer. I didn't drink beer, and I saved all my chits. Along with these—I won some gambling, and I also received quite a few for standing watch for different guys—I had enough beer chits to play Scrooge at an AA Christmas show.

I gave my chits to Swanson, and his fingers flew to the task. The way he threw himself into his work made me wonder about *him*. With the pleats, the shields, everything, he made me a lieutenant.

For a while it was just scuttlebutt that a WAVE was seen promenading forward at the fo'c'sle during the midnight watch. A number of guys who saw it didn't report it out of fear that they'd be given a Section 8 themselves. Finally one night I was doing my nautical Lady Macbeth when four guys, including the chief master-at-arms, jumped me.

I yelled, "Masher!"

Four naval psychiatrists worked over me at Newport Naval Hospital.

FIRST OFFICER: "Lenny, have you ever actively engaged in any homosexual practice?"

LENNY: "No, sir."

(An "active" homosexual is one who does the doing, and the "passive" is one who just lies back. In other words, if you were a kid and you were hitchhiking and some faggot came on with you and you let him do whatever his "do" was, he was an "active" homosexual because he performed a sexual act with someone of the same sex, and you are a "passive" homosexual if you allowed any of this to happen. You'll never see this in an AAA driving manual, but that's the way it is.)

SECOND OFFICER: "Do you enjoy the company of women?"

LENNY: "Yes, sir."

THIRD OFFICER: "Do you enjoy having intercourse with women?"

LENNY: "Yes, sir."

FOURTH OFFICER: "Do you enjoy wearing women's clothing?"

LENNY: "Sometimes."

ALL FOUR: "When is that?"

LENNY: "When they fit."

I stuck to my story, and they finally gave up. Only, it didn't work out the way I had figured it. They drew up an undesirable discharge.

At the last minute, though (this *does* sound like a fairy story, doesn't it?), the Red Cross sent an attorney who reviewed the case and saw that the whole thing was ridiculous. There were no charges against me. The entire division was questioned, and when it was ascertained that I had a good credit rating in virility—based upon paid-up accounts in numerous Neapolitan bordellos—I received an honorable discharge.

So everything worked out all right, except that they took away my WAVE's uniform. It bugged me because I wanted to have it as a sort of keepsake of the War. I wouldn't ever wear it, naturally—except maybe on Halloween.

Chapter
Six

The first place I went to when I got out of the Navy was back to the farm. I was anxious to show the Denglers my uniform and battle ribbons. And I wanted to see the Soapers down the road and the Ettletons across the way.

I got off the bus, and there were Mr. and Mrs. Dengler in the front yard, crating tomatoes. I ran over and threw my arms around Mrs. Dengler. She said "Hello" to me as if she had seen me only an hour before and I had just finished cleaning the stables.

I had written to them many times from overseas and had never received any reply, so I assumed they had sold the farm. I hadn't expected to see them now; I merely wished to find out where they moved. I couldn't believe they just wouldn't answer, because I'd thought our relationship had been so close.

"Didn't you get my letters?" I asked.

"Yes, thank you. We've been so busy we haven't even had time to do any canning."

I had expected . . . I don't know *what* the hell I had expected. Maybe some crying, or a big surprise cake; but instead Mr. Dengler simply climbed into the truck and his wife joined him.

"You put on some weight," she said. "Are you going to be around? Probably see you later."

And they drove off, leaving me staring at their dust.

Would I be around? I wept out of embarrassment. I felt like a clown in my uniform. The next train didn't go back to New York until 11 P.M.

I walked the six miles back to the station and just sat around, sort of half-hoping that Mrs. Dengler would come looking for me. She knew there were only three farmhouses in the area and only one train back to the city. She would go to each farm and inquire if I was there. Then she would rush off to the station and say, "Boy, you fell for the oldest trick in the world. You were really feeling sorry for yourself, weren't you? We were going to let you stay here another two hours just to tease you. I made a big surprise party cake for you, and all your friends can't wait to see you and hear all about how it was over there."

But no one came to the station.

I bumped into one kid I had known slightly, and he asked me if I was looking for a job. They wanted some beanpickers at the Ettletons'.

I knew then that this was all it had ever been: a job. Tom Wolfe was right when he said you can't go home again, but it's especially true when it was never your home to begin with. Still, you don't completely dissolve the fantasy . . .

Any minute that big black LaSalle would pull up, and my benefactress would make me secure with a sweater and a blow job, and the chauffeur would shake my hand and say, "Good show, son! It's grand to have the master home!" Then we would drive off to the little theater off Times Square, where Madame Chiang Kai-Shek would confide to me in the lobby that the Generalissimo hadn't taken off his stinking boy-scout uniform in 25 years; Franklin Delano Roosevelt would be standing up, pushing his wheel chair, screaming, "See the boardwalk in Atlantic City!"; my mother and father would be there—together—because they were never really divorced . . . they would kiss each other and say, "It's *all* over, Lenny, it was just a joke." Now everyone is seated, the lights come down, the conductor strikes up the last 32 bars of *Pins and Needles,* the curtains open, and there is Mema, reading a cereal box that explains what the big red-rubber bulb is for and telling the whole world: "It's Nobody's Business But Lenny's."

My mother had involved herself with a girl named Mary. In business, that is . . . my mother did not profess Will Rogers' paraphrased philosophy: "I never met a dyke I didn't like."

They taught ballroom dancing. My mother's name is Sally, so they combined names and came up with "The Marsalle School of Dance."

The school—a loft over Tony Canzoneri's liquor store—consisted of an office and a big room where their pupils (pensioners and other lonesome men that belonged to The Great Army of the Unlaid, but who were fortunate enough to be reaping the benefits of Mutual of Omaha) waited to learn the tango and the peabody.

The sad thing was that the women these men got to dance with were Mary and my mother.

There were lots of rooms over the dancing school that were condemned. The whole building, in fact, was condemned, except for the lower loft. I loved to hang out in my own special "condemned room." I would indulge myself in bizarre melodramatic fantasies, the spell usually being broken by my mother's request to empty the garbage.

If it was Monday I would take the garbage with me to the VA building, because to empty the garbage downstairs you had to separate the cans from the papers. The landlord insisted that you put the cans in one container and the papers in another. He was a real twisted nut in regard to his refuse-filing system.

"Miss Clark, check in the files of May 18, 1950, and bring me the eggshells and the coffee grounds and one orange peel . . ."

My reason for going to the Veteran's Administration (where I would just dump all the garbage, unsegregated, into a big wire basket) was the 52–20 Club. The Government gave all ex-GIs $20 a week for a year or until they could find a job. The accepted smart-thing-to-do was to find an employer who didn't report your wages or take out withholding tax, and then you could grab the $20 plus your salary.

I would fill out a report form, swearing that I had tried to find work that week. Which was true. I had asked my mother and Mema and two guys that sat next to me in a movie if they knew of any jobs.

When I finished filling out the weekly report, I noticed ink all over my fingers from one of those scratchy post-office pens. The man who invented them is the same guy who invented the wax napkins they give you with hot dogs. It doesn't wipe the mustard off; it rubs it in —like flavored Man-Tan.

I used a piece of newspaper to wipe the excess ink off my fingers. It contained a glowing account of Father Divine and all the money he was making. I stared at his picture and the amount. Then I went back to my "condemned room," carrying the work light from the dancing school. There was no electricity above the school floor; you just plugged in downstairs and carried up the extension.

I had my Fred Astaire fantasy, dancing up the steps with the light in my hand.

One day, while my mother was going through her "stuff"—four or five earrings that didn't match; six pairs of platform shoes in simulated lizard that she never wore; numerous bras with broken straps that she intended to mend some day; and, always, five or six crumpled-up Kleenex with traces of lipstick—she told me that she had decided to study eccentric dancing.

It was called "Legomania" or "Rubber Legs."

There was a fellow by the name of Joe Clooney who rented the studio to limber up early in the morning, for which he gave my mother a couple of dollars. After a while, he started trading her Legomania lessons for limbering-up space.

Within six months, Joe and my mother were doing an act together.

They started out by working hospitals and benefits, and then progressed to Saturday-night joints in Brooklyn; on Bergen Street, Ocean Parkway, or Coney Island. A short time later, Joe left the act and my mother was doing a single. The shows consisted of a comedian—master of ceremonies, a girl singer, a ballroom team, and my mother.

On one particular night, at the Victory Club on Ocean Parkway, the

master of ceremonies didn't show up. He had trouble with his car . . .
they found half-a-pound of pot in the trunk.

The owner asked my mother to m.c. She was petrified. She had never
spoken a single line on the stage before. Moreover, audiences were not used
to seeing a woman m.c. I had seen the master of ceremonies lots of times,
so I asked my mother if I could do it—what was so hard about, "Say, how
'bout a nice hand for the so-and-sos, folks?"

What with a quick meeting with the boss, and the law of supply and
demand, I was given my entree into show business.

It was about 15 minutes before showtime. I went into the men's room to
comb my hair. I pushed my pompadour as high as I could get it, and I put a
little burnt match on the mustache that I was sporting at the time. I was
really dap, with my sharp brown-suede shoes from A.S. Beck and a one-
button-roll suit from Buddy Lee's. It was *bar-mizvah* blue. I had a Billy
Eckstine collar, a black knit tie, and a five-point handkerchief, hand-rolled,
made in the Philippines, with the sticker still on it.

Should I wear my discharge button? No, I'll make it on talent alone.

Then I suddenly realized—I don't have any make-up! My first show and
no make-up. The men's-room attendant (sign, MY SALARY IS YOUR TIPS,
THANK YOU) had a can of white after-shave talc. I put that on, and in the
rush I dropped it and spilled it all over my brown-suede shoes. I don't know
if you've ever tried getting white talcum off brown-suede shoes, but it's worse
than trying to use leaves in the woods.

The men's-room attendant started getting nervous and staring at me. I
laughed it off and exited with my now brown-and-white-suede shoes.

The bandleader who was going to introduce me was doing a warm-up and
getting laughs. Loud laughs. He was using his clarinet in a manner that was
beyond mere phallic symbolism; he was swinging it between his legs and
singing "He's My Queer Racketeer . . ."

The cashier asked, "You nervous—want a brandy before you go on?"

"No, thanks. I don't know what the hell everybody is worrying about.
I've m.c.'d a million shows."

The ballroom team gave me their cues for applause. "Now, when I drop
the one knee, she comes up . . ."

Suddenly my feet began to get cold, and I was in the men's room, throwing
up. I was scared to death, and the attendant was flipping. It was five
minutes before showtime, all the waiters had been alerted, and a few of the
"regular" customers had developed anticipatory neurosis.

My mother looked at me from the opposite side of the room and pantomimed: "Your shoes are dirty!"

I again retreated to the men's room, but the attendant blocked my entrance
this time, and I threw up on a customer who was exiting.

I heard the strains of "Hi, Neighbor"—one of the standard night-club music intros—and I fled to the wings. My mother took one look at my powdered face and took me by the hand. I bolted away from her and into the ladies' room for one last purge.

I felt a wave of self-pity and identified with Aruzza, Manolete, Belmonte, and every other bullfighter—scared not of the bull but of the crowd. A crowd that waits: to be entertained, to view, *to judge*.

I heard the bandleader:

"Thank you, ladies and gentlemen. As you may know, our regular master of ceremonies, Tutti Morgan, is ill, due to a service-connected injury. Luckily, folks, show business has a big heart. A friend of his, Lenny Marsalle, a famous comic in his own right, who was in Guadalcanal with Tutti Morgan, is here in town to do the Ed Sullivan show, and when he heard that Tutti was sick he came right over to fill in—so how about it, folks, let's hear it for a great comedian and a great guy—Lenny Marsalle!"

I wiped my mouth with the square sheet of toilet paper that came in the container marked Onliwon, and made my grand entrance onto the stage direct from the ladies' room.

Actually, my function was quite simple. I was going out there and I was merely to say "Good evening," do a few straight lines and introduce the girl singer. But why did that bandleader have to say I was a "great comedian" and all that dishonest stuff about the Ed Sullivan show? Now they were all waiting for a great comedian.

But he also said I was a "great guy." Maybe, I hoped, that was more important to the audience, my being a "great guy" stuff. Maybe I could have my mother go out and say, "He's really a 'great guy' " and everybody would believe her because a mother knows her son better than anyone.

I saw a strange, silver, rather grotesque looking ball in front of my nose. It was a microphone. I was onstage.

"Good evening, ladies and gentlemen——"

"Bring on the broads!" cut me short. Oh, my God, a heckler! The angry request came from one of two guys standing near the bar; with them were two Lerner-clad ladies with the let-out hems, brown-and-white spectator pumps and whoopee socks, cloth coats with silver-fox collars that were a little too tight, and the final unique touch: lipstick on their teeth.

It shocked me into reality.

I looked at my mother and I saw a helpless smile. Her son, her baby that she nursed through chicken pox, working as a maid to sustain the both of us. Her child was in trouble and she couldn't help him.

Ma, help me; that boy hit me, Ma; gimme a quarter, Ma; I'm in trouble, Ma; I'm alone, help me, Ma . . .

"Bring on the broads!"

This time the request was more positive and energetic. The heckler must have sensed a weak, inexperienced prey. The two girls and the man with him bathed in his reflected glory. His friend joined him and they screamed in unison: "Bring on the broads!" Their lady friends shrieked with ecstasy.

"I'd like to, but then you wouldn't have any company at the bar."

My first laugh.

It was like the flash that I have heard morphine addicts describe, a warm sensual blanket that comes after a cold, sick rejection.

I was hooked.

My mother looked at me and really *schepped nachis* (which is the Jewish equivalent of "That's my boy!").

I introduced the first act, and an hour later, at the end of the show, when I was bringing my mother back for an encore, I said, "How about that, folks, Sally Marsalle—isn't she great?"

How about that for *silliness?* I'm telling a group of strangers: "Isn't my mother wonderful?" I had a dangerous desire to extend the tribute: "Yes sir, folks, not only can she dance, but she makes great chicken soup, and sweet lima beans, and when I'm sick she rubs my chest with Vicks."

When the evening was over, to my surprise the owner did not assume the Eduardo Ciannelli posture with the dialog that I had been conditioned to expect in the movie scene where the novice succeeds. Lyle Talbot always nods to Eugene Pallette: "You've done it again, Mr. Florenzo, this kid's sensational! We'd better sign him up before the Tio Bamba gets him."

I received no such gratification. As a matter of fact, he charged me for a meat-ball sandwich and ginger ale.

And when I stood on the subway platform and reached into my pocket for a dime, I found that the men's-room attendant had gotten even. I won't go into the scatological details; I threw the coat into the trash can.

But I'd had a smell of it and the aroma lingered.

Well, that's show business.

Chapter
Seven

I began to make the rounds of agents in Manhattan, and got in with Buddy Friar, an amateur agent with an office in the Roseland Building, now torn down.

There were 15 or 20 clubs—such as Squires in Long Island, the Clay Theater in New Jersey, George's Corners in Greenwich Village, the Blue Haven in Jackson Heights—that would put on amateur shows to fill in on slow nights. Supposedly, people from the audience would be called on as contestants. Actually, we were the forerunners of the rigged quiz shows.

The prizes were $100, $50, and $25. We "amateurs" would sit around the club, and when they called for volunteers we would get up. We were paid $2 apiece, carfare and, if we won, an empty envelope.

One of the other "amateurs" was a waiter from the Bronx who always sang *Sorrento*. When he reached the last four bars his face used to get red and his neck blue. I think he got a hand from the audience just for the fact that he lived through the number.

There was also some nut from Rye, New York, whose act consisted of standing on a chair, jumping straight up into the air and then diving and landing square on his head. Not on his hands, mind you; they were held tight to his sides. No, he would land smack on his goddamn head. It was a short act but it certainly was a hell of an opener.

There was another guy who played the sweet potato, doing a medley of patriotic songs like *The Caissons Go Rolling Along*. Then there was a performer known as "Al Jolson, Jr."—he was about 65 years old. And there was a girl acrobatic dancer who used to come to the club with all her lights, costumes, props, and her mother. I always wondered why no one ever caught on. Did they think that she just happened to drop in that night lugging all her paraphernalia?

Sometimes legitimate amateurs would try to get on, but they would be told that there wasn't enough time.

The winner was selected by holding a hand over the contestant's head and asking for applause. I never won. The sweet potato usually did. He had a limp and wore a double-size ruptured duck he had made especially for himself: you could see it from anywhere in the house. This gave me an idea for the first bit of material I ever did that caused controversy.

My agent had a pro date to fill on a Saturday night in Staten Island, at a place called The Melody Club. Since it had struck me funny that anyone who had been in the service would use that fact to gain rapport with the audience, I had a picture taken of all my campaign ribbons and medals (including a Presidential Unit Citation), had it enlarged, and put it on. I had the band play a big fanfare and *Anchors Aweigh*. Then I came out and said, "I stole this routine from Dick Powell and Ruby Keeler."

Right away one guy wanted to punch me in the nose for making fun of the ribbons. It was the first time I felt real hostility from an audience. And they'd missed the point.

The owner asked me to take the bit out for the second show. I tried to explain that I was trying to make fun of a guy who would do such a thing, not of the ribbons. He replied, "When in Rome do as the Romans do."

"OK, but I'll never play Rome again."

And I haven't played Staten Island since.

After four or five months of these amateur gigs, I wrote a little act for myself which eventually refined into the Hitler bit, wherein the dictator was discovered and handled by MCA. And I did all the standard impressions—Cagney, Lorre, Bogart—in double-talk German.

Marvin Worth, who later became a writer on the *Steve Allen Show*, had a lot of faith in my comedy prowess and decided to be my manager. He and his partner, Whitey Martin, and another agent, Bob Starr, got me on *Arthur Godfrey's Talent Scouts* show, which I won.

Within a few months I became "hot"—I was making $450 a week and working everything "good"—the Strand on Broadway, the Tick Tock in Milwaukee—and, around 1951, the consensus of showbiz opinion was, "Anybody can get a laugh with dirty toilet jokes; it takes talent to get laughs with clean stuff. You'll go a long way, Lenny, you're funny and clean."

Tears filtered through my lashes and rivered along each side of my nose. I was overcome with emotion—for I was blessed with talent; I didn't have to resort to dirty toilet jokes.

Then I started worrying . . . how dirty *is* my toilet?

I lay in bed, thinking about the "dirty-resort-to-anything-for-a-laugh" comedian. This could be the start of making the word "resort" dirty. Comedians who work resorts, entertaining people who go to resorts, are certainly resorting.

I couldn't contain my religious fervor. I exploded from the bedroom, thundered down the hall and threw open the door to that odious place—the "resort."

I screamed, "You dirty, filthy, stinky, crappy, Commie, dopey toilet! Thank God I don't have to resort to you to make people laugh. It's just a shame that there aren't laws to keep you and your kind out of a decent community. Why don't you go back where you came from? Take the tub and the sink and that jellyfish hamper with you! Even though their names aren't as dirty as yours, anybody who'd live with a toilet must be resort-addicted. Purists don't even go to the toilet. All I can say to you, toilet, is—it's lucky you're white!"

After theaters started closing and night clubs felt the absence of war, some show people couldn't get work and actually did have to resort to toilets. Not discussing them; cleaning them.

The first performers to feel the pressure were the magic acts. The agents' postwar cry was: "If I had a job, don't you think I'd be glad to give it to ya? They're not buying magic acts anymore. They're not buying dance teams anymore." The only place they could get a club date was at some broken-down Kiwanis hall, and even those were getting scarce.

What happens to people whose vocation becomes outmoded? (Elevator operators who are replaced by buttons—"What kind of a guy would want to be an elevator operator anyway?" Maybe some guy who just wants to return to a womb with a door he can open and close at different floors.)

Take Horace and Hilda, a dance team. They were a by-product of World War Two. Not a very good dance team; everything good was sent overseas to be killed. Horace handled the business, making the rounds of agents: Horace, fighting for breath in the abundance of the icy wind that trilled and wheezed around the Brill Building, echoing with the sound of a behemoth Goliath with bronchitis.

Horace and Hilda had met at the Arcadia Ballroom—"Dancing nitely, fun for all ages, no minors allowed." Hilda had been fortunate; she had a classical-ballet background received at the Borough Hall YWCA every Tuesday between eight and nine P.M., immediately after the public-speaking-salesmanship class.

She had a big keester and no nay-nays. She was built like a pear. Ballet helped her so she didn't have any fat. Rather, she was very muscular. A muscular pear. With shoes from Kitty Kelly's, net stockings that had been sewn so many times they looked like varicose veins, and black satin tights, the crotch not exactly split, but giving.

The top of her outfit was solid sequined—she loved it and the dry cleaner hated it. A tap dancer had sold it to her when Horace and Hilda were playing the State Theatre in Baltimore. The tap dancer said she wasn't going to use it anymore because a choreographer was planning to set a new number for her with college sweaters and megaphones, so Hilda got it at a steal for eight dollars. The hoofer had originally bought it from a drag queen she worked with at the Greenwich Village Inn when they had straight acts. They had female impersonators and then the straight acts would work in between. The drag queen said he paid $12 at Maharam's for the sequins alone.

Horace lived flamenco and spent all of his time in the rehearsal halls striking the classic flamenco pose. The way he stood looked to Hilda as if he were applauding his ass. Horace was a faggot, an out-and-out flaming faggot. He didn't swish but he was sort of like an old auntie. He was so obvious that everyone knew he was a faggot except Hilda and her family. They didn't know because they were very religious and Horace acted just like a lot of ministers she had seen in her formative years.

Horace had chosen show business because it was best for him since he was so obviously nellie; not that show people have more of a Christian attitude toward their fellow men and are less likely to look askance at one who is out of step—it's just that their egos are so big and they are so self-centered that they haven't the time to concern themselves with the individual and his problems.

As with drug addicts, Horace's homosexual traits were environmental. He wasn't "born that way." He was introduced to a group once that gave him *identity*. He was a stock boy at Macy's and after one summer at Atlantic City he came back a faggot. He could just as easily have come back a junkie or a water skier or a Jehovah's Witness—the point is, he came back as *something*.

"At least I'm something," is the keynote. "I belong to a group. I share their notoriety, their problems, their laughter." In a crowded arena, the cliché "It takes one to know one" is actually a profound philosophy.

At any rate, Horace blossomed in this anthropophagous society. He became poetic in his facility to relate in the argot of the citizens of Groupery in the county of Padded Basketdom—the esoteric delight in passing a complete stranger and shrilling, "Get you, Annie!"; the same idiomatic rapport of the nighttime junkie who is looking to score. Horace became a faggot simply because he wanted to belong.

Well, the Korean War weeded out some of the population and helped the housing problem, but it didn't leave the dramatic impact that World War Two did. As the impact lessened, so did the desire to escape lessen. And all the escape hatches—the bars, night clubs, theaters—felt it. And the people who depended economically upon these media also felt it.

Horace and Hilda were part of this milieu.

I was luckier. Comedy is an amorphous craft in the sense that there are no academies, there are no formulas. There are no books on comedy that can train an aspirant to command a salary of $200,000 a year, but it is a craft and it can be learned.

The reports on me were now: "All Lenny Bruce seems concerned with is making the band laugh." That should have been my first hint of the direction in which I was going: abstraction. Musicians, jazz musicians especially, appreciate art forms that are *extensions* of realism, as opposed to realism in a representational form.

The Club Charles in Baltimore was my last bomb, then. The owner asked me if I had any good numbers like "The Golf Lesson." This was sort of a devitalized Dwight Fiske routine, with nothing left but the subtle swish. I told the owner I didn't have any good numbers like that.

Jack Paar, Sophie Tucker, Joe E. Lewis and the other comedy performers of their generation grew up in our culture at a time when the discussion of sex was secretive and chic, so that the *double-entendre* comedian was considered quite daring. It delighted the customer to be "in"—"Ha, ha, you know what *that* means, don't you?"

My generation knows—and accepts—what *that* means, so there is no need for humor in that whoopee-cushion vein.

This is not an indictment of the performers of that era, for I know (and it disturbs me greatly) that soon I will be out of touch. I am 39 and already I can't relate to Fabian.

There's nothing sadder than an old hipster.

Chapter
Eight

In between the club dates, there were many theaters in the New York area that had vaudeville for one night. You got $17.50 for a single and a two-person act got about $25. All the acts were working these dates just to have a showcase; the money was secondary (because that's when the rent was due—on the second).

The announcement would read:

VODVIL EVERY FRI., SAT., SUN.
BINGO EVERY TUES.
FREE DISH TO LADIES
RKO Jefferson, Fourteenth Street.

Rehearsals were at 7:30 P.M., shortly after I got off the crosstown shuttle and cranked out a penny's worth of semifaded chocolate-brown nuts. How the hell did those nuts get faded in a vending machine down in the dark subway? Maybe they were nickel nuts that didn't sell in Miami because of a short season and they were shipped here next. I never knew the precise ingredients of the chocolate, but they were superior to M. & M.s—they wouldn't melt *anywhere*, let alone in your mouth.

(The vending machine on 42nd near Hubert's Museum was the best. It was integrated with engagement rings, wee harmonicas and teeny red dice.)

I washed down the peanuts with a Nedick's hot dog from the orange-drink stand next to the theater.

CLARK GABLE—SPENCER TRACY
BOOM TOWN
ROUGH, RAW, RIPPING!
MEN WITH HEARTS OF IRON
AND FISTS OF STEEL

The movie would be on and you'd just have a talk-over rehearsal with the five band guys in their room which was behind the pit, or sometimes in back of the screen. The backstage manager wasn't a kindly old man called Pop; he was a cranky motherfucker who kept yelling, "How many times am I going to tell you assholes there's no smoking back here!"

Prince Paul and Company, a brother-and-sister high-wire act, were bitching at their outdoor agent. They had never worked in the States. He had seen them at Wallace Brothers' Circus while they were touring in Canada and he was selling stocks in between bookings. He talked them into coming to New York with a promise of getting them on the Ed Sullivan show or a date at the Latin Quarter. They explained to him that they had never worked in any night clubs since their act required a 15-foot ceiling clearance after their rig was up. Altogether they needed about 53 feet.

For $25, the Prince had been sweating out 7 hours of rig assembly, reworking the antiquated floor plates that were in the theater; he completely severed the tip of his forefinger and badly bruised his knee with a miscalculated hammer swing; and he got fed up with Horace playing Florence Nightingale with his cold compresses and shrieks of "You're so *strong*."

With no cooperation from an unsympathetic theater manager who played 15 different acts a week, Prince Paul had just finished stripping a lug nut thread on the second guide wire when he heard the backstage manager yell, "What the hell do you people think this is, a goddamn rehearsal hall? You better make sure you clean up every bit of that crap after you're finished!"

The Prince kissed his severed forefinger, chucked Horace in the ass, walked over to the water cooler, picked up the stage manager and threw him directly through the center of the screen, just after Spencer Tracy had walloped Clark Gable on the chops, knocking him down. The audience thought the stage manager was Clark Gable getting up.

I wonder if somebody who saw him flying out envisioned at that moment the commercial potentialities and formulated the idea for Cinerama.

They took the Prince to the 36th Precinct, leaving his sister alone with the grim prospect of doing a nine-minute act with no partner. I can't describe the expression on her face when she looked up and saw the rig. From the top of the bar there was only three feet to the ceiling.

I crouched on my haunches in the wings as Prince Paul and Company was introduced as a double. I waited to see what the hell she was going to do as a single, with not enough room to recline, much less stand.

She went out and did eight minutes; she chinned herself 571 times.

During this post-War period, I was afraid I didn't have it as a comedian. I had the mental facility, but I didn't have the psychological capacity to accept rejection, which I sure got a lot of in those days. It was after work in one of those showbiz restaurants—the Hanson's of Baltimore, where everybody has his picture hanging on the wall—that I bumped into Tommy Moe Raft, who was a terrifically funny burlesque comic. I had seen him work several times and admired him immensely.

Sitting next to him was a stripper who was the most beautiful woman I had ever seen in my life.

She had long red hair that she actually sat on. She had a face that looked like a kindergarten teacher's. Since she was obviously a natural redhead, she wore very little make-up, stood about five feet, seven inches tall, and had strength-and-health-club measurements. Her firm alabaster breasts that were mapped with light, delicate blue veins, showed from her low-cut Frederick's of Hollywood dress, and I suddenly realized the attraction: Honey Harlowe was a composite of the Virgin Mary and a $500-a-night whore.

I sat with Tommy and he introduced us. Then he invited me to a party that she also was attending.

I took a cab there and walked up the stairs, heading for the door with the noise. The host was a manufacturer of aluminum awnings, and he "just loved show people." They used to give parties and get drunk, and then the husband would love *his* show people (the strippers and the girl singers) and the wife would love *her* show people (the acrobats and the m.c.s).

Everybody at this party was sober, and quite proper. Some people were exchanging cute little off-color jokes, and a few intellectuals were discussing the decadence and lack of culture in Baltimore. Honey and I just stared at each other and got hot.

Suddenly, right there on the sofa, in the midst of 20 to 30 people, we were hugging and kissing and rubbing and groping and embarrassing everyone at the party.

This was something special. I knew, and I didn't want to know it. Besides, who wanted "something special"? I was half-glad and half-sorry when I realized I wouldn't be around long enough to find out; I had made previous plans to ship out on a merchant ship after the Baltimore engagement. I was bored and depressed, so I had signed up.

If I had met Honey before, maybe I wouldn't have.

Chapter Nine

I was on the Luckenbach Line bound for Turkey, Greece, Marseilles, back to the Mediterranean I couldn't wait to get out of a few years before.

Two ships performed the same function—transporting men and objects across the Atlantic from one place to another; one place was Pier 92 on New York's West Side, the other was Marseilles—the two ships were the U.S.S. Brooklyn and the Samuel Brown. And I was on them both.

Samuel Brown might live in Brooklyn—but in Red Hook, not in Seagate. He alone could never attain the stature of all the individual little people in all the neighborhoods from Kensington and Bay Ridge to Bensonhurst and Coney Island who collectively make up the borough—rich, influential and powerful. That essentially is the difference between the merchant marine and the United States Navy. But though the merchant seaman commands less social esteem (there are no campaigns to write letters to the boys on tramp steamers and no USO shows at Christmastime), he makes more money and has an easier life, which are a pair of compensatory factors carrying no small weight.

Whereas in the Navy I scrubbed the decks aft of the 5th Division Fire Control Tower every morning—whether or not it was dirty—in the merchant marine the boatswain would say, "The deck around the forward hatch is getting mangy, Schneider. Grab some red lead and paint it." That was the prevailing climate: If it's dirty, paint it; if it's broken, "deep-six" it. "Deep sixing," although frowned upon by the ship's owners, is quite a common practice. This is the procedure, one which you will never find elaborated upon by Jack London:

A 300-foot steel cable, used for mooring, has become frayed and is in need of repair. Rope splicing is comparatively simple, but cable is a combination of threaded steel and hemp, and when it breaks under the strain, the seven-strand splicing is a wicked job. You can't work it properly with gloves, and without them, it is like trying to wrestle a barracuda.

I have struggled with four or five pretty husky guys, bending and twisting the hawser while it lashed around the deck as if it were alive. At the end of several hours our hands were so cut up that we looked as if we had butchered a cow in our blood-spattered levis. Everybody goes through this. Once you've *been* through it you are automatically inducted into the "Deep-Six Club." The initiation ceremony consists of simply throwing the cable into the ocean.

This fraternal rite cannot always be practiced in broad daylight without some sort of subterfuge, which usually comprises raising furious alarm in one part of the ship while the surplus goods are debarked over the side at another. In the Caribbean or anchored off Corsica, for instance, where the weather is warm and the water tepid, one Deep-Six Club member would volunteer to fall overboard. This was a drastic measure, to be sure, taken only when a whole set of lockers or bunks needed repainting.

"Waste not, want not" was not the merchant seaman's motto, then. Only those excluded from membership—the captain, the purser, etc.—disapproved of the Deep-Six Club. This was because they remained on the ship, whereas, for the most part, seamen sign on for one voyage and quit. Very few re-sign for the same ship. This is one indication of the character of men in this area of work. Their attitudes and relationships, personal as well as toward their work, are of a temporary nature. You may form friendships of remarkable intimacy, sharing the details of each other's lives, and then never see each other again.

I shared a compartment with two West Indian Negroes who were immaculate in their personal habits, and quite entertaining to listen to. They had a unique sound: "Mon, what de hell awr ye tawkin' about? You don't speek de king's Hinglish!"

They were marvelous seamen, and one of them with whom I became very friendly, Caleb Chambers, had been all over the world 60 times. It never failed to amaze me that he was as much at home in North Africa, Casablanca or Gibraltar as he was in San Pedro, California. It really knocked me out to hear him give directions. I've traveled the States extensively, but my knowledge of places is extremely limited. I can tell you how to get from the Civic Center in Los Angeles to Hollywood and Highland Boulevard, or how to get from O'Hare Airport in Chicago to Mister Kelly's on Rush Street, but so could Caleb.

He could also tell you how to get from the Medina in Casablanca to the Valleta in Malta, and advise you on the fastest, cheapest way to get there. But what really bugged me was that he was so familiar with everything everywhere that sometimes, when we would hit port, he wouldn't even bother going ashore. Imagine docking in Istanbul and staying on ship!

I have been to about 30 different countries and I'm ashamed to admit that my knowledge of the sights, culture, art and customs is on a par with the limited perspective of any other sailor. In Lisbon, the only place I know is the American Bar and Madame Krashna's. The same in Marseilles, Oran, Algiers, Izmir. The only place I know a little bit about is Libya. That's because the whorehouses are off limits. If you get caught in one of them, a fine and a jail sentence are mandatory.

I am enough of a snob to not mind having a record for jewel theft, embezzling or safecracking; but doing time for getting caught in a whorehouse would really be humiliating.

This is a warped concept, I realize. We Americans have a negative attitude toward prostitution that is not shared by foreign peoples. Even the words "French brothel" sound exotic, nearly romantic, compared to "cathouse." And they *are* more romantic. They cater to the imagination and the spirit as well as the body. Here, it's disgustingly cut and dried.

In Marseilles, for example, there was a place called Madame Claridge's that was delightful. They had an Arabian jazz trio, a bar and, of course, lots of girls. They charged admission, which I suppose you could call a "cover charge." Many guys used to go there just to drink and absorb a part of culture few American men ever experience.

If a guy walks into an American bar with the thought of picking up a girl, he will get an audible, hostile rejection from at least 90 percent of the women he approaches. And a painful physical rejection from the boyfriends of some of the other 10 percent when they return from the men's room. At Madame Claridge's, however, if you had a neurotic imagination, you could pretend that you were walking into an American bar and that every girl you tapped (you had your choice of 20 or 30 beautiful ladies) was willing to go upstairs with you.

"It seems I can't go into a bar anymore for an innocent glass of sherry without a dozen women begging me to take them to bed. I'm really devastating. All right, all right, if you insist, one at a time . . ."

Their return English is always questioning, in the few broken phrases they know: "How much you got?" "Short time?" "All night?" "Costume show?"

The costume show is an institution that might well be studied by clinical psychologists. Although I assume none of these girls has ever read Krafft-Ebing, I am sure they are instinctively cognizant of the many erotic fetishes that men have and are willing to pay for in order to have them catered to.

The costume show cost 1000 francs extra, which in those days was about $20. This might seem expensive, but we were getting $10 a carton for cigarettes that we bought tax-free for about 50 cents a carton.

You had a choice of basic settings—rooms complete with the particular decor required by the girl in costume to play her part.

1. *The Housewife Room.* The room was decorated like a homey kitchen. The girl wore a white cotton dress, an apron, no make-up, her hair pulled back simply in a bun. I didn't understand French, but since she had a complete routine memorized I called in a friend to translate for me. "Ah, Antoine, you naughty boy, you are late again. Tsk, tsk, tsk. You are making your poor mother gray with worry. Ah, *quel dommage,* you look disturbed,

my son. Here, sit by Momma. There, that is better, no? See, I'll massage your back. But don't do anything naughty to me. Antoine! Antoine! What are you doing? I am your mother! In a moment I will have to ask you to stop . . ."

2. *The Seminary.* This cost 2000 francs, but it was worth it. The room was a bare monastery cell with only a wooden table, some straight chairs and a straw pallet. Religious statues, pictures and candles were everywhere. The "towel girl" led me in and left me alone there, and as I looked about I was furious that when I would tell my friends in the States about it, they would think it was a lie. Not only that but they might have me committed. And I was at least as sane as the hundreds of men who visited this place *seriously,* men who we would consider decadent and degenerate, and more than that, in some twisted way, fanatically religious.

In a moment my thoughts were interrupted by a beautiful "nun," complete in her habit, white starched headpiece, cross around her neck, gold wedding band and all. I was so excited that I offered her a 2000-franc tip if she would just sit and talk to me in her broken English; that was a twist—a nun confessing to me. I was fascinated with her description of the operation. Some of her stories made my hair stand on end. But she really threw me into a laughing fit when she told me that a large percentage of her customers were priests. It's true that my philosophy is antiorganized religion but I am not making this up.

She told me that she'd had a few rabbis, too.

3. *The Nursery.* This was a sunny little room with small furniture, and an actual crib, with animal pictures and Mother Goose characters painted on the walls. There were all sorts of toys, a rocking horse, a music box, and lots of dolls. The girl was dressed in a little starched white organdy dress, and she acted as if she were no more than 12 years old. One of the musicians, who was her fiancé, told me later that she made more money than all the other girls put together. Especially in tips from men who got gratification from ripping the clothes off her, literally tearing her outer and undergarments to shreds. Of course it put a lot of physical strain on her because most of these men demanded that she struggle, for they desired not the sexual act so much as the illusion that they were violating her.

4. *The Torture Chamber.* Again, macabre though I be, I am not making this up. If this were a production of the Grand Guignol it would have in the program, "Sets and costumes by the Marquis de Sade." The walls were blood red and adorned with whips and instruments of torture of all descriptions. There were pictures of men and women in every conceivable pose of suffering and debasement. A record played the *Danse Macabre.* When the girl entered, made up in a satanic manner, wearing a long black Dracula cape, I really shuddered. She bolted the door. She meant business! How could I tell her I was only window-shopping?

She took off the cape purposefully. Underneath she wore only brief black panties and a push-'em-up bra, arm-length leather gloves, and what looked like hip-length leather-laced stockings with spike heels that were easily six-inches high. She walked toward me and menaced me with a riding crop, raised it over her head and screamed something in French, baring her sharp white teeth. Just as in nearly every other delicate situation in my life, I began to laugh. She got quite insulted and threw me out.

I had laughed myself right out of a beating.

What do you suppose would happen to a nonconformist in an American cathouse?

Chapter
Ten

When I talk on the stage, people often have the impression that I make up things as I go along. This isn't true. I know a lot of things I want to say; I'm just not sure exactly when I will say them. This process of allowing one subject spontaneously to associate itself with another is equivalent to James Joyce's stream of consciousness.

I think one develops a style like that from talking to oneself. I don't actually talk to myself out loud—"Hello, Lenny, how are you today?"—rather, it's a form of *thinking*. And out at sea you have a lot of time to think. All day and all night I would think about all kinds of things.

Sometimes I would talk out loud up on the bow, where tons of water actually bend the shield plate. You would never figure water to be so hard that it could bend steel, but I've seen it happen.

In the spring, however, the Atlantic Ocean is very pleasant, and the trip isn't so bad. The first land you sight is a thrilling experience. I must have played Columbus hundreds of times. It was really fun, standing those bow watches all alone.

I always felt that the Azores were going to sink, because on the map they're just a bunch of little dots. And everything that's *on* the Azores is shipped in. There was even a Turkish seaman who had gotten an attack of appendicitis on board his ship, and they had let *him* off at the Azores, where we picked him up.

He bunked with Caleb and me. He had a little leather bag in which he kept all his worldly possessions. He didn't speak any English, but when he sat down on the bunk, I tried to communicate with him anyway, asking him what had happened to him, although we already knew.

People are the same the world over. Just like an old lady from the Bronx, he proudly showed us his appendix scar.

I gave him two candy bars which he devoured immediately, and Caleb gave him soap and a towel. He scowled at us, and I guessed that probably in his country a towel and soap meant only one thing—that you were in *need* of same. I tried to explain in sign language. I sniffed him and smiled, in order to show that we *all* have towels and soap to keep in our lockers *if* and *when* we need them.

He wrote his name in Turkish for us, and we wrote our names in English for him. It seemed to be turning out like a Richard Halliburton story.

But then he opened his little bag and offered us something. I didn't know what the hell it was. It looked like bunches of strips of leather. I asked Caleb if he knew what it was, and he said maybe it was some sort of "good-luck leather." He took a piece and pushed it toward my face, and I pantomimed to the Turk: "Should we eat it?"—and then it dawned upon him that we didn't know what it was.

He gestured for a knife and a cigarette. He took the cigarette and opened it up, dumping the tobacco out on the bench; then he started chopping up the leather and the cigarette tobacco, until he had it evenly mixed. He took a pipe from his bag, filled it, and lit it. Oh that was it—some sort of religious ritual like the Indians have on first meeting—a peace pipe.

The tobacco was rather strong, and we passed it around several times, but when the pipe came to me the fifth time, for no apparent reason Caleb looked hysterically funny to me, and I started to laugh, and Caleb started to laugh, until we were carrying on like a couple of damned idiots.

"Oh, my God, this son of a bitch has us smoking hashish!"

As soon as I got the word out, he nodded and laughed, too. We smoked some more, and when it came time to go on watch, the relief man came and said, "Time to go topside," and I thought that was the funniest goddamned thing I'd ever heard in my whole life.

We laughed so hard that it scared the relief man, and he went away and didn't bother us anymore.

Within a week I could communicate perfectly with Sabu (the name I'd christened him). I made Harpo Marx look slow. I'm sure Vincent Price would have been honored to have me on his team on the TV version of charades.

No matter how hard I tried, though, I couldn't make Sabu believe that it was against the law on American ships to smoke dope. He wanted to know why, and I honestly couldn't tell him. He asked me what I used to get high, I told him whiskey, and he was horrified.

Since then, I've learned that Moslems do not drink. But they sure smoke a lot of that lovelorn. It's based on their religious-health laws. Imagine that: religious laws to smoke dope. But here's the capper: They're right. Alcohol is a caustic that destroys tissues which cannot be rebuilt. It is toxic, and damages one of the most important organs in the body—one that cannot repair itself or be repaired—the liver. Whereas, for example, no form of *cannabis sativa* (the hemp plant from which marijuana is made) destroys any body tissue or harms the organs in any manner.

This is a fact that can be verified by any chemistry professor of any university in the United States. Nevertheless, the possession of marijuana is a crime:

PUBLIC DEFENDER: Your Honor, I make a motion that the prosecution's statement, "Was involved and did encourage others to partake in this immoral degenerate practice" be stricken from the record. The word "immoral" is entirely subjective and not specific.

JUDGE: Objection overruled. Existing statutes give this word, in the context used, legal credence. Can counselor refer to an existing statute that labels marijuana users as moralists?

PUBLIC DEFENDER: Which moralists are we using as criteria? Sherman Adams? Earl Long? Jimmy Walker? Or does the court refer to the moralists who violated Federal law—segregationists, traitorous anarchists that have given ambiguity to the aphorism, "Of the people, by the people, for the people. . . ." Or the moralist who flouted Federal law—the bootleg coffers flowing with billions, illegal whiskey drunk by millions. A moral standard that gives mass criminal rebellion absolution? In the realm of this subject, the Defense requests that the six men on this jury be disqualified on the grounds of unfitness.

JUDGE: Can the Public Defender qualify this charge?

PUBLIC DEFENDER: The Defense submits these qualitative and quantitative documents in answer to the Court's query.

JUDGE: (Reading the documents aloud.) ". . . And these six jurors have sworn in the presence of a notary that their daily alcoholic consumption, martinis for lunch and manhattans before dinner, totals an average of a half-pint per day. Jurist also stated motivations for drinking: 'Gives me a lift.' 'Need a boost once in a while.' 'After a frustrating day at the office a couple of belts lift me out of the dumps.' " I fail to see the merit in your plea to disqualify. What is your point, succinctly?

PUBLIC DEFENDER: One cannot cast the first stone—if already stoned. (Dissolve to interior of jury room and new set of jurors.)

FIRST WOMAN: You know, I was thinking, that Public Defender was right. A crutch is a crutch no matter if it is made of wood or aluminum.

SECOND WOMAN: A couple of those jurors gave me the creeps anyway. That one with the thick fingers looked like a real moron.

THIRD WOMAN: And the other one with those sneaky eyes. I can always tell a person's character by his eyes.

FIRST WOMAN: To serve on a jury in a civil case is easy, but when you're dealing with drug addicts it's rough. This damned jury duty has me a nervous wreck. I had to take five sleeping pills to get some rest last night. You build up a tolerance to the damned things so quickly. I feel miserable today. I'm really dragging.

SECOND WOMAN: Here, take one of these Dexies.

FIRST WOMAN: What are they for?

SECOND WOMAN: They're amphetamine, Dexedrine Spansules. My doctor gave them to me for depression and fatigue. They really give you a lift. I take them all the time except when it's "that time of the month"—then I take Demerol.

THIRD WOMAN: (*Rummaging through her purse and producing a handful of pills.*) Do you know what these red-and-white ones are? My neighbor's doctor gave them to her to try out. They're supposed to be for nerves. Better than Miltowns.

SECOND WOMAN: Oh, these are Deprols. Umm, no, wait a minute, I think they're phenobarbs.

(*An elderly woman juror, silent until now, turns and speaks.*)

ELDERLY WOMAN: Come on, ladies. We need a verdict. What are we going to do with this man?

FIRST WOMAN: Oh, yes—the dope addict. How does a person sink that low?

So I do not understand the moral condemnation of marijuana, not only because of its nontoxic, nonaddicting effects as contrasted with those of alcohol, but also because, in my opinion, caffeine in coffee, amphetamine, as well as all tranquilizers—from Miltown to aspirin to nicotine in cigarettes—are crutches for people who can face life better with drugs than without.

Part of the responsibility for our indiscriminate use of drugs is the doctors'. How often does a patient say to his doctor, "Doc, I have this cold coming on—can't you give me a shot?" And the doctor does, although the patient might just as easily get over the cold without it. One of the reasons for this is that the doctor realizes that most people do not feel that they've gotten their money's worth if they haven't gotten "a shot."

But the doctor also knows that constant inappropriate usage of penicillin and aureomycin and other antibiotics is breeding strains of bacteria that are resistant to these drugs, so that not only will their protective qualities be lost in the future if ever they are desperately needed, but more and more people are suffering from dreadful drug "reactions"—swelling, itching, and sometimes even death. And every day the ads and the TV commercials bombard us with new things to swallow so we can take the modern way to normal regularity—things to drink, chew, gargle, stick into ourselves. It's Nature's way . . .

Surprisingly enough, there are actually psychotics in high public places that have been reported to have *sympathetic* feelings concerning the stiff penalties received by the marijuana users and narcotics offenders. Judging from the newspapers and movies, one would believe that drug users are sick, emotionally immature, degenerates, psychos, unstable. They are not right in the head. They are *weirdos*. So, I would assume, they belong in jail with all the other crazy people.

Or do you believe all that crap about mental-health programs? I mean, you don't actually believe there *are* crazy people, do you? You don't actually believe people are emotionally unstable, do you? A person is only bad because he wants to be. You can do anything you want. Anything. You can memorize 12,000,000 different telephone books—all the names inside them.

Or *can* you do anything you want? Do you perhaps believe in the *existence* of mental illness, but still feel that treatment for the mentally ill should be duplexed? Good nuts, the ones who blow up trains with 300 people or repeatedly try to kill themselves, should be sent to Bellevue or other institutions equipped with mental-health programs; but bad nuts, who try to kill themselves with heroin or other narcotics, should be sent to jail.

After all, what's the sense of sending a heroin addict to a hospital for intensified therapy and perhaps curing him in three years, when you can have him in and out of jail three times over a period of *ten* years? Then, the last time, you've got him for good!

I don't know about you, but I rather enjoy the way tax money is spent to arrest, indict, convict, imprison, parole, and then re-imprison these people. I'd just piss it away on beer, anyway.

I must admit that, since a certain incident, I've never given a penny to mental health. I shan't mention the city in which this occurred because I have no desire to cause any trouble for the individual involved (although, what with his being a genuine masochist, he might *love* the trouble). And certainly I have no moral judgment to bestow on him—which others certainly would, if they recognized him from my description.

I discovered the truth about this guy through a friend of mine, this chick who was a hooker; the guy was one of her tricks. Anyway, this *noffka* told me about a trick who didn't want anything but a good beating. He was willing to pay from $100 to $500, depending upon how ingenious and sadistic the amusement she devised for him was each evening.

She described the guy in detail to me: his home, his personal appearance, right down—or up—to his toupee.

Then, another hooker, who, I'm positive, didn't know the first chick, told me about this same trick one night and said that he had asked her to bring her boyfriend along to help work him over. She was a little wary about asking her boyfriend to do this because he was a rather surly type and inclined, perhaps, to get a little carried away with his work, which was important to avoid, because this trick insisted that he was never to be hit above the shoulders. He was an important man and had to travel in respectable business circles, and couldn't afford to have his scars seen in public.

She asked me if I would accommodate her that evening and punch him around a bit. Somehow, I didn't feel quite up to it—I don't know, maybe I'm just a sissy—and I graciously declined her offer. I was sorry about it afterward, because the next day she saw me and complained that they hadn't been paid because, sure enough, her boyfriend had gotten a little overexuberant and given the trick a black eye and a swollen jaw.

Now here's the capper, and I swear it is true. That afternoon there was a meeting of the heads of the mental-health campaign, and I had been asked to contribute my services as a performer to a fund-raising show they were organizing. I attended the meeting with the other acts, planning the billing and staging, and so forth, and we had to wait for about ten minutes for the president of the committee to arrive. I had met the gentleman before, a very imposing, robust businessman with a brusque good nature and a toupee that nearly matched the graying hair at his temples.

Till the moment he walked in, I had never connected him with that trick, nor would I have in a million years. But there he was, black eye, swollen jaw and all. It was like a cheap old Charlie Chan movie; the chief of police turns out to have committed the series of brutal murders.

Immediately everyone displayed great concern over him. "What happened?" "You poor thing!" "Oh, my God, George, look at your eye!"

He sat down wearily and told his tale:

"I was coming out of the Plymouth House last night, about two in the morning, meeting with the board from the United Fund, you know, and in the parking lot there were these two chaps attacking a young girl. Well, I grabbed one of them and knocked him out and clipped the other one, when six more jumped out from behind a car. You see, it was a setup: the girl was in on it—part of the gang, I guess. The next thing I knew, I was flat on my back. I mean I couldn't handle them *all*."

"Were there any witnesses?" I asked.

"No. At two o'clock in the morning, I might just as well have been alone in the jungle."

"Weren't there any cops around?"

"No. Isn't that the damnedest thing, Len? It's always that way—when you want a cop, you can't find one. They're too busy giving out tickets."

"Well," piped up the inevitable cliché expert, "it's a lucky thing you didn't get killed."

"Yes," he agreed philosophically, "I guess I am lucky, after all."

I thought to myself: He probably would *love* to get killed, if only somehow he would be able to live through it to enjoy it.

I am not trying to project an image of myself as pure, wholesome and All-American. Again, I certainly am not making any value judgment of others and attempting to put myself on a high moral level above anyone else. As I have said, I have indulged myself in houses of prostitution.

I try to keep in mind that the only difference between a Charles Van Doren, a Bernard Goldfine, a Mayor Curley or a Dave Beck, and me, is that they got caught. I am always offended by a judge or district attorney with an Academy Award sense of moral indignation. I have great respect for the offices of law enforcement and preservation, but I'll never forget that William O'Dwyer was the D.A.

I love my country, I would give allegiance to no other nation, nor would I choose any other for my home, and yet if I followed a U.S. serviceman and saw the enemy bind him, nude, face down, and then pour white-hot lead into a funnel that was inserted in his keister, they wouldn't even have to heat another pot for me. I would give them every top secret, I would make shoeshine rags out of the American flag, I would denounce the Constitution, I would give them the right to kill every person that was kind and dear to me.

Just don't give me that hot-lead enema.

So that's how low I am. That's what I would resort to, to keep that lead out of my ass. I spent four battle years in the Mediterranean and saw starving priests, doctors and judges. I saw ethics erode, again, according to the law of supply and demand.

So I am not offended by war in the same way that I am not offended by rain. Both are "motivated" by need.

I was at Anzio. I lived in a continual state of ambivalence: guilty but glad. Glad I wasn't the GI enjoying that final "no-wake-up-call" sleep on his blood-padded mud mattress. It would be interesting to hear his comment if we could grab a handful of his hair, drag his head out of the dirt and ask his opinion on the questions that are posed every decade, the contemporary shouts of: "How long are we going to put up with Cuba's nonsense?" "Just how many insults can we take from Russia?"

I was at Salerno. I can take a lot of insults.

War spells out my philosophy of "No right or wrong"— just "Your right, my wrong"—everything is subjective.

After we resolved our conflict with the villainous English, the Indians were next. They had some absurd notion that since they were here before us, they had some claim upon the land.

Setting a precedent for Nazi purging, we proved to those dunderhead Indians the correctness of the aphorism "Possession is nine tenths of the law." If you have any doubts about that, if you're ever in Miami, drive to the one tenth: the Seminole Indian reservation, in the mosquito-ridden, agriculture-resistant Everglades swamps.

The next suffering people we had to liberate were the Mexicans. We took Texas and California. But we always maintained a concept of justice. We left them a land where holy men could walk: the desert.

Later, continuing with our hollow, rodomontade behavior, we involved ourselves in the war to end all wars.

After going out on a limb like that, there were wars that followed nonetheless, especially the one that took courageous Americans, heroic Russians, invincible Englishmen, and the indefatigable French, who shared moral unity, having God and Irving Berlin on their side, and censuring those who offended the principles of Christianity—the Italians.

The Pope, possessing the clairvoyance of a representative of the Deity, did not flee to Argentina, thereby escaping the fate of Adolf Eichmann.

Where was I? Coming out of a whorehouse in Marseilles—the mental-health official would have been so happy in *The Torture Chamber*.

Sometimes when I work onstage I make these stream-of-consciousness transitions so smoothly from one point to another that the audience doesn't realize until later that I have forgotten to tie up the idea I began with. More than once, someone has come back to the club and tried to get back in, demanding to find out the ending.

Something unusually emotional was happening to me during the merchant marine time. I found that the longer I stayed away from Honey Harlowe, the more involved I became with her. It was so new to me—what others had called "being in love"—and I discovered that I actually enjoyed abstaining: a sort of selfless sacrifice. I just was not interested in participating in sexual relations with anyone but Honey.

It was an amazing experience for me. I was 25 and I had dated at least 200 girls and been promiscuous with twice that number (since this included those I never "dated," in dressing-room bacchanals, chorus girls and strippers who had nothing else to do till their nails got dry). It was an inescapable fact: I was hooked on Honey.

When our ship hit Spain I took all of the money I had saved and called Honey. It took me a long time to trace her, from one club to another, and finally to her mother, but then at last I heard her voice.

I told her I loved her and I was coming home.

Chapter Eleven

Honey and I got married . . . I was wed to a stripper!

Strippers were only a step above hookers, even as late as 1951. The first great break-through—or, rather, breakdown—of society's nudity/lewdity guilt-by-association was the now-famous Marilyn Monroe calendar. Marilyn's respectability when she died was based principally upon her economic status, which is, in the final analysis, the only type our society really respects.

There were a number of other steps which she took to climb down off the barbershop mirror and up the ladder of acceptability, the chairmanship of the board of directors of her own corporation. Joe DiMaggio was the first rung in that ladder. In marrying all America's all-American, she challenged society to condemn its own honored image of the red-blooded hero prototype. After all, would Jolting Joe ever take as a wife someone whom we could not admire?

After she had thus won the "workers' vote," she copped the intellectuals' approval in a tour de force by becoming Mrs. Arthur Miller. (He's a brilliant fellow—would he demean himself by climbing into bed with someone who was not his equal? She reads Dostoievsky!)

Other bovine ladies began to bare their chests for a frank and honest appraisal of their inner spiritual qualities. I have in mind that picture of Sophia Loren sitting in a public restaurant, quite exposed herself, in a gown of delicate décolleté, but staring at Jayne Mansfield's naked nipple peeking out of her low-cut sheath as if to say, "Now, why didn't I think of that?"

Marilyn Monroe was PLAYBOY magazine's first Playmate of the Month. PLAYBOY's Editor and Publisher, Hugh M. Hefner, has cleverly accompanied these center foldouts with capsule biographies emphasizing that the Playmate is *not* necessarily a professional model, but the very antithesis: a secretary, a coed, a waitress, a social worker. You Too Can Take Off Your Clothes and Succeed.

Archaeologists a thousand years hence will indeed be confused by the slew of would-be PLAYBOY imitators, and even *Pageant* (the Legion of Decency's PLAYBOY) and other like magazines with their articles interspersed with sweet young Oklahoma lasses who are kept from being overexposed by bulky-knit Italian sweaters that never quite do the job.

If a girlie book was all that was left as a document of this generation, an anthropologist of the year 2965 would logically assume that this culture seemed to be identified with the religious concept: "God made my body and if it is dirty, then the imperfection lies with the Manufacturer, not the product. Do not remove this tag under the penalty of law."

Meanwhile, back at the strip show, I knew that according to all true Christian standards nudity in itself was certainly not lewd, but burlesque— with its "subtle" charades of grabbing, "floor work," pulling and touching— *was* lewd. Lewd in the sense that there was a woman on the stage whose chief aim was to get the audience horny. I knew that my wife would have to stop stripping unless I could rationalize being a halfway pimp.

I decided to develop her other talents. Honey had a fairly good voice. I spent two years doing a double with her, working all sorts of joints so that we could be together, but after about the first month, I realized I would have to have more money to make her a singer than I was making as a comedian.

How to make some quick money and stay out of jail . . .

If Father Divine could do it, why couldn't I!

Of course—that would be the gimmick—I would become a priest or a rabbi or a monk or whatever the hell was necessary to perform miracles such as taking money from someone else's pocket and putting it into mine, still remaining within the confines of the law. I had no qualms about the sinful aspect of my aspiration because I felt—and still do feel—that all so-called "men of God" are self-ordained. The "calling" they hear is just their own echo.

I knew, of course, that becoming a rabbi or a priest would be a slow process. Churches and synagogues were probably hard to come by. I've never seen one for rent, and they don't ever seem to go out of business. The amazing thing about churches and synagogues is that they never complain about a bad location. I suppose they have a lot of walk-in trade.

No, that would be too slow a process for me. First renting the building, then putting ads in the papers, "Grand Opening, Free Prizes and Blessings to the Kids!" Then I would have to hire an organ player, one that would be responsible and show up for the gig. And then I would have to decide if I would be the m.c. or would I hire one, and what would be the theme of the show—would it be Fire and Brimstone, or Ivy-League Reform?

The big problem would be the breadbasket holders. Most good ushers were working, I assumed, and the ones who weren't working had probably been busted for gelt-grabbing.

So a house of worship wasn't the answer. What I needed was some disease which hadn't been exploited yet. Cancer, muscular dystrophy and tuberculosis had been run through the wringer. Most people had benefited from their contributions—they had the same catharsis of guilt for their own health that Nobel, the man responsible for the killer, dynamite, must have had when he instituted the Nobel Peace Prize.

I needed a disease.

Bronchitis? No, that's such a unhip disease. At least consumption has a sexual connotation to it; bronchitis is sort of poor and Jewish. "I've got bronchitis, I want a *challah* and some sweet butter."

Cholera is Midwest–Protestant–Nelson Algrenish.

Pellagra has class. "Yeah, I got pellagra—uh huh, we brought it up from Southampton with us." You can even make out with chicks. "Yeah, baby, cool it with him if you want to. I'll just pellagra it up here. I'll stay in the pad alone. . . ." That'll get her.

The clap! No one had ever exploited the clap! When the guy comes to your door for the Community Chest or the United Fund, do you ever say to him, "Hey, wait a minute, I'm gonna give you a donation, but how much of my buck is going to the clap?" And actually, it's way up there on the charts. Or are you like a lot of subintellectuals who would say, "Well, no, I wouldn't ask about the clap because only bums get it. And Communists." Sure, 7,000,000 war heroes that are bums and Communists.

You can talk about leukemia all day long, because there's no specific cure, but the clap—you could whack it out in two days with all the antibiotics, so how come it's there and stays up there? Don't even say the *word* clap, man. "It's all right, Mrs. Sheckner, you've just got a little discharge." Because you get leukemia in a respectable way. But how do you get the clap? By *doing it,* and anybody who does that dirty thing obviously *deserves* to get the clap.

Why do you think Ben-Hur's mother and sister got leprosy? Because they didn't put paper on the seat.

Now, if your daughter dies in the back of a taxicab bleeding from a bad curettage because she had a baby in her belly and therefore she's a tramp because the witch doctor didn't put a hoop on her finger, is it any easier for your son to come to you and tell you he has the clap?

If he's lucky, he may go to some *schmuck* who sweeps up the drugstore.

"Hey, Manny . . . you'll mop later, can I talk to you for a minute?"

"Whaddaya want?"

"Listen, I got the clap."

"Oh, yeah—where'd you get that?"

"From painting the car, *schmuck*—what's the difference? I got it, all right?"

"So whaddaya want from me?"

"Some pills. You work in the drugstore here."

"All right, I'll give you some pills. Dexedrine Spansules."

"Is that any good?"

"Yeah, they're all the same. These are good. They keep you awake so you know you've got it."

"How do I know when I get rid of it?"

"Well, if your knees don't swell up and you don't go blind, I guess you're OK."

"The reason I want these pills is, I finally got a good job."

"Oh, yeah? Where you working?"

"In a meat-packing plant, and I don't want to lay off because I'm sick with the clap. You want some steaks?"

"No; no, thanks."

I envisioned my campaign. . . . "She's got it, by jove, I think she's finally got it!" And then the chorus would sing, to the tune of "See the U.S.A. in your Chevrolet," "Curb the Clap Today in the U.S.A., it's a job that's never been done before!" What a thrill it would be to produce the first Clapathon on TV. Instead of little children being exploited, coming out with their little crutches, you could have glamorous movie stars: "Folks, we've raised $680,000 tonight, $680,000 that will be spent for research and treatment; no longer will men have to suffer the indignity of putting it on the window sill and slamming the window on it." A big ad campaign—"Remember, an ounce of prevention, the most important quarter inch!"—and then perhaps a beautiful dramatic actress would give a testimonial:

"Ladies and gentlemen, I have been helped by this wonderful organization; thanks to these brave people, we have been brought out of the dark ages. We have had the clap in our family for years and never knew it. My husband and I sensed there was something strange about the size of Ronnie's head—he was our first son—but like many others we were too ashamed to ask our doctor about it. Then we read the literature, *Curb the Clap Today,* and we brought it to our family doctor. He read it and to his amazement he discovered that he had the clap, too . . ."

But I was only fantasizing again, making stuff up for my own amusement. Then one day I was looking through my scrapbook and I came upon a feature story on myself that had appeared in The Detroit *Free Press:*

FRIEND TO FOUR HUNDRED
Entertainer Conducts Aid Drive
For Lepers
By Ralph Nelson
Free Press Staff Writer

Ashore in Trinidad in 1944, while his ship was being refitted with guns, a 27-year-old Detroiter began a friendship with a colony in British Guiana that remains strong and warm.

The people of the colony number about 400 lepers at Mahaicony Hospital, East Coast Demerara, British Guiana, a handful of missionaries and six American Sisters of Mercy who care for the sick.

Leonard Bruce, of 1347 Selden, was then a turret gunner aboard the U.S.S. Brooklyn, a light cruiser that saw action at Casablanca and Salerno, and won a Unit Citation at Anzio.

"We put in at Trinidad for new guns and repairs from shell fire," Bruce said. "It was there I first found out about lepers, and how completely forgotten they are by the world."

Bruce said that the greatest strength for good at the tiny colony is a 61-year-old Unitarian missionary, himself a leper.

"The care and Godliness that Adam Abrigo, himself incurably ill, spread among the sufferers was wonderful," Bruce said. "I cleaned out the ship of all we could spare in the way of old clothing, shoes and food, and I've been sending the colony things ever since."

Bruce admitted that his private welfare project is getting out of hand.

"There are about 400 lepers there, including 50 small children who are stricken," he said. "Their need for toys, with Christmas coming, underclothing, jackets, candy and food, is overpowering. The colony is very poor."

Bruce pointed out that sunglasses are a great boon to the sick, as leprosy strikes at the eyes, making the equatorial sun unbearable.

Bruce and his wife, Harriet, both well-known Detroit entertainers, will leave January 15th, with a USO group headed for Korea, for a 10-week stay.

"Before we go, I hope we can reach into the hearts of enough Detroiters, with a few toys or old clothing to spare, to make a good Christmas for the inmates of the leper colony," Bruce said.

"Twenty-four-pound packages are the largest that are permitted, and it will take a lot of bundles to go around to the 350 people and those little children."

Letters to Bruce from Father Abrigo bear mute testimony of the need and gratitude of the colony for gifts Bruce had sent on his one-man crusade of help.

"Just a package, to the Medical Superintendent of the Mahaicony Leprosarium, East Coast Demerara, British Guiana, South America, will do more for these people than anyone can ever know who has not been there."

Now this article had been factual and I had been proud of it. But for the first time it seemed to me that even *I* had been exploited. The reporter, a nice enough guy, was hard up for a human-interest story around Christmastime and *that* was the reason he had written it. He had to make some kind of a living, like everyone else. It was just practical. So my lepers and I got used.

Actually, the article didn't hurt anybody; it helped people. As a direct result of the article, a wealthy man donated 30,000 pairs of sunglasses. The people who received the donations, as well as those who gave them, benefited. They felt very generous and noble and gratified.

But more important—to me, that is, at that particular moment—was the fact that the reporter had helped *himself*. "God helps those who help themselves," I remembered.

Until then my theological knowledge had been limited to the lives of Christ and Moses, which I had read many times. I had been touched deeply by what I understood. I really loved Christ and Moses. I related very strongly to them because it seemed to me that I thought so much like them in so many ways. They had a deep regard for education and they continually gave, with no motivation other than to give.

Which is where we were to differ.

I felt that modern-day priests and rabbis were doing about the same thing as that reporter, and no one saw anything wrong with it. Maybe this is the sort of thing I was cut out for. I could assume the role of a "priest" and raise money for the leper colony. It would be better than going about it in the amateur manner I had previously employed.

The lepers would benefit, and so would the good people who contributed. And I would keep 50 percent for my efforts. It was no more—and certainly much *less*—than the majority of charitable institutions take out for *their* efforts. They hire professional collecting organizations, advertising agencies, fellows who really know how to get the gelt. I might even employ some novice "priests" myself if business got good.

Of course it was dishonest and corrupt, and I don't fool myself by saying there are degrees of corruption. Just as the old cliché goes, "There is no such thing as being a little bit pregnant," stealing is stealing. But, I rationalized, what is the difference between a real priest and me?

Instinctively, I knew that for a *true* man of God with a crystal-clear set of ethics, there could be no compromise.

There are people living on the verge of—and dying of—starvation in this country. In New York City, in the vicinity of Lexington Avenue and 110th Street, there are ten or twelve people living in one rat-infested room. This is not copping out on the "starving masses of India and China," although that, too, is nonetheless true, but it is too far removed for people to grasp the horror of children eating out of maggot-infested garbage cans somewhere else in the world.

Conditions of unspeakable poverty, filth and humiliation exist right here in "the richest country in the world." This country, which magnanimously balms its conscience by helping Greek orphans and buying bonds for Israel, but manages to pass up the appeal for bail-bond money needed desperately

57

by sixth-generation Negro Americans fighting for their human rights.

The Daughters of the American Revolution have supplied enough status and respect due to people for such an honorable heritage; well, some of the Negroes now serving time in jail for the terrible offense of wanting to sit at lunch counters are sixth-generation Americans, too.

Nikita Khrushchev, when he visited the United States in 1959, received obsequious, oversolicitous treatment wherever he went, but my fellow Americans who fought and died for their country are denied the privilege of using a toilet if it is not in the proper geographical location.

I did not doubt for a moment then that if Christ were to come down at that moment, he would go immediately to headquarters and ask the Pope, "What are you doing wearing that big ring? What are those gold cups encrusted with diamonds and other jewels for? Don't you know that people are starving all over the world? At this very moment a poor pregnant Negress is standing with swollen ankles in the back of a bus in Biloxi."

And if Moses were to come down, wouldn't he order all the rabbis in their Frank Lloyd Wright *shuls* to sell their *tallith* for rags and melt down the *mezuzahs* for bail money for all the Caryl Chessmans that sit in gas chambers or electric chairs or walk in the blue-gray shadow of the gallows? Would not Moses say to them, "Why have you mocked the Ten Commandments? What is your interpretation of 'Thou Shalt Not Kill'? It's not, 'Thou Shalt Not Kill *But . . .*'"

I knew in my heart by pure logic that any man who calls himself a religious leader and owns more than one suit is a hustler as long as there is someone in the world who has no suit at all.

So I made up my mind. I would become a priest.

Chapter
Twelve

I spent two weeks hanging around a rectory, trying to observe the mannerisms of the Holy Men.

I noticed that the priests had the same attiude toward their lessers as do most successful businessmen: they treated them like illiterate children, not by kissing them and giving them ice cream, but rather by giving them the kind of treatment which makes the receiver feel as though he had graduated from third grade only with the help of political influence.

And then, too, they had their friends with whom they would have a few beers when they were off duty. They even enjoyed telling each other off-color stories.

With others, they were able, chameleonlike, to fit into the Pat O'Brien stereotype.

I found an ingenious method of hanging around the rectory without being picked up for vagrancy. I sold *The Watchtower*.

Daily, I learned more about how to behave in the manner of men who have the world by the tail . . . no income tax, no traffic tickets, you live in a world on its best behavior, a wonderful, rosy world . . . instead of cursing, everybody pours his soul out to you.

I would stand there every day watching visitors go in and out, and I observed, sadly, that most of them were little old ladies; the ones who actually needed help—soothing love—would never come. And, since the priests didn't go out looking for needy cases, the purpose and the end result seemed quite paradoxical to me.

After a couple of weeks of observation, I realized that I couldn't bring myself to start the basic operation; because of years of moral conformity I couldn't bring myself to break into a church and steal the uniforms.

And, unfortunately, Klein's didn't stock them.

But, as I pondered this problem, I noticed something else about priests that made my uniform-heisting task much easier—both morally and technically. Their attitude with strangers was similar to any successful, busy merchant—curt and direct. This was the direct opposite of the behavior pattern that Christ was supposed to have followed. So, not only was their life like the successful businessman's, it was even a little better: Everything was delivered.

On Monday, Carmelo the barber would come.

On Tuesday, the Peerless Laundry man would come.

On Wednesday, the Paris Dry Cleaners man would come. This visit interested me most of all. The man from Paris Dry Cleaners was a rather nondescript chap with a strong Boston accent. He would rap sharply on the door with a two-bit Leonard Bernstein tempo, an overture that was the cue for a cheerful, red-faced father to appear with a bundle of soiled holy garments. The man from the dry cleaners would come at nine A.M. sharp, every Wednesday.

A week later, at ten minutes to nine, I appointed myself as Guest Conductor, substituting my own knock—da de da, da de da da da (the opening bars to *Joe and Paul,* a dirty Jewish folk song)—for the regular pickup man's "shave-and-a-haircut" rapping. I waited a moment, and a handsome young priest appeared with a bundle of priest uniforms that he would never see again.

He studied me quizzically, then said, "Haven't you been selling *The Watchtower* in front of the rectory?"

"Yes," I said, "but I didn't agree with their editorial policy, and I got a job instead with the Paris Dry Cleaners."

I noticed his white collar. Where the hell would I get white collars? They weren't included in the bundle of soiled uniforms.

Being an inventive, if corrupt, genius, I said, "Father, do you know the owner of the Paris Dry Cleaners?"

"No, I can't say that I do."

"Well, it's supposed to be a surprise, Father, but he wants to present Monsignor Martin with a dozen handmade Irish-linen collars."

"Well, isn't that lovely—I'm sure he will appreciate them."

"Now, if you'll excuse me, Father, I don't want to be pushy," I said, jamming my head between the oak sill and the copper binding of the door, "but Mr. Kepnews, the owner, wanted to use Monsignor Martin's collar for a sample."

"Oh, that would be impossible. To touch anything in the Monsignor's room is unthinkable. However, you could ask Father Langford. He is the same size as Monsignor Martin." He pointed to a cottage at the end of the rectory yard.

As my feet crunched the gravel, I imagined it turning into red-hot coals. I saw Walter Huston, the Devil himself, laughing at me from above, where he was sitting on a tree limb.

I was about to knock at Father Langford's door when I noticed a brass plate that announced the residence of Monsignor Martin. The door was ajar. I strolled leisurely in, whistling *Ave Maria,* and was in and out before you could say, "Blessed are they who give . . ."

I had a neat haul: twelve collars and, believe it or not, seven of the farthest-out *Tillie and Mac* books I'd ever seen, plus one of the numbered editions of Henry Miller's *Black Spring*.

I left the grounds with movielike timing. I heard the disbelief in the voices of the real man from Paris Dry Cleaners and the priest as they exchanged the dialog that always follows the discovery of an unusual theft: "Why would anyone . . . ?" "How could a person be so . . . ?" "Now *if* they had some *use* . . ." "This is just a case of wanton stealing for *no earthly reason* . . ."

I had learned my first important lesson in theology: *Always insist on an official receipt for your dry cleaning.*

The next few weeks were spent with a battery of lawyers getting a charter from New York State which legalized the Brother Mathias Foundation. This licensed me to solicit and disburse funds to the leper colony—which was not at all illegal, for I meant to *do* just that . . . after "operating costs" had been deducted.

I had it made: a priest with a disease—an unbeatable combination.

The first place in which I chose to solicit funds was Miami Beach. Honey was stripping there, at the Paddock Club, and I was working at the Olympia Theater in Miami. We were living at the Floridian Hotel.

Honey was in bed, eating a breakfast that consisted of an orange pop and a hot dog with Everything on it. I had had Monsignor Martin's pants taken in at the seat and the legs let out. I had three suits all nicely tailored, cleaned and pressed. They fit perfectly. They hung in lovely incongruity: the clerical costumes and the G string, side by side.

The sun poured through the room and bounced off the beaded G string. The prism formed a halo as I walked out of the room in my somber black outfit.

I was just about to get into Honey's 1949 convertible Chevrolet with the leopardskin seat covers when I heard it for the first time, loud and clear: "Good morning, Father."

The voice came from a sensual-looking, buxom woman of about 35. They bounced when she walked. Ooooh, Daddy! I stood looking at her, both reverent and horny at the same time.

"I'm Mrs. Walsh," she said. "Are you at the Floridian, Father?"

"Yes, I'm with the Brother Mathias Foundation, and we're in this area to collect money for the poor unfortunate lepers in British Guiana."

"Well, I don't have my checkbook with me——"

"Oh, no," I interrupted, "a donation was the farthest thing from my mind."

"I know that, Father, but I want to give you something. I'm going to my room—417. When you return, give me a knock, won't you?"

"Well, yes, if you insist."

I watched her do her little-girl pout. Some women can pout so that it looks as if they're putting in a diaphragm at that very moment.

"You won't forget, will you, Father?"

"No, I shan't forget."

With all the sublety of an exhibitionist exposing himself in a subway station, she telegraphed: "My husband better not keep sending me down here alone."

I drove away as Honey scowled out the window, devouring another one with Everything on it.

I started to drive north from the Floridian, heading my winged chariot, which had a conventional shift that stuck, toward the wealthy homes.

A priest driving a convertible with the top down would cause a lot of comment in Boston, but here, in the domain of David and Celia, I went unnoticed. I whizzed past the markets which proclaimed "Goodman's Noodles" and "Hebrew National," past the theater which advertised "Saturday Night Only—Cantor Rosenblatt, Naftula Brandywine, Yetta Stwerling, Direct from Second Avenue, in *A Mema's Hartz*—Jewish Drama."

Always the same problem with a little plot twist, like a pretzel. The Jewish girl marries a gentile boy and the Jewish girl's family immediately goes into mourning. The gentile husband stays drunk and beats her throughout the entire second act. The third act has the usual happy ending, where the girl gets pregnant, the drunken husband leaves her, and she goes blind working in a sewing-machine factory. The child grows up to be a brilliant physician who naturally, is a genetic representation of his mother's side; but he stutters terribly because of the gentile blood in him. At the end of the third act, his kindly old Jewish grandmother, who has been searching for him, meets him unexpectedly while sitting on a bench waiting for an offstage bus. He kisses her and whispers stutteringly in her ear, "I love you"—in Hebrew . . . but the evil gentile part of him comes out and he bites her ear off as the curtain falls on the little theater off Times Square. About 40 blocks off Times Square.

As I stopped for a pedestrian to pass, a rabbi drove by and gave me a friendly wave. I wondered, do rabbis and priests always wave at each other, just like people in sports cars?

I reached a wealthy section a few blocks away which, interestingly enough, was inhabited almost exclusively by gentile families. I parked the car at the curb and knocked at the first door.

If you have ever done any door-to-door selling, whether it be encyclopedias, siding, shingles, baby pictures, or Avon cosmetics, you know that you receive rejection 95 percent of the time. I've always assumed that one would have to be a dedicated masochist to pursue this type of employment.

As a kid, I studied the color transference of a buttercup while lolling on a lawn retreat between soliciting subscriptions for the *Long Island Daily Press*. I would commune with nature to recoup my stamina and morale between houses. Actually, I was a door-to-*lawn* salesman.

It sure was uncomfortable standing on a porch, looking through a screen door at a shadowy figure bent over struggling with a mohair davenport while the roar of an unattended vacuum cleaner bellowed and wheezed. A nine-year-old salesman hasn't learned the refinements of the game . . .

The first telephone call: "Hello, Mrs. Harding? I hope I'm not disturbing your dinner. . . . Ha, ha, ha—well, I won't keep you a minute; I know it must be delicious. My name is Schneider. Your neighbor, Mrs. Wilson, gave me your number. Now, before you hang up, don't get the idea that I'm trying to *sell* you anything. Certainly not! You are very fortunate, indeed, because my company is engaged in a market-research project and, providing you qualify according to our strict specifications, I *may* be able to offer you a most valuable service, free of charge—absolutely free—which will not cost you one single penny . . . that is, of course, *providing* you do pass our strict qualifications . . ."

The strict qualifications being that she doesn't hang up.

But I cannot indict the system. It is no more corrupt than any other form of selling. The term itself, "selling," implies talking the customer into purchasing an article he has not previously had any need or desire for.

When I was nine years old, I would find myself standing on a strange and unfriendly porch, getting the breath scared out of me by some dopey chow dog who always leaped out at me from nowhere. Luckily he would just miss me by the six-inch strain on his chain. Dogs seem to take a particular delight in scaring nine-year-old boys. I think it's really a game with them, harmless enough, like fetching sticks, because they are certainly capable of killing you if they wanted to. They don't, though; they just nip at your heels when you ride past on your bike. It's all in fun. For *them*. I didn't understand the rules of the game when I was nine years old. I was a prepubic spoilsport.

I must admit that when you stand on that porch and they leap out, it does serve some useful function. If you have sinus trouble, your nasal passages are cleared up in seconds. I imagine that's what the cave men must have done instead of taking nose drops. If a kid's nose was stuffed up, they just stood him in front of a cave until a dinosaur stuck his head out.

By 1951 I had considerably refined my sales approach. I still had no "opener" telephone call to ease my introduction, but I did have a uniform.

A uniform is an important means to instant acceptance.

A man is no longer just a man; he is part of an institution—milkman, postman, diaper man—he has conquered the suspicion of being a stranger by acquiring a kind of *official* anonymity. He is associated with a definite mission. He means business.

I learned that from my experience in the Navy, the merchant marine and, of course, the WAVEs. Now, my priest uniform overshadowed General Eisenhower's in commanding respect.

I walked up to that $90,000 bay-front home with the yacht parked in the back, and the chow dog lay down just the way Daisy used to in the *Blondie* movies. That's what preacceptance does for you. Androcles had achieved it for me thousands of years before, taking that thorn out of the lion's foot.

The door opened even before my foot touched the first step. A flustered maid, wiping her hands on her apron, gulped: "Good morning, Father, won't you come in? Mrs. McKenery will be right down."

The house was immaculate. The maid led me to the music room. In the center was a beautiful Baldwin grand, the grandest piano I had ever seen. It probably hadn't been played since the little girl whose picture stood on top of it had grown up.

I conjured up a mental picture of the mistress of the house. People usually look like their homes. This house was spotless, but not the crisp, white-kitchen cleanliness with yellow-flowered curtains and a cute Donald Duck–clock decor with which some reflect themselves. This house smelled of wood polished with linseed oil.

Some women are Clorox scrubbers; others are dusters or straightener-uppers. Mrs. McKenery was a banister polisher.

She entered, a woman in her 60s, with slightly oily skin, satiny as the furniture. She probably used some expensive monkey-gland preparation for the purpose of preservation, and it certainly served its function; all of her wrinkles were well-preserved.

Within half-an-hour, all I was able to contribute to the conversation was, "I am from the Brother Mathias Foundation, and we are in this area receiving contributions for the unfortunate lepers in British Guiana. . . ." And I had to fight to get *that* in. She had taken a deep breath when she sat down and didn't stop for another one as she treated me to the most intimate revelations of her life. First she related the details of all the Good Work she had ever done—the organizations to which she gave unstintingly of her services. Then she concentrated on her *real* sacrifices—being married to an insensitive, cruel man and remaining with him only for the sake of their daughter so that she could have a normal upbringing.

Of course I had to agree that she, Mrs. McKenery, had wasted her life so that her Dolly could have a mother and father and not suffer the indignity of "a broken home." I inquired where Dolly was, and I was not overly surprised to find that she was at the analyst.

After Mrs. McKenery cataloged all the sacrifices she had made since her marriage, she described how she had been raped "by a nigger farm hand Daddy had fired." She was only seven years old when it happened, but she related the Sabine scene to me in intricate detail; detail that is acquired only by constant retelling. It was in the Poe Classicist manner. "We lived on a two-hundred-acre estate—do you know where that big new store downtown is? Daddy used to play croquet with me there—it was our front yard."

She went on and on and on, into the ghastly description of the lynching of her attacker who, incidentally, had never actually "touched" her, but had been drunk and was merely boasting to others of his intentions.

"What if he *had* gotten to me? I still shudder when I think about it."

After the confession of her early traumatic sexual experiences, she discussed frankly her husband's lack of manliness. "He was *never* an affectionate man." She sighed deeply, but before I could take advantage of this opportunity to make my pitch, the maid interrupted: "Excuse me, madam, but Mr. Madison is here."

I was introduced to Geoffrey Madison, "a brilliant young poet" who was acquainting Mrs. McKenery with the Greek classics and teaching her to appreciate tragedy. He was taking her to the opening of the first espresso house in Miami Beach.

She explained to this sensitive fellow the purpose of my visit—the wonderful work I was doing for the poor lepers in—"Where was that place?"

Madison smiled askance at me. One hustler to another.

He reminded Mrs. McKenery that they had only 15 minutes to get to the art exhibit, and she hurriedly wrote me a check, putting in the amount and signing it, telling me to fill in the name of my organization. She kissed my hand and left me alone with the maid, who had been raped, too. When she was 14.

I don't know if I have an extrasensory gift for divining violated virgins, but of all the women I interviewed, nearly 80 percent had been raped. The other 20 percent had either been hurt on a bicycle or horseback riding, or fallen accidentally on a fence. Their big problem was that their husbands never believed them.

The maid gave me an envelope, and I couldn't wait till I got out of the house to the car so that I could open it and peek at the amount on Mrs. McKenery's check; I was too discreet to conduct such an investigation on the premises. The envelope contained a poem Mrs. McKenery had written about Saint Agnes, also a clipping from the Seventh-day Adventist paper about the tea cozy she had made for the Korean Orphan Drive, and the check. When I looked at the amount on it, I thought there must have been a mistake. I saw the number 750 in the upper-right-hand corner and figured she had forgotten the decimal point; but there it was spelled out: "Seven hundred and fifty and no/100 dollars."

I knew then that I was on my way to being the highest-paid analyst on Miami Beach.

In two days I made only nine calls. The sessions got longer and longer. I got only one rejection and collected $5300 in cash and checks. All from the purest, most self-sacrificing women who were unfortunately married to insensitive, unaffectionate husbands, and who would all be virgins to this day if it weren't for what seemed to be the same lustful rape artist or a fence whose height had been just a little underestimated.

I was mildly annoyed because I never got the chance to discuss religion, which was my official sphere of interest. I had done a lot of reading in preparation, and it was all being wasted.

The only trouble I had was from Honey. When I came home that first night, she wouldn't believe that I had gotten "all that money just for nothing." She insisted, "No woman's going to give you $750 just for *talking*."

She would go through all my clothes for lipstick traces; she would sniff me all over for the scent of powder or perfume.

I never did anything but shake hands with any of these women, but there were times during our marriage when I kissed other girls, and I had found it much safer to leave the lipstick on and explain it away with, "I couldn't help it, this tipsy old lady just grabbed me and kissed me, she said I looked like her son who was killed in the War, she must've been about seventy . . ."

If you've ever tried to rub lipstick off, you know that even if you remove it all, your mouth is twice as red as it was when you left it alone.

When Honey and I had first started going together, she had told me: "I know how men are, like butterflies going from flower to flower. I understand that from time to time you may kiss another girl, and I don't mind, as long as you tell me. I just never want to hear it from anyone else."

And I believed her.

And I did tell her.

Just once.

"I'm glad you told me," she said, and began a slow burn. Within half-an-hour, she had broken every record I had—including my Gramercy Five 78s—and ripped up all the pictures I had of anybody I knew before we were married, and demanded that I tell her the girl's name and that we go together to her right then at four A.M. and "have it out." She ended with: "OK, if you can have a good time, I can have a good time, too!"

For weeks after, every time I came home from, say, the drugstore, she would say, "How's your girlfriend?" Whenever I talked to anyone on the phone, or on the street, or in a store—even a salesgirl—Honey would charge over or, following me in the car, pull up to the curb and challenge: "Is that her?"

Three days after my confession she saw me talking to the secretary of an agent who was trying to get me a booking. This, incidentally, was a woman so ugly I would *never* have kissed her. Somehow Honey got her name, traced her number and called up her husband. She introduced herself and told him. "It's not my husband's fault, he's very weak-minded." Therefore, his wife was to blame, and he probably knew she was a tramp, but if he wanted her "in one piece" for himself when his turn came, she'd better keep her hands off me!

The funny thing was that the secretary had been giving her husband all kinds of hell for cheating until then. It really created a lot of confusion. He was very sympathetic to Honey and invited her over to hear the whole story. When she went over there, he was half-looped and made some pretty strong advances, figuring that they would console each other, and she was struggling with him when his wife walked in.

Honey came home with her blouse ripped and her lipstick smeared, and I really gave *her* hell.

The next day I "made" the stores on Lincoln Road. Honey happened to be in one of the shoe stores and heard me give the manager my pitch. After that, she believed me. He gave me a check for $100, which was considerably less than the average, but, after all, he had never been raped.

Chapter Thirteen

One afternoon as I left a big house on Palm Island with $250 in cash warming my pocket, I beheld a sight that made my heart stop just as it did that day so many years ago when my father walked in on me while I was stroking it. A cop on a motorcycle pulled up to the curb, kicked the prop stick in place, and said: "Can I talk to you for a moment, Father?"

"Yes, my son, what is it?"

He was a nice young man with a polite but straightforward approach. "We've had complaints from residents in this area concerning soliciting. It's just a matter of form, but I have to ask to see your permit."

"Permit?"

"Yes, your permit."

"Oh, yes, my permit . . . oh, yes . . . hmmmm."

He just stared and repeated: "Yes, your permit."

"Gracious, let's see, did Brother Leon take care of that matter? I know I spoke to the Cardinal about it after Mass . . ."

I kept mumbling until my voice was choked off by the sight of a squad car cruising down the block. It stopped about 20 yards from us, and the police inside the car motioned to the motorcycle cop in a grandiose manner. He walked over and exchanged a few words with them, while I stood there not knowing what to do.

"Hey, you! C'mere! You! Hey! Get the hell over here!"

I looked all around me as if I could not believe that anyone could possibly address me in that tone of voice.

The officer in the car got out. I don't think I have ever seen such a huge man, before or since. He was about 60 years old, must have weighed about 250 pounds, and was easily six feet, eight inches tall. White hair, crewcut. Not one ounce of fat.

Just then another car came wheeling around the corner and slammed up right in front of us. It was a stripped-down 1951 Ford. Obviously two plainclothesmen.

Paul Bunyan walked over to them and conferred with them as four more motorcycles blasted up, their sirens screaming.

By this time, all the people were pouring out of their homes. Within ten minutes there were four police cars, six motorcycles, and three kids yelling "Bang! Bang!" while rolling in the dirt.

No one had said a word to me since "Hey, you!"

They just stood off a few paces and eyed me with a sort of take-him-dead-or-alive look.

The giant spoke his line again: "Hey you!"

I attempted to preserve my dignity in front of my parishioners, who were watching anxiously.

"Sir?"

"You heard me, jackoff. Take the shit out of your ears!"

Those past few days, sipping tea from bone china with ladies and nibbling Ry-Krisp and watercress, had made me feel quite pious. I actually shocked myself when I heard my voice come out with: "I see no reason to use vulgarity, my son."

Two elderly ladies came to my aid, shaking their fists at the giant's hip pockets. He actually apologized to them for his outburst, but when I looked at him with benevolent forgiveness, he got hot all over again.

I edged over behind the old ladies.

"Get in the car," he commanded. One old lady got so frantic she had her prayer beads skipping around as if she were doing a hula.

"We're not going to let them take you, Father," said one benefactress, "They belong to Satan's army."

An officer tried to grab my arm but one of the plucky old dolls came up with her purse which must have had nothing less than a brick in it, because it knocked him squarely on his butt. As a reflex, the sergeant came up and kicked the old woman in the ass, not hard, but hard enough to bring a Doberman pinscher bounding seemingly out of nowhere. In retaliation, he took a good piece out of the sergeant's hip.

It wasn't long before I heard more sirens, and soon enough we were drawn up in battle lines. On one side were about 50 policemen, paddy wagons, tear-gas guns, riot-quelling equipment, and the fire department, whose men were beginning to screw the fire hose onto the hydrant.

On the other side of No Man's Land I held my ground with my army of elderly ladies and our K-9 Corps, Brutus the Doberman.

Although we were no more than 25 feet apart, the captain in charge picked up one of those electric speakers you see in prison pictures, where the warden always says, "Give up, Dutch, we have you surrounded!"

My ladies had formed a Red Cross unit and were passing out hot coffee to the ranks.

The mechanical voice boomed over the megaphone. "This is Captain Goldman! Give up now and no one will be hurt! You will be given fair treatment, whether you are a priest or not! We just want to take you down for questioning! If you have any Christian feelings, you will surrender yourself and spare this mob the tear gas and fire hose which we will use if they do not disperse!"

I looked at my forces and my heart swelled. There were nearly 50 women, the youngest about 80 years old. They stood at attention, awaiting the decision of their leader.

Everything was orderly and disciplined except the kids. There were dozens of them yelling "Bang! Bang!" "I'm Hopalong Cassidy!" "I'm Bishop Sheen!" as they rolled over in the dirt, creating the impression of a genuine skirmish.

But my ladies stood fast. I like women in that age bracket, because they're the only ones who still wear rouge. I looked sadly at my troops and said, "I had better go."

A cracked cracker voice behind me spoke up determinedly. "If you don't want to, we're behind you, Father!" And I heard the click of what sounded like . . . and to my amazement, it was indeed . . . she had cocked the breech of a monstrous-looking elephant gun.

"We're behind you," another cried. And she started to hum, then all joined in singing, "I'm brave when He walks with me . . ."

The police stood across the way and gaped, dumfounded.

For one crazy moment, I thought, "How nice, Honey and I will move into this neighborhood and I will be their pastor."

"You have ten seconds!" The voice boomed over the loudspeaker. The ladies pressed together around me in a solid phalanx. Brutus pricked up his ears. "One . . . two . . ." I saw the firemen ready the hose.

"Beat your swords into plowshares," I said gently, raising my hand in peace, and walked away from my blue-haired battalion toward the enemy.

The captain whispered in my ear: "Don't make any dramatic gestures to those biddies or I'll crease your head with this club."

"Incitement to violence is not the path of righteousness, my son," I assured him.

They took me in the squad car. Instead of going directly to the police station, we pulled up at a Catholic church. The captain intended to assure himself that I was a fraud before they booked me. The Monsignor came out. We spoke for half-an-hour.

The arrest report describes the result of that meeting: I was booked on a charge of vagrancy.

They searched my hotel room, found the charter of the Brother Mathias Foundation, and realized that everything was in order. They wired New York to find out if I was wanted there. When I came up clean, they released me.

In court the next morning I was found not guilty.

The law had taken a close look at me and recognized my occupation as legitimate. It was Easy Street from now on. I went home and counted my receipts. I had collected about $8000 in three days.

I made out a check for $2500 to the lepers and kept the rest for operating expenses; it would take a lot of gas to get us to Pittsburgh.

My vision mathematically calculated the numbers on the highway signs. U.S. 101 . . . PENN. 42. (101 plus 42 is 143.) Peripherally I read the impersonal directions: TRUCK ROUTE; DETOUR; GO SLOW; SCHOOL ZONE. Did the guys who had painted those signs wonder where they would be placed?

How tragically ironic that most of these signs are made and painted in prisons, perhaps by life-termers who would never have the opportunity to see their handiwork in "action."

How sweet and truly Christian it would be if every priest, minister and rabbi would be responsible for a lifer and take him out for just one day so he could see his artwork on a sign or perhaps on a license plate and be able to say to himself: "I made that." Just one day out of his cage.

Goddamn the priests and the rabbis. Goddamn the Popes and all their hypocrisy. Goddamn Israel and its bond drives. What influence did they exert to save the lives of the Rosenbergs—guilty or not? Again, the Ten Commandments doesn't say "Thou Shalt Not Kill *Sometimes* . . ."

So the Pope has his secretary issue a statement about not executing Chessman. What is that? With the tremendous power of the Church I don't believe they could not have exerted pressure enough to get him off if they had really wanted to. But they didn't. He was an agnostic. He did not ask for forgiveness. He might have had a chance if he hadn't been so stupid as to continue claiming he was innocent.

Why don't religious institutions use their influence to relieve human suffering instead of sponsoring such things as the Legion of Decency, which dares to say it's indecent that men should watch some heavy-titted Italian starlet because to *them* breasts are dirty?

Beautiful, sweet, tender, womanly breasts that I love to kiss; pink nipples that I love to feel against my clean-shaven face. They're clean!

I say to you, Legion of Decency—you, with your dings scrubbed with holy water and Rokeach soap—you're dirty!

Why doesn't the Legion of Decency say: "It's indecent that men should stand by and watch cyanide gas administered to human lungs in a death chamber!" The answer is because in their philosophy life is not as important as death. If death and the imminence of death serves the purpose of bringing a person to his knees before the Church, then it is worth using as a positive instrument of propagating the faith. The Church therefore condones capital punishment.

They went a long way toward refining its methods themselves during the Crusades and the Inquisition.

Of course I disagree with them and of course they have a right to believe whatever they do; all I want is for them to come out and admit it and stop issuing sanctimonious bulls saying one thing while they pursue the opposite.

And since they condone capital punishment, I want them to stop bitching about Jesus getting nailed up.

The Burma-Shave signs whizzed past and suddenly Pittsburgh sprang up and yelled "Boo!" as the dark broke. It looked so dramatic, the city in the dawn, that I felt a twinge in the pit of my stomach. I don't know exactly what it is, but any city at that time of day gives me the feeling I used to get when I swallowed the contents of a Benzedrine inhaler and chased it with Coke. It really *was* "The Pause that Refreshes."

I guess I feel funny about the city because it's so big and alone. I was always alone when I was a kid.

Chapter
Fourteen

Pittsburgh was all alone, too. Like a tough Polish kid with a homemade haircut, cap, knickers, and a broken tooth.

Honey and I checked into the Milner Hotel.

Those Milner Hotel rooms were beautiful, with high ceilings and fake fireplaces and the mirrored pictures with the flamingo bird. "A Dollar a Day and Servicemen Welcome."

We always got a special rate for a double. There was no toilet in the room—it was at the end of the hall—but there was a sink in the room. Needless to say, I never washed my face in it.

The thing I especially liked about Milner Hotels is that they always had real pillows with chicken feathers in them. I hate those foam-rubber pillows. You can't bend them over. They keep bouncing up. Nothing is more obscene to me than a foam-rubber pillow covered with a clear plastic polyethylene zipper bag, even more so when it starts to turn brown; it looks like the burnt isinglass in a potbellied stove.

I'm probably the only one who ever really looks at the mattress in hotels. There always seems to be a brown stain around one button. I've never stained any of these mattresses, and I've asked a lot of people who are very truthful and have no inhibitions, and they've told me *they* never stained any either. There must be some guy who stains these mattresses before they leave the factory.

I finished examining the mattress and then I double-locked the door. Honey had the dopiest thing about always making sure the door was locked. I used to tell her, "What the hell, I'm in the room, nobody is going to bother you." But she would go through the whole ritual, going outside the door, having me lock it from the inside and making sure no one could get in.

I used to really put her on. When she was locked out I'd start screaming and yelling to her as she tried the door. "Get away! Leave me alone, you horny broad! You're a nymphomaniac! I'm all sore, I can't do it anymore!"

Honey gets embarrassed if she coughs in an elevator. She hates anything loud, and although she is a sensitive and delicate lady, she gets me hotter than any woman I have ever known. When I finally let her back in the room, she was angry, so we made up.

Later we decided to get the rest of our stuff out of the car. To my consternation, the car was gone. Stolen? The audacity! I had a sign on the windshield which clearly read: CLERGY. What a sin—stealing a holy automobile! Should I call the police? No, I would call headquarters. "Hello, operator, give me Rome—IVMLV."

Honey, being more earth-bound than I, hustled me off in a cab in the direction of the car pound. She noticed that we had been parked the wrong way on a one-way street on the no-parking side in front of a fireplug during a rush hour.

As we rode along, the wind blew her long natural-red hair across me so that it caressed my neck and shoulders. I took her in my arms; it was so luxurious, riding in the back seat as if I were Mr. First-Nighter with his own chauffeur. I held Honey tight. Every part of her was warm and sensual. She always dressed crisply and smelled clean. I don't know how long we had been parked in front of the car pound when the driver finally summoned up an "Ahem" and pointed to the meter, which was still running.

The officer in charge of the pound treated us to a brief lesson in morality. "What's the matter with you people—don't you believe in signs?"

I never understood what that was supposed to mean. "Don't you believe in signs?" Suppose you say, "No, I don't believe in signs." Will they let you go because in this country we're guaranteed freedom of belief? No man is to be forced to believe in something that goes against the grain of his conscience. "That's right, officer, I don't believe in signs." "Very well, brother, go in peace."

Anyway, we paid the fine and got the car out.

It was the black 1951 Chevy convertible that we had bought on time. That's such a cute way to put it, the implication being that you don't really have to pay money, you just sort of adopt it for a little while, keep it around, and it's yours.

I recently found my financial records and looked up the figures. There was no record on the Chevy, but the Cadillac I bought right after it originally cost only $161 a month. I took a loan on it and had it refinanced to payments of $63 a week. It was new when I bought it in 1951, and when I sold it in 1957—still making payments of $254 a month—I still owed $1200 on it. I got only $900 for it and had to scrounge around to make up the difference of $300 in order to stay out of debtors' prison for the right to ride the bus.

Honey and I were on a tight budget in 1954—$17 for groceries, $6 for insurance, $4 for the Laundromat, rough-dried and folded. Laundry was always a big problem. Honey figured out that when the baby came, our laundry bill would be doubled and we could save a lot of money by getting a washer-dryer combination which was advertised by the appliance store for only a dollar down "on time." That's all she could see: "It's only costing us a dollar, the Laundromat is paying the rest." Instead of $20 a month to the Laundromat, we paid $21.06 to the appliance store. We were going to save what would otherwise have been "doubled" when the baby came.

I knew intuitively that it was a mistake. But Honey always had a way of explaining things to me so that it looked as if the *store* was taking a big screwing. We took advantage of more stores—it's a wonder they're still in business.

JUST $1 DOWN . . . ONLY $21.06 A MONTH
NO   HIDDEN   CHARGES . . . NO   GIMMICKS

And they were telling the truth. Your only investment *was* a dollar—that is, if you were willing to use your washing machine in their store. They wanted $36 for trucking charges to deliver.

"Are you kidding—$36? I'll get a couple of guys, we'll have it out of here in a minute . . ."

The first step in exploiting your friends into doing manual labor is to get them to admit they're not doing anything first.

"Hi, Manny, what's happening?"

"Nothin'—we're just hanging around the pad here."

"Listen, you want to have some kicks? I got a new Kenny Drew Album and Joe Maini is on it and he really sounds good. When will you be over? In about ten minutes? Oh, wait a minute, I got a wild idea. Listen, I've got to talk soft. Honey is in the kitchen. I saw a nutty-looking chick in this downtown store who's a real balling freak. And I hit on her and she's a nut for bass players, so I told her that I'd bring you over. It'll be perfect; I can sneak out on Honey because I've got to go over there anyway to pick up something."

This operation is quite successful with the average satyr who is always "ready." The girl-in-question has always conveniently taken the day off when you get there, and after your friend recovers from the disappointment of the vanishing phantom lady, you march him to Appliances.

I shared his second shock. It was a big white monster that was designed to "wash 'n' dry" in one cycle. It really was quite a wonderful machine. It could do everything but get through the goddamned door.

"A little this way." "Up on this end." "Easy now, easy now, *easy now,* goddamnit!" "Oh-oh, one sure thing, we can't take it back now." "Well, we're lucky it's just scratched in the back."

Of course, there are always hallway superintendents that hit you just when you are in the worst position, when you're going down the stairs with it. One guy's fingers are slipping, and it has your shoulder pinned against the fire extinguisher, and you have to go to the bathroom in the worst way—and he hits you with encouraging words like "Are you guys kidding? You'll never get that thing out of here!"

And there is *still* one guy who asks, "You got a match?" And would you believe it, I invariably *reach* for one.

With the help of a young, willing kid we got the machine into the street. Young boys are sincerely godlike in attitude. A young kid will always help. I think the motivation is for adult acceptance, and the sweet part about it is that you know it's never profit motivation, because when you go to give them some money, they always say in a shy, awkward manner, "No, that's all right, mister." And when you force it on them, they're quite embarrassed.

What happens to sweet, willing young boys? What happens to all of us? We never stop anymore and say, "Can I help you, mister?"

My musician friend had a 1940 Pontiac convertible, and the washer-dryer just fit in the back seat. The edge of the machine pushed the driver's seat way forward, leaving my friend pushed tightly against the wheel. As we drove along, he looked very intense because of his position, as racing drivers used to look before they got stand-offish, hugging the wheel.

We were talking and laughing about the dirty trick I had pulled on him, but the conversation stopped at every bump and I would just hear *whoosh,* as the machine inadvertently served for an artificial respirator.

We got to the house, and the car couldn't make the steep driveway, so we had to lift the machine out of the car and carry it 60 feet. As we were carrying it, I thought this would be a great torture device to give to the Secret Service.

The landlord looked on apologetically, and then said, "I would like to help you"—he was one of those guys—"but, you know, I'm not supposed to lift anything."

The final *coup de grâce* that I had anticipated with fear now became a reality: the kitchen door was too small. But you still keep thinking that no one would design a product that couldn't fit through an average door.

We finally got it through the living-room door. By this time, my thumbnail and my index fingers were Mediterranean blue. My friend's back would never be the same.

We set the machine down with a thump on the living-room floor, taking a breather before we attempted to lug it into the kitchen. It was such a cute little kitchen. The house was really a cute little house. A cute little gingerbread kitchen with a cute little door, six feet high by two-and-a-half feet wide. Now I don't care who you are—even if you're the mover who did William Randolph Hearst's San Simeon job—you're not going to get a washer-dryer, four feet high by four feet wide, through that door.

What the hell, a lot of people have washer-dryers in their living rooms.

They also have pigs and chickens, but they're Indians, and they live in Mexico. That's it, goddamnit, the majority rules. If I were a Mexican or an Indian, and all our neighbors were Mexicans or Indians, we'd think nothing of having the washer-dryer in our living room.

As I sat with a glum look on my face, wondering whether we ought to move to Mexico with the washer-dryer, Honey started with, "What the hell are you so grouchy about? Boy, you take the fun out of everything. I have to sit here all day by myself, and you've been gone three hours."

Yeah, that's it. I'm just selfish. Manny and I, we're having all that fun, smashing our fingers and putting our backs out of whack. But I never went into this with Honey. I just thanked her, grateful for the laughs she gave me.

We couldn't decide where to put the washer-dryer; perhaps next to the sofa, or better yet in a corner, since the living room was a little overcrowded anyway. Honey considered making a coffee table out of it, but then we would have to build up all the couches and chairs. Of course, we could have made a "coffee counter" out of it.

But what the hell, we were saving money. Luckily, we hadn't sent the weekly car payment in yet, because it cost that much plus $10 to have the plumber come in and connect the machine.

It really looked wild . . . those two big, long black hoses going out of the living-room window into the yard . . . like the laboratory where Frankenstein's monster was born.

Everything worked fine, until the neighbors started watering the lawn. It had something to do with the pressure. When Honey was washing clothes, the owner would stand there holding a watering hose in his hand with just a trickle coming out.

We got the plumber back to do some more fixing and pipe changing. Now Honey could do the washing, and the landlord could water the lawn—but suddenly his wife screamed out the window: "The toilet won't flush!"

Whenever anyone flushed the toilet, you couldn't wash clothes or water the lawn. Which worked pretty good, except for those of us who had problems because of early toilet training and suffered from anal repressions, since it was necessary to yell at the top of your lungs, "I'm going to the bathroom! Stop washing and watering!" Then you could flush the toilet.

For those of us who found this announcement too traumatic, there were proxy announcers. I learned, also, that the landlord, who was quite a timid soul, was using the facilities next door.

The dopey dryer part of the machine was gas-operated, and it had a pilot light that kept going out. The pilot was right on the bottom, *one inch* from the floor, so you couldn't see it, you had to feel it. You had to reach in with your fingers, press down a button and light a match; then you had to hold it for at least 30 seconds till it took. I don't know what kind of matches the inventor of the machine used, but in 30 seconds, the matches *I* used always burned my fingers—or else, because of the fact that most floors carry a bit of a draft, the matches burned out in 15 seconds.

But the machine had a "guarantee." Of course, like all guarantees, it only covered parts. The particular part that was giving me trouble cost 38 cents, but the son-of-a-bitch who had to come in to replace it cost $26. It wasn't bad enough that I had been exploited by the department store, but now a mechanic, too.

That's something which has always bugged me. Radios, automobiles, whatever—you're really at the mercy of the repairman, because when they look in "there" and throw a lot of mechanical terms at you, you really feel like an idiot. It's the same with a broken watch. When the guy tells you that you need a new blah-blah-blah, you can't say, "Why, that blah-blah-blah is in *perfect* condition."

Maybe some day I'll write a *Manual of Stingmanship*. It will contain one completely esoteric reference to apply to each mechanical device the average guy owns, so that the repairman will assume that you're a genius and that you know twice as much as he does.

For example: You take your radio in to be repaired. Before the guy unscrews the back, you say: "I don't know what the hell it is—those new low-impedance osculators haven't had quite the filtration powers that the old X72103 set had. I'd check it out myself, but I've got to rip down that damned radar installation I put up last month in the Radon Valley."

After you give the repairman your name and address, leave immediately, before he has a chance to ask you if this radio is A.C. or D.C., which, if you're like I am, you wouldn't know. All the *Manual* would contain would be one or two good sentences for every appliance.

I wonder where that washer-dryer is today.

I've always wondered about things like that. When I look at a refrigerator that I figure must be 30 years old, I know that the couple who first bought it loved it dearly and shared many personal experiences with it. Probably it was already there in the house at the arrival of their first-born. It probably held the formula for all their children.

And then what? Sold. Perhaps to some guy who had a Boat, Dock and Fishing Equipment Shack; and the butter, milk, eggs, Jell-o and leftover spaghetti was replaced by frozen bait and cans of beer.

Then maybe, in between homes and people, it stands in a Used Appliances store. You've seen them: big, bare stores with maybe 50 or 60 refrigerators, old and new, with descriptions scrawled on them in black crayon: "As Is," "Perf. Mechanical Cond.," "Beauty, Clean," "Repossessed."

Are they happy there, all the refrigerators together? Do they talk to the gas stoves? Are electric stoves snobs?

There they are, an army of refrigerators, expensive ones and budget jobs, rich and poor. If one of them were socialistically minded, he might indeed say, "Some of us are old and some are quite modern with roll-out trays and automatic cube dispensers, but while we are here, we are all the same . . . because we're all defrosted."

Chapter
Fifteen

Living from one crazy disaster to another, Honey and I were always laughing, kidding, teasing, loving each other. Nothing could really hurt either of us because we were always together, and when one of us was down the other would pick the both of us up.

I had never enjoyed sleeping as much as when I slept with Honey. She just seemed to fit so nice, and I would really sleep soundly. It was funny, because when we first got married, I had never slept with a woman before. I had *schtupped* plenty of women, but I had never *slept* with one. I was fairly promiscuous, but I always went home "after," so it took me awhile to get used to sleeping with someone. I remember, about the second week of our marriage, Honey was heartbroken because I asked for a room with twin beds. But little by little, I got used to sleeping with her, and after a while I couldn't sleep without her.

I was like that kid in *Peanuts* with his dopey blanket

Honey was the most ticklish person in the world. All I had to do was *look* at her and say, "I'm going to tickle you now, I'm going to give you the worst tickling you've ever had," and she would really get giggly. I would just have to touch her side, and she'd laugh so hard the tears would come to her eyes.

She really made me laugh and did all kinds of bits for me. As I've said before, she had the most beautiful hair I'd ever seen. It was naturally red, and she could sit on it. When she wears it down, some women are so catty that they come up to her—in a hotel lobby, a shopping market, a movie theater—and say, "Oh, what lovely hair you have!"—and then they always touch it and give it a little yank; Honey wised me up as to their motivation—some women wear things called "switches," long pieces of store bought hair that fit in their own hair and match it in color, by which device they can make their hair look about a foot longer than it really is. I had never seen anyone with hair as long as Honey's; to hear others talk, though, 80 percent of the women in the world had hair that long, but they just cut it last week. "Oh, when I see your hair that long, I could just shoot myself. My hair was just as long as that, and I cut it, like a damn fool."

If I were depressed, Honey would even use her hair to try to cheer me up—tickling me playfully with it, or even making a mustache out of it.

We were driving happily along the streets of Pittsburgh, as silly as a couple of kids, sitting squeezed up tight to one another, deliciously in love, and laughing about my plans for the Brother Mathias Foundation.

We approached an intersection and came to a stop. It was dusk. There was a large truck a block-and-a-half away, coming along at about 40 miles an hour. I saw that we had plenty of time and nosed out to make it across. But as I pulled out an old Packard touring car whipped around the truck, passing it at breakneck speed. It was a convertible—as it came on us I could see the sudden terror in the driver's eyes. He involuntarily screamed, "Ma!"

I felt a rough substance coarse against my lips. It was cement. I had been thrown out of the car, and my mouth bit into the pavement, the curb connecting with my head with the thud of a coconut cracking. I found out later that my skull had been fractured, but I stood up immediately with that superhuman strength that people always have when "My life was saved by Eveready flashlight batteries."

To my horror I saw the Packard ramming my car down the street. The seats were empty and both doors flapped like mechanical wings of death. I saw the back wheels go over Honey's soft young body. I heard her hips crack like the sound of a Chinese fortune cookie. The next moment the truck, coming behind the Packard, also ran over her.

I raced to her and threw myself upon her. I felt something warm and wet, and looked down. It was her intestines. Oh, my sweet wonderful baby, my wife, every combination of everything, my mistress, my high priestess, I love her so much, please God let this only be a nightmare.

Her face was gray and there were puddles of blood around her. I yelled, "Oh God, why are you punishing her for my sins, why?"

I kissed her cold face and shouted into her ears, "I love you, take me with you!" I prayed and cried and wished for death, and all at once I realized we were in the center of a huge circle of people. I looked up into the faces of the crowd that had gathered and I knew I had been punished.

I sat on the curb and wept as the siren of the ambulance became louder.

"Oh, dear God, how ashamed I am, not ashamed of sinning, but ashamed that I have fallen into the mold which I despise. I am the image of the men I hate, the debauched degenerate that all men are who only in last resort find religion. How shallow you must think me, God, for surely if I were *your* God, I would say 'To hell with him. When he needs me, then he prays. But when he doesn't need me I never hear from him.' I cannot say I am sorry that I posed as a priest, but I can tell you this, if you let Honey live I'll rip up the charter and never do it again."

Four months later, Honey took her first step. The doctor said that with proper care, exercise and rest, she would regain her normal posture and health within a year.

I thanked God silently.

Thus ended the career that might have dwarfed those of Billy Graham and Oral Roberts and all the other evangelists who save. Save every goddamn penny they can lay their hands on.

The only hang-up now is, I wonder if God is a man or woman, or what color He is. Since the Bible could not be read if it weren't for printing, and the Chinese people were smart enough to invent printing, God must be yellow. What would His son's name be? Wong? Jesus? Or Christ Wing Fat? "Yea, I say to thee villilee." I know that God is not Japanese because *they* killed nuns at Pearl Harbor.

"Well," the theologians say, "I don't believe that God is a person. God is within me." Then He's a cancer, and all those scientists who want to cut Him out must hate God.

Or perhaps God is a transvestite who practices voodoo—the Father, the Son, the Holy Ghost. And I'm confused about the direction of Heaven. It's not *up* there, because the earth revolves, and sometimes you can go to Hell at 8:30, and Heaven at 12:06.

The Roman gods had naught to do with religion, except for Tuesday Night Wrestling & Christian-Eating. And the Egyptians before them didn't relate to Christianity; Rameses was the son of God, and he balled everybody in the kingdom including Moses' mother.

And Jehovah's Witnesses came to Atlantic City during the busy season and couldn't get any rooms. What is the answer? There is no God. *Dominus non sequitur.*

Certainly on an intellectual level I cannot buy the mysticism attached to any man-made religious object, whether it be the *mezuzah* nailed to the door sill—at least if they'd make it functional and put a chain on it, you could use it for a lock and kiss it at the same time—or the white plastic statues that Father Gregory from Louisiana has manufactured, the proceeds of which go to building segregated Catholic schools—they can make those white plastic statues functional, too, by tying them in electronically with the bumper and the windshield washer, so that when you do someone in, at the same time you can give him the last rites and baptize him.

With the money that Honey and I got from the accident, we bought a new Cadillac—a black four-door, really chic job that cost $4017. We drove to Arcadia, California, to see my father, who had remarried. We were going to go to Hollywood—"where my father is"—and then Honey would *really* get into the movies. My father wasn't really involved with the motion-picture industry; in fact what he *was* really involved with was a chicken farm.

We worked on the farm for two months. It was like being back with the Denglers. I really put the place into shape. Honey did the canning.

Then my father and I had a beef, and we left. We couldn't get jobs. California is a weird place—you've got to get booked from New York.

Until Honey and I started "winging"—that is, getting into a higher-income bracket—we always bought secondhand stoves and refrigerators. You could get a stove for about $35 and a refrigerator for about $75. When we were living on the Coast, I knew she wanted a new refrigerator, but I couldn't afford it.

At that time, I was working a burlesque club, and there was a TV producer from the show, *Your Mystery Mrs.*, who was a regular customer. Like most voyeurs, he needed a rationalization for watching the strippers. "The girls—are you kidding? Those old bags! I go to see the comedians!"

This was in part true. Somehow these guys have the misconception that the m.c. can fix them up with the girls. But the request—"Will you fix me up with so-and-so?"—is preposterous, unless a girl is an out-and-out hooker, which strippers are not; otherwise they would be hookers, not strippers.

Of course, there are some people who sell themselves for money. That "some" constitutes 90 percent of the people I've known in my life, including myself. We all sell out some part of us.

Any 19-year-old girl who is married to a wealthy, elderly guy . . . well, never mind that—just *anyone* who is married for security is a hooker. Two dollars for a short time, as opposed to a marriage license and a lot of two dollars for a longer time.

The point is that women, unlike men, cannot be "fixed up." With the exception of a hooker, you can't go up to any girl and say, "How about doing it with my friend?" For women to make it, there has to be a love motivation, or at least a chemistry that passes as love.

On the other hand, men are animals. Again, guys will make it with mud, dogs, cats, goats—ask any guy who has been unfortunate enough to spend time in an institution, or a place where men are deprived of women. Many of these men will practice homosexuality, never to return to it upon release.

Ironically, the way homosexuals are punished in this country is by throwing them into jail with other men.

I remember one of the funniest newspaper *shticks* I've ever read was this case where a Miami judge gave two guys 30 days in the county jail—are you ready for the charge?—for kissing each other and dancing in one saloon or another on Alton Road. He told them in court, "I realize that this is a medical problem, but I have to set a precedent at the beginning of the season."

You're allowed to kiss all the *petzies* you want in March, but don't *fress* in February.

Before I go any further, I had better explain what kind of show *Your Mystery Mrs.* was . . .

ANNOUNCER: In 1931, today's Mystery Mrs. lost her family in a mine explosion. Bravely she went on alone and through years of self-teaching and discipline, she was able to support herself. Where other women, used to the support of a husband, would live off the charity of relatives, your Mystery Mrs. studied day and night, came to New York City, and now has a wonderful job. She is an usherette at the Roxy Theater.

One night last month, in the line of duty, showing two people to their seats, she tripped and fell and has been incapacitated ever since. She has been too proud to accept any help. Our show heard about this plucky widow and decided to do something. There aren't many plucky widows, folks. How many of you out there can say you know a plucky widow? How many widows can say in all honesty, "I'm plucky!"

(*All the widows in the audience stand up and say "I'm plucky!"*)

ANNOUNCER: Our Mystery Mrs. has always dreamed of having her own set of matched luggage. We're going to make that dream come true. And our Mystery Mrs. is . . . (*Organ fanfare . . . camera pans to Mystery Mrs., seated in audience.*) . . . You, Mrs. Ralph Whoozis from Alberta, Kansas!

Mrs. Whoozis does her "surprise" take—sometimes referred to in the business as the "Does he mean *me*?" take. There are several accepted methods of creating expressions for the surprise. One is to clench the fist of the left hand, simultaneously drop the lower jaw, and in a split second bring up the left side of the other clenched fist so that the index finger lands between the teeth. Individuals who have seen a few neorealistic Italian films, where the "wronged" bites the index finger in anger, usually do well with this take.

The announcer waves both wrists limply but speedily to encourage applause. Mrs. Whoozis takes her luggage after shedding a few tears on the unbreakable, unscuffable, unfashionable crap they give her—and housewives at home sigh and identify.

Now, when the producer of this show was drooling at his favorite stripper, I never dreamed that a time would come when I would be involved with a Mystery Mrs. "You know, Lenny, you're a pretty creative guy," he said one night, having corralled me backstage, "because every time I come in here you've got some new material. You know, I'm pretty creative, too. I don't like to blow my own horn, but I'm a brilliant writer. The shame of it is, nobody knows."

"How's that?" I asked, looking at him as one looks at a desperate man standing on a ledge.

"Lenny, did you see *Your Mystery Mrs.* yesterday?"

"Hardly. It goes on at nine o'clock in the morning."

"I had on a widow that not only lost three sons in the War, but two husbands. And she's a blood donor. We got more telephone calls on this show than on any one we've had in two weeks. People from all over. Some furrier from the Bronx is going to send her a full-length sheared-beaver coat to keep her warm. The pitch was, she has given so much blood that now, by some strange quirk, she has low blood pressure."

"Amazing," I said. I always say that when I don't know what the hell else to say. When I don't say "amazing," I switch off with "Boy, some people," or sometimes an "I don't believe you." Another good phrase is "Can you believe that?" If the talker is bitching about being exploited, the best one for that is, "It seems some people, the better you treat them, the worse they are to you." Or, "It just doesn't pay to be nice to people."

After I gave out with two "Hmms" and a "That's one for the book," the producer laid it on me: "They eat it up, Lenny, you wouldn't believe it, but they eat it up. The cornier it is, the more they eat it up. And now are you ready Lenny? Are you ready for the bit? It's all bullshit, ya hear me? Bullshit with a capital K. I write it. Me—poor little, stupid me—is the one that makes 'em laugh and makes 'em cry. I make it all up!

"You know who that plucky little widow is? She's a waitress I met when I was in the Air Force. I bumped into her in a dancehall last week—now, mind you, I haven't seen her in over, let's see, the War was over in 1945, I came back to L.A., why, it's an easy 14 years—and I says to myself, 'Now I know that broad from somewhere.' Then it hits me. She's 'Go Down Gussie.' This broad was the greatest French job on the West Coast. Loved it. Couldn't get enough of it. I said, 'Hey, remember that place where you used to wait on me?' She looked at me for a minute and couldn't place me. I didn't have the toupee then and I guess I look different without it."

His toupee was the kind which had lace in the front that looks like a screen door cut out, and he always had it on a little crooked. I don't know who it could have fooled—maybe passed-out drunks or little babies. When he sweated, it used to curl up in the front.

Anyway, he continued: "We shot the shit for a while and then I told her what I was doing and asked her if she would like to be a plucky widow next week. 'What's in it for me?' she says. 'Nine inches,' I says. 'Always braggin', ain't ya?' she says. I says, 'Let's go up to your apartment and fix some grub, I'm starved.' She says, 'I don't got anything in the icebox.' "

Of all this degenerate flack he was throwing at my ears, the one thing that hit me was her icebox. How sad—the icebox again. I wondered where she got *her* icebox. Maybe it was one of those built-in iceboxes that Pullman kitchens have. Hookers' iceboxes always look the same: a jar of mustard, a Coke, maybe a lemon, and half an onion wrapped in wax paper.

The producer went on and on, describing in lewd detail how she had Frenched him. The poor French. There's an example of how one minority group has given a whole nation an erotic reputation. It could easily have been another country. He could just as well have said "She Polacked me."

He explained that the "widows" or "grandmas" or "have-a-year-to-livers" were all people who could be trusted—friends of his or the other writer for the show, or people those friends sent. They could have their choice of two deals: One, take a straight $50 and he would keep the prizes; or, two, if it was the "Basket Case" (the act which had the most dramatic impact), you would get $50 and split the prizes. The big prizes were a color-TV set, a washing machine, a set of silver, and an air-conditioning unit—all of which they got free from the distributors in exchange for plugs.

"You need anything, Lenny? Any appliances?"

"Well, I *could* use a new refrigerator . . ."

"You got it."

"I don't think I'd make a very convincing plucky widow."

"Look, Lenny, if you can get me an old lady about 60 years old that you can trust for next Wednesday, the machine is yours. And, let's see . . . er—if you can get me—yeah, that's it, get me a 60-year-old lady and her wedding picture, get the wedding picture as soon as you can so I can get it to the lab and have it blown up, and I'll give you a script Monday.

"She doesn't have to remember much. I never give them more than a few lines: 'I only wish the Mister was alive to see this!' Or, 'My boy is coming home from the Veterans Hospital, and this TV set will make all the difference in the world to him!' I gotta go, Len, I'll see you Wednesday at the office. Here's my card. Bring the wedding pic. I'd like to stay and see Princess Talja, but I gotta go. You know what they say, when ya gotta go, ya gotta go."

I've never known who the hell "they" are, but I'll bet they belong to the American Legion, have very white skin with real white legs, and wear Jockey shorts, and black shiny dress shoes with black stockings on the beach.

A 60-year-old lady?

Mema had a relative that she was pretty friendly with, and she called her on the phone and explained in Yiddish what she was to do. She said "Nix," but *she* had a friend who was a real *vilda chi* (wild one). She said this woman was perfect, she spoke very good English, etc.

I went over and met Mrs. Stillman. The woman was about 70 but looked about 55, had bleached-blonde hair, full make-up, and platform shoes—the highest I'd ever seen, about ten inches. With the platforms, she was about four feet tall. Some Jewish ladies look like little birdies to me.

I flipped when she showed me some sheet music she brought out. She was going to be on TV, so she was going to sing. She had all of the Sholom Secunda hits (He was the Yip Harburg of Second Avenue).

She said she also knew a few stories, but maybe they were a little *shmutsik* for TV. When I told her that the program wasn't exactly that type of format, she was visibly shaken. I was afraid I was going to lose her, so I started to pad—"But then, after you tell them about your *tsooris* maybe you'll sing your song." That made her happy. I figured after she told the story I would shuffle her off into a room and give her a quick con about overtime. The song she was planning to sing was *Bells Mine Schtatetala Bells.*

She gave me her wedding picture, and I got it over to the office. It was perfect. A real old tintype. The story was going to be a real basket case:

"Miss Whoozis was a spinster who searched her whole life for the perfect man. She has always been lonely and unhappy. Two months ago, on a boat from Greece, came a man who was her ideal type. They met at Horn & Hardart's Cafeteria, by the silverware section. He was confused by some of the food, the chow mein in particular. They met every day and fell in love, but sadness struck our happy couple.

"George Polous was unemployed and the Immigration Department was going to send him back. But he has a lot of money coming to him, if only he can find his Uncle Nicholas who has $7000 of his inheritance. This is a wedding picture of Uncle Nicholas and his wife. *Your Mystery Mrs.* did a great deal of research and was saddened to discover that George's Uncle Nicholas had passed away. But his wife was alive, and his wife had the money put away for George."

And guess who the aunt was going to be, boys and girls—that little Jewish bird lady, my aunt's friend. Her wedding picture would be shown on a TV screen. There was Mr. and Mrs. Nicholas Polous in their wedding picture—as played by Mr. and Mrs. Stillman.

It was two days away from the show when Mrs. Stillman called me and asked me to come over immediately. It was about the show. On the way over, I figured the worst. Maybe she wanted a trio in back of her when she was singing.

She looked pleasant as she sat me down on the polyethylene-covered furniture. "Mr. Bruce, I want you should feel very relaxed wid me; efter all, you and I boat know things about life."

I thought to myself, Christ, who is going to believe this Hebrew National is a Greek? Well, maybe they would introduce her as a symbol of brotherhood. A Greek who lives in an old Jewish neighborhood and has assimilated.

"What I'm gettin' et, is, you are dishonest cheating me."

"Oh?" I said. After all, her prize was supposed to be a refrigerator-freezer combination, a washing machine and a TV set. I was going to get the refrigerator, she would get $50, and the producer would get the rest of the prizes.

"Don' ect tricky wid me, Sonny."

"Tricky? What the hell are you getting at?"

"One tousend dollars, that's what I'm getting at . . . I talked to my son in Westchester dis mornin', end I told him to watch me on the telewision. He sed to me, 'I'm so heppy for you, Momma, how much are you getting?' I told him $50. Vell, he's leffing so hard, I said, 'Oh, I'm a comedian?' He says, 'Momma, you are de beggest sucker in de world, people are always teking edventage of you.' Well, that is the trut, Mr. Bruce, people hev always made a good-time Benny out of me.

"He told me that Shirley Beck, who lived downstairs from us when we lived in Laguna Beach last year—was it last year now, let me see, Vera was 32 years old, and Helen was pregnant in June, yes, last year—Shirley was on the Groucho Marx show and got $1000, and Mr. Bruce, $1000 is not $50."

"Is that right, Mrs. Stillman—$1000 is not $50? Do you realize that if this information gets into the wrong hands, our country could be in great danger? Now, look, I don't know what you're trying to prove, but *gonsa geschikta*"—which means 'the whole thing'—it's always good to throw in a couple of Yiddish words when you're debating with a member of the older generation—"is for our refrigerator, which I need, and that's the reason I'm getting you on the show. And for doing this for me, I want to *give* you $50 from my own pocket. The rest of the prizes are a washing machine and a TV set that the producer wants for letting *me* get *you* on the show in the first place. Now, I don't know where any $1000 is going to come from."

"Vell, dat's your headache already. I'm not doing it for a penny less than $1000."

I left her house a beaten man. I'm such an impulsive nut that as soon as I had heard about getting the refrigerator, I had promised ours to a couple who had just been married, and they were so happy about it. . . . I told Honey the bad news. She said, "That's all right, Daddy, the old one is plenty good."

"Yes, but I promised to give it away, and I can't disappoint these people."

"Why do you have to use Mrs. Stillman? Get another woman."

Of course! It still wasn't too late. I was supposed to bring Mrs. Stillman down to the studio to sign her release the next day. Honey knew a woman of about 60 who made most of the strip wardrobe for the girls. She was very good-natured. We called her on the phone and she was perfect.

The only slight problem was that they already had the wedding picture of Mrs. Stillman blown up ten feet high by four feet wide; and Mrs. McNamara, the seamstress, was about five feet, nine inches tall and weighed 160 pounds.

I briefed her, and then we met the producer. "This is Mrs. Stillman," I said, "our basket case."

"Well, she doesn't look too much like her wedding picture. How the hell tall is her husband?"

"Oh, he was a big man," she said without missing a beat.

The show was 36 hours away.

And then I got a call from one of my best friends, a saxophone player. He was broke, and he had a chance to make some bread in a recording session, but he needed $50 to get his alto out of hock.

It came to me in a flash.

"Joe," I said, "your mother's going to give you that fifty dollars."

"Are you kidding, Lenny? She hasn't got fifty cents. And if she has, she's already spent it on wine." Joe's mother was the sweetest, best-natured woman I've ever met, but she did like her Napa Valley.

I explained the TV deal to Joe, and he called his mother and then called me back, saying that it would be a perfect deal. Joe's mother would be Mrs. McNamara, posing next to Mrs. Stillman's picture, who was supposed to be Mrs. Polous, who was going to give to her Greek nephew—who was going to be deported—$7000 that she had been saving for him ever since his Uncle Nicholas had died. Then George and his Horn & Hardart sweetheart could be married, and I would get my refrigerator, and Joe's mother could have $5 for wine (which I gave to her as an advance), Joe could have his $50 to get his alto out of hock, and the producer could go straight to jail if anything went wrong.

At 8:30 on the morning of the show, Joe's mother and I met the usher as we had been directed to do, and he sat her in a special seat, with me next to her. The people who were going to be "surprised" always had to be seated in the right seats so that the cameraman knew where to pick them out.

Luckily, the producer of *Your Mystery Mrs.* came late, and when he saw Joe's mother sitting next to me, clutching her brown paper bag twisted into the definite shape of a wine bottle (and she really was boxed—I had never seen her so drunk—and just think, she'd be on television in ten minutes), he kept staring at her with a what-the-hell-am-I-losing-my-mind-is-that-the-same-woman-who-was-up-in-my-office? look.

Before the program started, a warm-up master of ceremonies told some disgusting water-closet-humor jokes. Then he explained about the applause. And then the show was on:

"Somewhere in this fruitful land, someone nice needs a helping hand . . . and we present, with love and kisses (*Organ fanfare.*) . . . *Your Mystery Mrs.!*"

The first act was a light, what they call humorous, bit. Four men were onstage behind a rig with their pants rolled up to their knees, so that you could see only their legs. If this woman could pick her husband's legs, she and her husband could win a round trip to Holland to attend her father's funeral.

I heard a strange sound and my heart stopped. Joe's mother was snoring. I gave her a good pinch and brought her out of it. When the announcer said,

"And it's lucky you, Mrs. Nicholas Polous!" the camera panned to her just in time to see her kissing the brown paper bag. I whispered, "Go ahead on up there, please. Don't forget, you're not doing this for Joe's alto but for my icebox."

It took her two years to get up to the stage.

The m.c. observed very quickly that his next guest was drunk. "Mrs. Polous is certainly a brave woman, folks. She was just discharged from the hospital this morning, and against doctor's orders she's here. I'm going down to help her." This got the audience's sympathy, and his quick thinking turned round one into a winner.

They flashed the wedding picture on the screen, and you would have had to be blind not to have seen that this was not Mrs. Polous. There was a weight difference of about 80 pounds—which difference you might buy; people do lose and gain weight. But they don't grow seven inches. Mrs. Stillman was a little tiny woman. Joe's mother was even bigger than Mrs. McNamara.

But when they flashed the picture on, all the women in the audience gave one of those "Oh, isn't that sweet?" sighs. The announcer reminisced about the wonderful life that Mr. and Mrs. Polous had shared, and how brave she was, and how he knew that she was comforted by the memories of her late husband.

And all Joe's mother kept saying was, "Yeah, he was a hell of a man!"

The m.c. didn't quite believe what he had heard the first time, and he sort of laughed to cover up, but she kept saying it: "Yeah, he was a hell of a man!" He sensed she was going to go into a stream of profanity, and when I looked up inside the glass booth, I saw the producer staring down at me, nodding his head slowly and mechanically.

All of a sudden I saw a cue card that the audience saw, too: "GET TO THE PRIZES AND GET HER THE HELL OFF!" This certainly confused the studio audience. A brave woman like that, who had just gotten out of the hospital? Is that way to talk about her? Get to the prizes and get her the hell off?

". . . And a beautiful refrigerator with a double deep-freezer compartment will be sent to your home . . ."

The show was over, and I hustled Joe's mother into a cab, after she insisted I go back and get her the wine she had left under her seat.

I came home with a bottle of champagne and two hollow-stemmed glasses. Honey loved that kind of glass, and she loved champagne. She was standing in the doorway with an I've-got-bad-news look on her face.

"What's the matter, sweetheart?"

"I just got a call from guess who—Mrs. Stillman. Her son in New York watched the show and saw her picture being used. He called his lawyer and they're suing for invasion of privacy."

And sue they did. But everything turned out OK. I got the refrigerator,

Joe got his alto, his mother got her wine, and Mrs. Stillman settled out of court.

Naturally, though, the producer lost his job. I felt sort of bad about that, but soon enough he was producing a show twice as big as the *Your Mystery Mrs.* package. And this one is still running; still successful.

All of which goes to prove the old adage, "You Can't Keep a Good Crook Down . . ."

Chapter Sixteen

It was starting to get desperate for us financially, and Honey said, "OK, I've got a chance to strip."

"Oh, Christ, no. I don't want you to go back to stripping!"

"Well, I'll just go stripping for two weeks, and that'll be it. I'll play Las Vegas."

The thing was just to get enough money to make payments on the car—$120 a month. I had it all figured out. I got a room for seven dollars a week. I ran an ad in the paper: "LENNY THE GARDENER—LET ME EDGE, CLEAN AND MOW YOUR LAWN FOR $6.00."

And I lived, just for the hell of it, on 15 cents a day. I cooked for myself. I was making $90 in a burlesque joint, plus the money I got from gardening. I had Honey's picture up and flowers in the window of my room, just like a shrine.

I had never been separated from her before, and I just couldn't wait for the two weeks of stripping in Vegas to end. But the night she was supposed to come home, she called up and said she had a chance to stay over for two extra weeks.

"Are you kidding? Come home."

I begged and begged and begged, but she stayed there anyway. That was a telltale sign of where I stood in the marriage. I started eating more crap and more crap. I was a complete slave. I was really hung up on her.

Eventually, Honey and I were to get divorced.

I finally had some guts and got rid of her. She left me.

We kept breaking up and going back together at my insistence. She was always better at holding out.

After you break up and go back again enough times, you get hip to one thing: the time of day you break up is very important. If you run away in the middle of the night, there's no place to go. You can't wake your friends up, and in a small town you're *really* screwed. It's best to break up on your day off, in the afternoon. You get out and you go to the movies. Otherwise, like a *schmuck,* you're standing on the lawn at three o'clock in the morning with a pillowcase full of clothing and the door locked behind you.

That's when you're *not* proud that you've "lived next door to someone for 15 years and didn't even know their name."

When I got divorced, a couple of major magazines, like *Time,* asked me, five years later, that dumb question: "What happened to your marriage?" I figured I would throw a real stock line and they would know I was putting them on and they would cool it.

"What happened to my marriage? It was broken up by my mother-in-law."

And the reporter laughed—"Mother-in-law, ha, ha, what happened?"

"My wife came home early from work one day and she found us in bed together."

"In bed—that's perverse."

"Why? It was *her* mother, not mine."

One thing about getting divorced, it gave me about an hour's worth of material. That's not bad for an eight-year investment.

But I didn't know how screwed up I was over Honey until one night she came into the club where I was working and sat ringside with some guy. I completely fell apart, and was able to do only a nine-minute show.

Guess who I saw today, my dear . . .

How can I ever get married again? I'd have to say the same things to another woman that I had said to Honey. And I couldn't say the same things to another woman because somehow that would be corrupt to me.

I wrote half a musical, and I did blues from it on the Steve Allen show:

All alone. All alone.
Oh, what joy to be all alone.
I'm happy alone, don't you see.
I've convinced you, now how about me?
All alone.

I'll get my own pad. I'll really swing. If you can't live with them and you can't live without them, I'll go one better: I'll live with a lot of them. I can really fix up a pad. I'll get hi-fi stereo, a bullfight poster, a black coffee table—no, I'll get a coffee table and make a door out of it—and a pearl-white phone. And sit back and relax and finally be all alone. All alone.

Honey used to look so good standing up against the sink. I don't want a sharp chick who quotes Kerouac; I just want to hear my old lady say, "Get up and fix the toilet, it's still making noise."

All alone. All alone.
I'll just sit in my house all alone.
Ah, but it's better to be all alone.

No more taking out the garbage,
Hear her yakking on the phone.
I gave her everything,
Even my mother's ring.
But to me she was so petty.
She didn't know her best friend.
Sometimes I wish she were dead,
But it would probably take her two hours to get ready.
When she's old she'll be sorry.
Her future spells a murky gloom.
I'll be rich and famous
And she'll live in a furnished room.
It'll be too late, I won't hear her moan.
I'll be living in my Nob Hill mansion,
Rich and all alone.
All alone. All alone. I'll be happy and rich,
And all alone.

Yeah. I'll be an old man in an empty hotel suite, and nobody'll want me to co-sign.

Four years of working in clubs—that's what really made it for me—every night: doing it, doing it, doing it, doing it, getting bored and doing it different ways, no pressure on you, and all the other comedians are drunken bums who don't show up, so I could try anything.

The jazz musicians liked me. I was the only hippy around. Because I was young, other people started to work the same clubs for nothing, just to hang out, the way you do when you're young. Hedy Lamarr would come to see me work, and Ernie Kovacs. Every joint I worked, I'd start to get a sort of following.

"You should get out of this place," I would be told, "you're too good for these shithouses." But I knew I wasn't ready yet. I was still thinking in terms of "bits"—you know, "I've got my so-and-so bit, and I've got this other bit. I've got two complete shows."

Then, after a while, instead of just getting material together, little by little it started happening. I'd just go out with no bits.

"Hey, how come you didn't do any bits that show?"

"Well, anything is a bit if I do it twice."

And I really started to become a craftsman, where I could just about structure anything into humor.

Up until 1957, I had never gotten any write-ups. I had worked all these burlesque clubs, where they just had the ads for the club—the names of the girls in the show, and then on the bottom they had:

Lenny Bruce, Master of Ceremonies
Three Shows Nightly 9:30, 11:30, 1:30
Ladies Invited, Plenty of Free Parking

Now, when I went to San Francisco I stopped working these burlesque clubs and I worked the so-called straight clubs, such as Ann's 440, where I would be the only act.

Ordinarily an opening at a small club—and Ann's 440 was a damned small club—would get no attention at all. But when I opened there, the press got wind of it, and I really blew the town apart.

Hugh Hefner heard about me, and he came to San Francisco to hear me. He arranged for me to come to Chicago and work at The Cloister. They offered me $600, but I had been working Ann's 440 on a percentage and getting $750 a week (not bad after coming from a room where I was making $90), so I asked for $800 at The Cloister, and if they held me over, I would get $1250 a week.

I hadn't realized till then how much material I had, because here were places where I wasn't merely m.c.ing between 15 strippers. I could just wheel and deal for hours and hours. And the same people started coming every night, and there was always something different, and it would really drive them nuts. I had a whole bagful of tricks which I'd developed in the burlesque clubs.

There was already this "in" kind of thing with all these musicians who had heard of me, but the controversy that actually did, let's say, "make" me was the bit I called "Religions, Inc."

I had gotten a job as a writer at 20th Century-Fox. They were working on a picture called *The Rocket Man,* and Buddy Hackett told them, "Lenny's very good, he's funny and he can create and everything. Why don't you let him have a crack at it?"

So they told me to read the script over the weekend.

The average writer knocks out 15–20 pages a day. I went and did about 150 pages over the weekend and I came back and really impressed the hell out of them. They changed the whole theme of the picture.

The story was about these kids in an orphan asylum. It was just a cute little picture. Nothing unusual. I added to it—there was a Captain Talray who had a space show for kids. He goes to the orphan asylum and he gives the kids all these toys. And Georgie Winslow is the last kid he sees, and he doesn't have a toy left for him, and so the kid is really sad. But then a space gun appears—*Pchewwwww!*—a magic gun.

Georgie Winslow starts using this gun—like when a car's going to run over him—*Pchewwwww!*—he stops the car. And that was the whole different twist I gave the picture: the magic space gun.

They gave me a contract and I was so proud. My God, a writer at 20th Century-Fox! My own secretary! Man, I just couldn't believe it. It was one of the most thrilling things in my life, because all the other things that have happened to me have happened gradually.

Anyway, I wanted to produce my own picture. At the time I was sort of swept up with the story of Christ—this big, beautiful man—and the picture I had in mind was about a handicapped bum who wore a hearing aid. His whole ambition in life was to save enough money to buy a black-leather motorcycle jacket. Some day the motorcycle, but first he just wanted to get enough money together to buy the jacket.

There was to be a scene in the picture where he was really disappointed, and his hand was caught in the door and had to be all wrapped up in a bandage, and he was struggling with his suitcase . . . and he passes this statue of Christ. It's a beautiful statue. It doesn't show Christ being crucified; it shows him very stately, on top of the world, standing there, and he's King of Kings.

The shot was to be this: I walk up to the statue, pass it, look back, gaze at it for a while. There are some flowers on the ground at the foot of this ball which is the earth. I pick up the flowers. I can just about reach His toes, and I put the flowers at His feet, and then I just sort of fall on the globe, embracing it. When we go back to a long shot, showing my arms outstretched while I'm falling there, it looks like a cross.

Now I had searched and searched for a statue of Christ. It took me two days to find the right one. I found it outside in this big churchyard, on Melrose and Vine Streets in Hollywood.

I still had a concept of priests that stemmed from all the Pat O'Brien movies. You know: you're in trouble, they just come and comfort you.

Well, I couldn't get to talk to one of them.

So I went directly to the headquarters, on Alvarado Street, the center where all these different priests go.

At the rectory, I got this kind of answer: "It's not my parish."

They'd all close their windows, and they wouldn't even talk to me. True, I was dressed as a bum, because I was doing the picture, but still. . . . They just wouldn't talk to me.

Finally—and this part didn't actually happen, but I made a joke out of it on the stage that night—I said: "I tried to find a statue of Christ today, and I tried to talk to priests, and no one would talk to me, but I finally got a chance to talk to one, and he sold me a chance on a Plymouth."

That was the first joke I ever did on religion. It was only a joke, but it really related to the rejection and disappointment I had felt that day.

Then came the extension. I abstracted to: "The Dodge-Plymouth dealers had a convention, and they raffled off a 1958 Catholic Church."

And that was the beginning of Religions, Inc.:

And now we go to the headquarters of Religions, Inc., where the Dodge-Plymouth dealers have just had their annual raffle, and they have just given away a 1958 Catholic Church. And seated around the desk are the religious leaders of our country.

We hear one of them. He's addressing the tight little group in Little-town, Connecticut (Madison Avenue is getting a little trite). "Well, as you know, this year we've got a tie-in with Oldsmobile. Now, gentle-men, I don't expect any of you boys to get out there in the pulpit and hard-sell an automobile. That is ridiculous. But I was thinking now. What do you say to this? If just every once in a while, if we'd throw in a few little terms, just little things like, uh, 'Drive the car that He'd drive!'—and you know, you don't have to lay it on, just zing it in there once in a while and then jump maybe to the Philistines."

In December of 1962, I was arrested at The Gate of Horn in Chicago for "obscenity." But, according to *Variety*, ". . . the prosecutor is at least equally concerned with Bruce's indictments of organized religion as he is with the more obvious sexual content of the comic's act. It's possible that Bruce's comments on the Catholic Church have hit sensitive nerves in Chicago's Catholic-oriented administration and police department . . ."

And actually I had *praised* the Catholic Church.

"Remember the freak shows," I asked—"the alligator lady and the guy who could typewrite with his toes? The irony is that the generation now that is really offended by 'sick humor'—talking about people that are deformed —they're the generation that bought *tickets* to see the freaks: Zip & Pip, the onion-head boy, Lolly & Lulu, all these terrible, bizarre-looking freaks.

"Now," I said, "dig the difference between the generation today and my father's generation. These young people today, the ones who are 'going to hell in a basket,' they're really better Christians and more spiritual than that last, perverse generation, because this new generation not only rejected but doesn't support freak attractions—that's not their entertainment *shtick*—they like rock 'n' roll as opposed to the freak shows. But, Thank God for the Catholic Church, there'll still be freaks—the thalidomide babies—they'll grow up and get a good tie-in with Barnum & Bailey."

*A group of my North Bellmore schoolmates
who may someday turn up on a jury.*

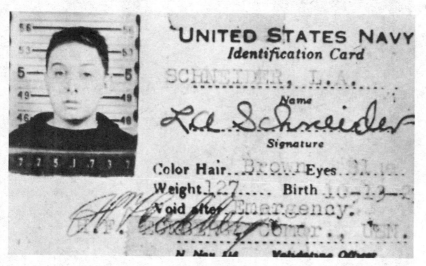

UNITED STATES NAVY
Identification Card

SCHNEIDER, L.A.
Name

Ld Schneider
Signature

Color Hair...Brown...Eyes...Bl...

Weight 127..... Birth 10-13-2

Void after Emergency.

*"How come your name is Schneider and you use the name Bruce?"
Because Leonard Alfred Schneider sounded too Hollywood.*

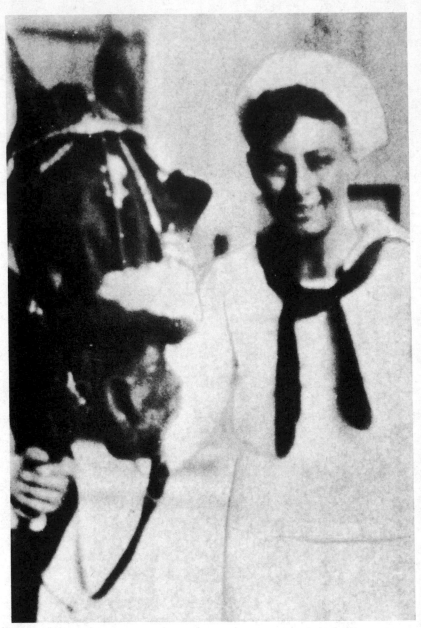

A girl in every port.

Portrait of a post-War vagrant. I wanted to look like Warner Baxter or Roland Young but, alas, the comment from Aunt Mema was: "You look like a pimp."

This Sabu shot was taken during my mystical period—so mystical I can't even remember where or why it was taken.

At last! My name in lights: S·T·R·A·N·D . . .

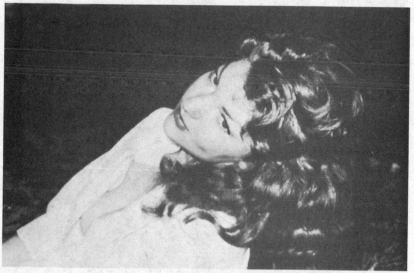

*Honey Harlowe was the most beautiful woman
I had ever seen in my life . . .*

. . . and she still is.

But the week that I met her, I shipped out in the merchant marine.

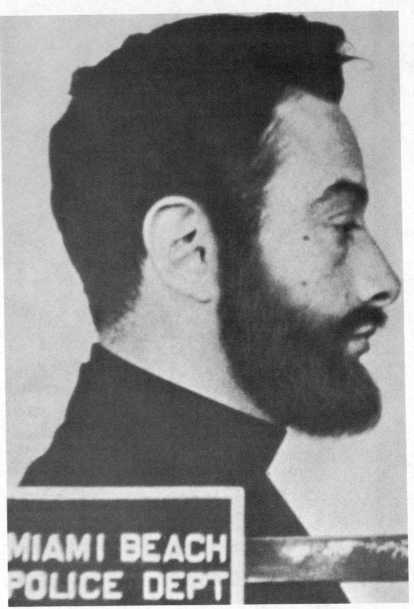

The fuzz figured a priest in Miami Beach had to be up to something.
But it was OK—I had a license to practice.

ARREST REPORT

Place of Arrest: ___48 Street & Alton road___
Time of Arrest: ___1:40 P.M.___   Date ___April 23, 1951___
CHARGE: ___Vagrancy (Investigation General)___
        ___Pan Handling___

Arresting Officer (S)
             ___L.H. Oodood___

Prisoner (No. 1) ___LEONARD SCHNEIDER___
Address ___Floridian Hotel___
Prisoner (No. 2) ___54 Livingston Street BKLYN.N.Y.___

Make of Car (If any) _____
Present Location of Car _____
License Tag _____ State _____
Hold For: _____

Prisoner (No. 3) _____
Prisoner (No. 4) _____

STATE COMPLETE DETAILS OF ARREST AND WHY INVESTIGATION IS WANTED

         Received a call to investigate a man dressed as a priest soliciting funds for a lepor colony.

         Found subject at the corner of 48th street & Alton road, dressed as a priest, subject stated to the undersigned that he was soliciting funds for some non-sectarian organization that had sponsered a lepor colony.

         Subject had no identification of any nature on his person, and stated that he was not working, but that maby he would go to work this week end. Subject stated that he was a comedian on the stage and appeared localy in night clubs under the name of LENNY BRUCE.

         Subject was interrogated several times and the more he was questioned the more confusing his story became. Subject was taken by St. Pat's and questioned by one of the priests there and he inturn could not arrive at a definate decision as to subjects true object of work.

         Subject states that he is the founder of the organization which is behind this lepor colony and that there is 4 other beside himself, but that the other 4 are still in New York, and that the organization is a chartered one in the state of New York.

Released. OR
   u.C.N

Respectfully submitted :
        Reporting Officer ___L.H. Oodood___

They charged me with panhandling...

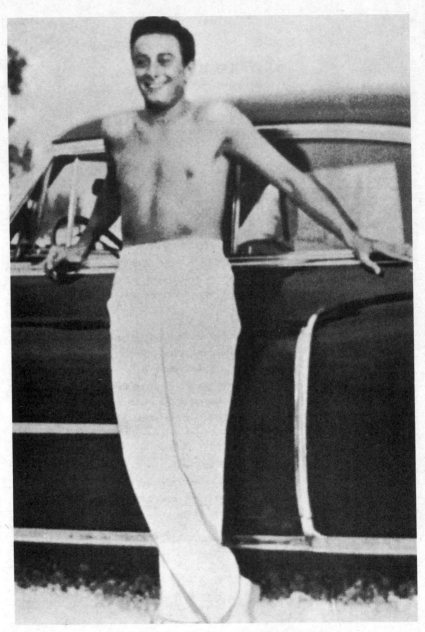

...I ask you—is this the pose of a panhandler?

Honey was making it as a singer, at last, and we were doing fine.

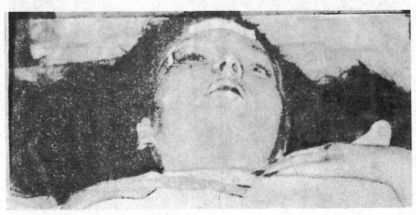

Singer Injured in Auto Crash

Night Club Artist Badly Cut, May Have Fractured Skull After Collision in Lawrenceville

A night-club singer and her comedian-husband were injured yesterday evening in a two-car collision in Lawrenceville, minutes after they had retrieved their car from the City towing garage where it had been held for being illegally parked.

Mrs. Harriet Bruce, appearing chelle, suffered severe lacerations of the forehead, multiple bruises, contusions and a possible fractured skull.

Remains in Hospital

She was detained at St. Francis Hospital. Her husband, Lenny, also appearing at the Monte Carlo, was treated for severe head lacerations and released. He went back to the club to go on with the show, but his head began to bleed before curtain time so he returned to St. Francis.

The Bruces, who make their home in Brooklyn, paid $8 to get their car out of the City towing garage at 6 p. m. Thirty minutes later the car was back in the garage, its front badly wrecked.

Other Driver Unhurt

At Twenty-ninth and Smallman Streets, Lawrenceville, the car, driven by Mr. Bruce, and one which police said was driven by Raymond Schreiver, of ____

LENNY BRUCE

Serious auto injuries may mar Honey Michelle's bea____

Monte Carlo management said Harvey Bell of Miami and S____ it was feared the titian-haired Rosemary O'Reilly, a local beauty might be lastingly "Bell had happened to scarred.

That was the day I left the priesthood.

Honey didn't take another step for four months.

Here I am in my famous impression of a faith healer. Yes, friends, drop your bread in the collection box or I'll throw this right in your faith.

*Hefner? Hefner? I can't seem to find your name
in my dance card.*

*Clowning for the camera in one of my grave moments,
I cross up a friend.*

Another in my series of famous impressions. Red Buttons?
Eddie Cantor? Jonah describing the whale?

Here I am in my guise as a mild-mannered charity promoter.

I forget who the other two guys are, but that's not Shirley Temple on your right. For years I dreamed of a situation like this, but I finally had to set up my own cop and judge. P.S. I was acquitted.

*We Americans love nonconformity and often
award it the metal of honor.*

An introspective moment: Isn't it about time I weaned myself from the bottle?

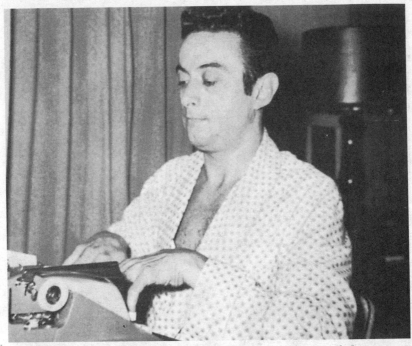

Writing this historic opus, I thought it appropriate to wear a period costume.

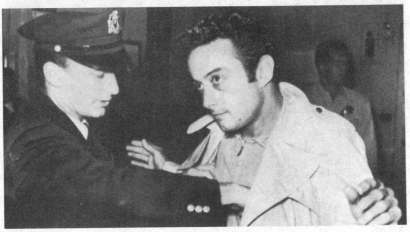

Here I am, living up to my public image. A true professional never disappoints his public.

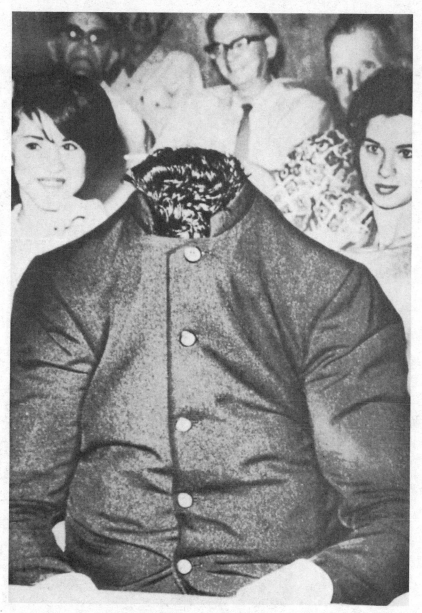

*Ever since I started using that greasy kid stuff,
my head keeps slipping out of sight.*

*My love for California is flagging. Attempting to escape
autograph hounds, I employ a standard ruse.*

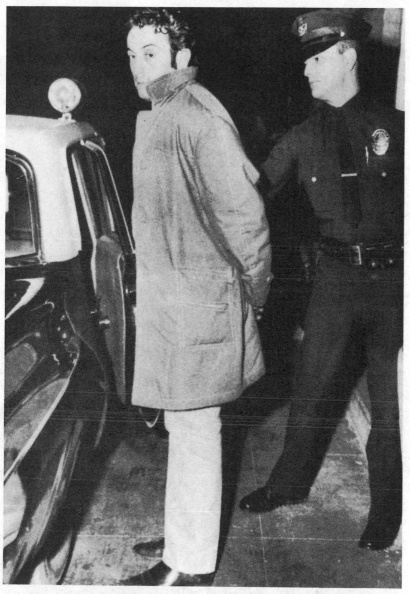

The efficient gas-station attendant, at right, has not only Simonized my car, but cleaned out the back seat as well; I wonder what the service charge will be.

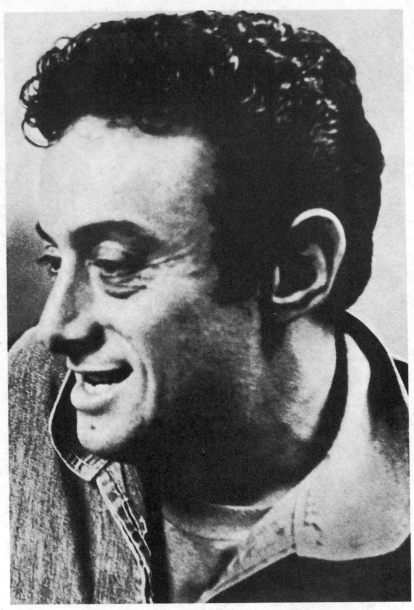

"Whaddaya mean, that's aspirin on your dresser," the fuzz said. What's the needle for? I can't stand the taste of the stuff.

Chapter
Seventeen

"Are you a sick comic?"

"Why do they call you a sick comic?"

"Do you mind being called a sick comic?"

It is impossible to label me. I develop, on the average, four minutes of new material a night, constantly growing and changing my point of view; I am heinously guilty of the paradoxes I assail in our society.

The reason for the label "sick comic" is the lack of creativity among journalists and critics. There is a comedy actor from England with a definite Chaplinesque quality. "Mr. Guinness, do you mind being called a Chaplinesque comic?" There is a comedian by the name of Peter Sellers who has a definite Guinnessesque quality. "Mr. Sellers, why do they say you have a Guinnessesque quality?"

The motivation of the interviewer is not to get a terse, accurate answer, but rather to write an interesting, slanted article within the boundaries of the editorial outlook of his particular publication, so that he will be given the wherewithal to make the payment on his MG. Therefore this writer prostitutes his integrity by asking questions, the answers to which he already has, much like a cook who follows a recipe and mixes the ingredients properly.

The way I speak, the words with which I relate are more correct in effect than those of a previous pedantic generation.

If I talk about a chick onstage and say, "She was a hooker," an uncontemporary person would say, "Lenny Bruce, you are coarse and crude."

"What should I have said?"

"If you must be specific, you should have said 'prostitute.' "

"But wait a minute; shouldn't the purpose of a word be to get close to the object the user is describing?"

"Yes, and correct English can do this; 'hooker' is incorrect."

The word has become too general. He *prostituted* his art. He *prostituted* the very thing he loved. Can he write anymore? Not like he used to—he has *prostituted* his work.

So the word "prostitute" doesn't mean anymore what the word "hooker" does. If a man were to send out for a $100 prostitute, a writer with a beard might show up.

Concomitant with the "sick comic" label is the carbon cry, "What happened to the healthy comedian who just got up there and showed everybody a good time and didn't preach, didn't have to resort to knocking religion, mocking physical handicaps and telling dirty toilet jokes?"

Yes, what *did* happen to the wholesome trauma of the 1930s and 1940s—the honeymoon jokes, concerned not only with what they did but also with how many times they did it; the distorted wedding-night tales, supported visually by the trite vacationland postcards of an elephant with his trunk searching through the opening of a pup tent, and a woman's head straining out the other end, hysterically screaming, "George!"—whatever happened to all this wholesomeness?

What happened to the healthy comedian who at least had good taste? . . . Ask the comedians who used to do the harelip jokes, or the moron jokes—"The moron who went to the orphans' picnic," etc.—the healthy comedians who told good-natured religious jokes that found Pat and Abie and Rastus outside of Saint Peter's gate all listening to those angels harping in stereotype.

Whatever happened to Joe E. Lewis? His contribution to comedy consisted of returning Bacchus to his godlike pose with an implicit social message: "If you're going to be a swinger and fun to be with, always have a glass of booze in your hand; even if you don't become part swinger, you're sure to end up with part liver."

Whatever happened to Henny Youngman? He involved himself with a nightly psychodrama named Sally, or sometimes Laura. She possessed features not sexually but economically stimulating. Mr. Youngman's Uglivac cross-filed and classified diabolic deformities definitively. "Her nose was so big that every time she sneezed. . . ." "She was so bowlegged that every time. . . ." "One leg was shorter than the other . . ." and Mr. Youngman's mutant reaped financial harvest for him. Other comedians followed suit with Cockeyed Jennies, et al., until the Ugly Girl routines became classics. I assume this fondness for atrophy gave the night-club patron a sense of well-being.

And whatever happened to Jerry Lewis? His neorealistic impression of the Japanese male captured all the subtleties of the Japanese physiognomy. The buck-teeth malocclusion was caricatured to surrealistic proportions until the teeth matched the blades that extended from Ben-Hur's chariot. Highlighting the absence of the iris with Coke-bottle-thick lenses, this satire has added to the fanatical devotion which Japanese students have for the United States. Just ask Eisenhower.

Whatever happened to Milton Berle? He brought transvestitism to championship bowling and upset a hard-core culture of dykes that control the field. From *Charlie's Aunt* and *Some Like It Hot* and Milton Berle, the pervert has been taken out of Krafft-Ebing and made into a sometimes-fun fag.

Berle never lost his sense of duty to the public, though. Although he gave homosexuals a peek out of the damp cellar of unfavorable public opinion, he didn't go all the way; he left a stigma of menace on his fag—"I sweah I'w kiw you."

I was labeled a "sicknik" by *Time* magazine, whose editorial policy still finds humor in a person's physical shortcomings: "Shelly Berman has a face like a hastily sculptured hamburger." The healthy comic would never offend . . . unless you happen to be fat, bald, skinny, deaf or blind. The proxy vote from purgatory has not yet been counted.

Let's say I'm working at the Crescendo on the coast. There'll be Arlene Dahl with some New Wave writer from Algiers and on the whole it's a cooking kind of audience. But I'll finish a show, and some guy will come up to me and say, "I—I'm a club owner, and I'd like you to work for me. It's a beautiful club. You ever work in Milwaukee? Lots of people like you there, and you'll really do great. You'll kill 'em. You'll have a lot of fun. Do you bowl?"

The only thing is, I know that in those clubs, between Los Angeles and New York, the people in the audience are a little older than me. The most I can say to people over 50 or 55 is, "Thank you, I've had enough to eat."

I get to Milwaukee, and the first thing that frightens me to death is that they've got a 6:30 dinner show . . . 6:30 in the afternoon and people go to a night club! It's not even *dark* out yet. I don't wanna go in the house, it's not dark yet, man. If the dinner show is held up, it's only because the Jell-o's not hard.

The people look familiar, but I've never been to Milwaukee before. Then I realize—these are the Grayline Sight-seeing Bus Tours before they leave— this is where they *live*. They're like 40-year-old chicks with prom gowns on.

They don't laugh, they don't heckle, they just stare at me in disbelief. And there are walkouts, walkouts, every night, walkouts. The owner says to me, "Well, I never saw you do that religious bit . . . and those words you use!" The chef is confused—the desserts aren't moving.

I go to the men's room, and I see *kids* in there. Kids four years old, six years old. These kids are in awe of this men's room. It's the first time they've ever been in a place their mother isn't allowed in. Not even for a minute. Not even to get something, is she allowed in there. And the kids stay in there for hours.

"Come out of there!"

"No. Uh-uh."

"I'm going to come in and get you."

"No, you're not allowed in here, 'cause everybody's doing, making wet in here."

In between shows I'm a walker, and I'm getting nudgy and nervous. The owner decides to cushion me with his introduction: "Ladies and gentlemen, the star of our show, Lenny Bruce, who, incidentally, is an ex-GI and, uh, a hell of a good performer, folks, and a great kidder, know what I mean? It's all a bunch of silliness up here and he doesn't mean what he says. He kids about the Pope and about the Jewish religion, too, and the colored people and the white people—it's all a silly, make-believe world. And he's a hell of a nice guy, folks. He was at the Veterans Hospital today doing a show for the boys. And here he is—his mom's out here tonight, too, she hasn't seen him in a couple of years—she lives here in town. . . . Now, a joke is a joke, right, folks? What the hell. I wish that you'd try to cooperate. And whoever has been sticking ice picks in the tires outside, he's not funny. Now Lenny may kid about narcotics, homosexuality, and things like that . . ."

And *he* gets walkouts.

I get off the floor, and a waitress says to me, "Listen, there's a couple, they want to meet you." It's a nice couple, about 50 years old. The guy asks me, "You from New York?"

"Yes."

"I recognized that accent." And he's looking at me, with a sort of searching hope in his eyes, and then he says, "Are you Jewish?"

"Yes."

"What are you doing in a place like this?"

"I'm passing."

He says, "Listen, I know you show people eat all that crap on the road. . . ." (Of course. What did you eat tonight? Crap on the road.) And they invite me to have a nice dinner at their house the next day. He writes out the address, you know, with the ball-point pen on the wet cocktail napkin.

That night I go to my hotel—I'm staying at the local show-business hotel; the other show people consist of two people, the guy who runs the movie projector and another guy who sells Capezio shoes—and I read a little, write a little. I finally get to sleep about seven o'clock in the morning.

The phone rings at nine o'clock.

"Hello, hello, hello, this is the Sheckners."

"The people from last night. We didn't wake you up, did we?"

"No, I always get up at nine in the morning. I like to get up about ten hours before work so I can brush my teeth and get some coffee. It's good you got me up. I probably would have overslept otherwise."

"Listen, why we called you, we want to find out what you want to eat."

"Oh, anything. I'm not a fussy eater, really."

I went over there that night, and I *do* eat anything—anything but what they had. Liver. And Brussels sprouts. That's really a double threat.

And the conversation was on the level of, "Is it true about Liberace?"

That's all I have to hear, then I really start to lay it on to them:

"Oh, yeah, they're all queer out there in Hollywood. All of them. Rin Tin Tin's a junkie."

Then they take you on a tour around the house. They bring you into the bedroom with the dumb dolls on the bed. And what the hell can you tell people when they walk you around in their house? "Yes, that's a very lovely closet; that's nice the way the towels are folded." They have a piano, with the big lace doily on top, and the bowl of wax fruit. The main function of these pianos is to hold an eight-by-ten picture of the son in the Army, saluting. "That's Morty, he lost a lot of weight."

The trouble is, in these towns—Milwaukee; Lima, Ohio—there's nothing else to do, except look at stars. In the daytime, you go to the park to see the cannon, and you've had it.

One other thing—you can hang out at the Socony Gas Station between shows and get gravel in your shoes. Those night attendants really swing.

"Lemme see the grease rack go up again," I say. "Can I try it?"

"No, you'll break it."

"Can I try on your black-leather bow tie?"

"No. Hey, Lenny, you wanna see a clean toilet? You been in a lot of service stations, right? Did you ever see one this immaculate?"

"It's beautiful."

"Now don't lie to me."

"Would I lie to you about something like that?"

"I thought you'd like it, because I know you've seen everything in your travels——"

"It's gorgeous. In fact, if anyone ever says to me, 'Where is there a clean toilet, I've been searching forever,' I'll say, 'Take 101 into 17 up through 50,' and I'll just send 'em right here."

"You could eat off the floor, right, Lenny?"

"You certainly could."

"Want a sandwich?"

"No, thanks."

Then I start fooling around with his condom-vending machine.

"You sell many of these here?"

"I don't know."

"You fill up the thing here?"

"No, a guy comes around."

"You wear condoms ever?"

"Yeah."

"Do you wear them all the time?"

"No."

"Do you have one on now?"

"No."

"Well, what do you do if you have to tell some chick, 'I'm going to put a condom on now'—it's going to kill everything."

I ask the gas-station attendant if I can put one on.

"Are you crazy or something?"

"No, I figure it's something to do. We'll both put condoms on. We'll take a picture."

"Now, get the hell out of here, you nut, you."

I can't help it, though. Condoms are so dumb. They're sold for the prevention of love.

As far as chicks are concerned, these small towns are dead. The cab drivers ask *you* where to get laid. It's really a hang-up. Every chick I meet, the first thing they hit me with is, "Look, I don't know what kind of a girl you think I am, but I know you show people, you've got all those broads down in the dressing room, and they're all ready for you, and I'm not gonna . . ."

"That's a lie, there's nobody down there!"

"Never mind, I know you get all you want."

"I don't!"

That's what everybody thinks, but there's nobody in the dressing room. That's why Frank Sinatra never gets any. It's hip *not* to ball him. "Listen, now, they all ball him, I'm not gonna ball him." And the poor *schmuck* really sings *Only the Lonely* . . .

It's a real hang-up, being divorced when you're on the road. Suppose it's three o'clock in the morning, I've just done the last show, I meet a girl, and I like her, and suppose I have a record I'd like her to hear, or I just want to talk to her—there's no lust, no carnal image there—but because where I live is a dirty word, I can't say to her, "Would you come to my hotel?"

And every *healthy* comedian has given "motel" such a dirty connotation that I couldn't ask my *grandmother* to go to a motel, say I want to give her a Gutenberg Bible at three in the morning.

The next day at two in the afternoon, when the Kiwanis Club meets there, then "hotel" is clean. But at three o'clock in the morning, Jim. . . . Christ, where the hell can you live that's clean? You can't say hotel to a chick, so you try to think, what won't offend? What is a clean word to society? What is a clean word that won't offend any chick? . . .

Trailer. That's it, *trailer*.

"Will you come to my trailer?"

"All right, there's nothing dirty about trailers. Trailers are hunting and fishing and Salem cigarettes. Yes, of course, I'll come to your trailer. Where is it?"

"Inside my hotel room."

Why can't you just say, "I want to be with you, and hug and kiss you." No, it's "Come up while I change my shirt." Or coffee. "Let's have a cup of coffee."

In 50 years, coffee will be another dirty word.

Chapter
Eighteen

The first time I got arrested for obscenity was in San Francisco. I used a ten-letter word onstage. Just a word in passing.

"Lenny, I wanna talk to you," the police officer said. "You're under arrest. That word you said—you can't say that in a public place. It's against the law to say it and do it."

They said it was a favorite homosexual practice. Now that I found strange. I don't relate that word to a homosexual practice. It relates to any contemporary chick I know, or would know, or would love, or would marry.

Then we get into the patrol wagon, and another police officer says, "You know, I got a wife and kid . . ."

"I don't wanna hear that crap," I interrupted.

"Whattaya mean?"

"I just don't wanna hear that crap, that's all. Did your wife ever do that to you?"

"No."

"Did anyone?"

"No."

"Did you ever say the word?"

"No."

"You never said the word one time? Let ye cast the first stone, man."

"Never."

"How long have you been married?"

"Eighteen years."

"You ever chippied on your wife?"

"Never."

"Never chippied on your wife one time in eighteen years?"

"Never."

"Then I love *you* . . . because you're a spiritual guy, the kind of husband I would like to have been . . . but if you're lying, you'll spend some good time in purgatory . . ."

Now we get into court. They swear me in.

THE COP: "Your Honor, he said blah-blah-blah."

THE JUDGE: "He said *blah*-blah-blah! Well, I got grandchildren . . ." Oh, Christ, there we go again.

"Your Honor," the cop says, "I couldn't believe it, there's a guy up on the stage in front of women in a mixed audience, saying blah-blah-blah . . ."

THE DISTRICT ATTORNEY: "Look at him, he's smug! I'm not surprised he said blah-blah-blah . . ."

"He'll probably say blah-blah-blah again, he hasn't learned his lesson . . ."

And then I dug something: they sort of *liked* saying blah-blah-blah. (Even the BAILIFF:) "What'd he say?"

"He said blah-blah-blah."

"Shut up, you blah-blah-blah."

They were yelling it in the courtroom.

"Goddamn, it's good to say blah-blah-blah!"

The actual trial took place in the early part of March 1962. The People of the State of California *vs.* Lenny Bruce. The jury consisted of four men and eight women. The first witness for the prosecution was James Ryan, the arresting officer. Deputy District Attorney Albert Wollenberg, Jr., examined him.

Q. . . . And on the night of October the fourth did you have any special assignment in regard to (the Jazz Workshop)?

A. I was told by my immediate superior, Sergeant Solden, that he had received a complaint from the night before that the show at this club was of a lewd nature, and that some time during the evening I was to go in and see the show and find out what the complaint was all about . . .

Q. And during the course of his act did any . . . talking about an establishment known as Ann's 440 arise?

A. Yes . . . during this particular episode at the 440 he was talking to some other person, who, as near as I can recall, I think was either his agent or another entertainer. And during this conversation . . . one person said, "I can't work at the 440 because it's overrun with cocksuckers."

Q. . . . Now, after this statement, what then occurred?

A. A little later on in the same show the defendant was talking about the fact that he distrusted ticket takers and the person that handled the money, and that one of these days a man was going to enter the premises and situate himself where he couldn't be seen by the ticket taker, and then he was going to expose himself and on the end of it he was going to have a sign hanging that read, WHEN WE REACH $1500 THE GUY IN THE FRONT BOOTH IS GOING TO KISS IT.

Q. . . . Now, subsequent to the statement about hanging a sign on a person exposed, was there any further conversation by the defendant while giving his performance?

105

A. Yes. Later in the show he went into some kind of chant where he used a drum, or a cymbal and a drum, for a tempo, and the dialog was supposed to be . . .

MR. BENDICH (my attorney, Albert Bendich): I'll object to what the witness infers the conversation or dialog was supposed to import, your Honor. The witness is to testify merely to what he heard.

THE COURT: Sustained.

MR. WOLLENBERG: . . . Can you give us the exact words or what your recollection of those words were?

A. Yes. During that chant he used the words "I'm coming, I'm coming, I'm coming," and . . .

Q. Did he just do it two or three times, "I'm coming, I'm coming, I'm coming"?

A. Well, this one part of the show lasted a matter of a few minutes.

Q. And then was anything else said by the defendant?

A. Then later he said, "Don't come in me. Don't come in me."

Q. Now, did he do this just one or two times?

A. No. As I stated, this lasted for a matter of a few minutes.

Q. Now, as he was saying this, was he using the same voice as he was giving this chant?

A. . . . Well, this particular instance where he was saying "I'm coming, I'm coming," he was talking in a more normal tone of voice. And when he stated, or when he said "Don't come in me. Don't come in me," he used a little higher-pitched voice . . .

Mr. Bendich now cross-examined.

Q. Officer Ryan, would you describe your beat to us, please?

A. . . . It takes in both sides of Broadway from Mason to Battery.

Q. And in the course of your duties, Officer, you have the responsibility and obligation to observe the nature of the shows being put on in various clubs in this area?

A. Yes, sir, I do.

Q. Would you tell us, Officer, what some of those clubs are? . . . Then I'll ask you some questions about the content of the work that is done there . . .

MR. WOLLENBERG: Well, that's irrelevant and immaterial, if your Honor, please, other than that they are on his beat, the content of the work done there.

MR. BENDICH: We're talking about community standards, your Honor.

THE COURT: (Mr. Wollenberg's objection) overruled. Now, the question is just to name some of the establishments. [The officer named several night clubs.]

Q. . . . Now, officer, you testified, I believe, on direct examination

106

that you had a specific assignment with reference to the Lenny Bruce performance at the Jazz Workshop, is that correct?

A. That's correct.

Q. Tell us, please, if you will, what your specific assignment was.

A. My assignment was to watch the performance of the show that evening.

Q. What were you looking for?

A. Any lewd conversation or lewd gestures or anything that might constitute an objectionable show.

Q. What were your standards for judging, Officer, whether a show was objectionable or not?

A. Well, any part of the show that would violate any Police or Penal Code sections that we have . . .

MR. BENDICH: . . . [You have previously described] the clubs that are situated upon the beat that you patrol, and among other clubs you listed the Moulin Rouge. . . . And would you be good enough to tell us, Officer Ryan, what the nature of the entertainment material presented in the Moulin Rouge is?

A. Primarily a burlesque-type entertainment.

Q. Strip shows are put on . . .?

A. That's correct.

Q. And, as a matter of fact, Officer Ryan, there is a housewives' contest put on at the Moulin Rouge with respect to superior talent in stripping, is there not?

A. I don't know if it just encompasses housewives; I know they have an amateur night.

Q. Now, Officer Ryan, will you tell us a little bit about what occurs during amateur night?

A. Well, just what it says, I believe. Girls that have had little or no experience in this type of entertainment are given a chance to try their hand at it.

Q. To try their hand at it, and they try their body a little, too, don't they?

MR. WOLLENBERG: If your Honor please, counsel is argumentative.

THE COURT: Yes. Let us not be facetious, Mr. Bendich.

MR. BENDICH: I will withdraw it. I don't intend to be facetious.

Q. Officer Ryan, will you describe for the ladies and gentlemen of the jury, if you will, please, what the ladies who are engaged in the competition on amateur night do?

MR. WOLLENBERG: If your Honor please, this is irrelevant.

THE COURT: Overruled.

THE WITNESS: Well, they come on the stage and then to the accompaniment of music they do a dance.

MR. BENDICH: And in the course of doing this dance, they take their clothes off, is that correct?

A. Partially, yes.

Q. Now, these are the amateur competitors and performers, is that correct?

A. That's correct.

Q. Tell us, please, if you will, what the professional performers do.

A. Approximately the same thing, with maybe a little more finesse or a little more ability, if there is ability in that line.

Q. And you have witnessed these shows, is that correct, Officer Ryan?

A. I have, yes.

Q. And these are shows which are performed in the presence of mixed audiences, representing persons of both sexes, is that correct?

A. That's true.

Q. Now, Officer Ryan, in the course of your official duties in patrolling your beat you have occasion, I take it, to deal with another club, the name of which is Finocchio's, is that correct?

A. That's true.

Q. And you have had occasion to observe the nature of the performances in Finocchio's, is that true? . . . Would you be good enough, Officer Ryan, to describe to the ladies and gentlemen of the jury what the nature of the entertainment presented in Finocchio's is?

A. Well, the entertainers are female impersonators.

Q. May I ask you to describe for the jury what female impersonators are?

A. A male that dresses as a woman, and the type of show they put on is, I guess, a pretty average show, other than the fact that they are female impersonators. They have songs that they sing, dances that they do, and so forth.

Q. . . . And can you describe the mode of dress, Officer, of the female impersonators in Finocchio's?

A. Well, they wear different types of costumes. Some of them are quite full, and others are . . .

Q. Quite scanty?

A. Not "quite scanty," I wouldn't say, no, but they are more near to what you'd call scanty, yes.

Q. "More near to what you'd call scanty." Well, as a matter of fact, Officer, isn't it true that men appear in the clothes of women, and let's start up—or should I say, down at the bottom—wearing high-heeled shoes?

MR. WOLLENBERG: Oh, if your Honor please, he's already answered that they're wearing the clothes of women. That covers the subject. We're not trying Finocchio's here today.

MR. BENDICH: We're certainly not trying Finocchio's but we are trying Lenny Bruce on a charge of obscenity, and we have a question of contemporary community standards that has to be established, and I am attempting to have Officer Ryan indicate what the nature of the community standards on his beat are.

THE COURT: . . . Well, ask him to be more specific.

MR. BENDICH: Very well. Will you please be more specific, Officer Ryan, with regard to describing the nature of the scantily dressed female impersonators in terms of their attire.

A. They have all different kinds of costumes. Now, which particular one—I never paid that much attention to it, really.

Q. Well, they appear in black net stockings, do they not?

A. I imagine they do at times.

Q. And they appear in tights, do they not?

A. On occasion, yes.

Q. And they appear wearing brassieres, do they not?

A. That's correct.

Q. I think that's specific enough. . . . Officer Ryan, in the course of your observations of the strip shows in the Moulin Rouge, have you ever had occasion to become sexually stimulated?

A. No, sir.

MR. WOLLENBERG: I'm going to object to this and move to strike the answer as incompetent, irrelevant and immaterial, if your Honor please.

THE COURT: The answer is in; it may remain.

MR. BENDICH: Were you sexually stimulated when you witnessed Lenny Bruce's performance?

MR. WOLLENBERG: Irrelevant and immaterial, especially as to this officer, your Honor.

THE COURT: Overruled.

THE WITNESS: No, sir.

MR. BENDICH: Did you have any conversation with anyone in the Jazz Workshop on the night that you arrested Mr. Lenny Bruce?

A. No.

Q. Officer Ryan, you're quite familiar with the term "cocksucker" are you not?

A. I have heard it used, yes.

Q. As a matter of fact, Officer Ryan, it was used in the police station on the night that Lenny Bruce was booked there, was it not?

A. No, not to my knowledge.

Q. As a matter of fact, it is frequently used in the police station, is it not?

MR. WOLLENBERG: That's irrelevant and immaterial, if your Honor please. What's used in a police station or in private conversation between two people is completely different from what's used on a stage in the theater.

THE COURT: Well, a police station, of course, is a public place.

MR. WOLLENBERG: That's correct, your Honor.

THE COURT: As to the police station, the objection is overruled.

MR. BENDICH: You may answer, Officer.

A. Yes, I have heard it used.

Q. Yes, you have heard the term used in a public place known as the police station. Now, Officer Ryan, there is nothing obscene in and of itself about the word "cock," is there?

MR. WOLLENBERG: I'm going to object to this as being irrelevant and immaterial, what this man feels.

THE COURT: Sustained.

MR. BENDICH: Just two last questions, Officer Ryan. You laughed at Lenny Bruce's performance the night that you watched, did you not?

A. No, I didn't.

Q. You didn't have occasion to laugh?

A. No, I didn't.

Q. Did you observe whether the audience was laughing?

A. Yes, I did.

Q. And they were laughing, were they not?

A. At times, yes.

Q. And no one in the audience made any complaint to you, though you were in uniform standing in the club?

A. No one, no.

MR. BENDICH: No further questions.

Mr. Wollenberg re-examined the witness.

Q. Now, Officer, when the word, "cocksucker," was used during the performance, did anybody laugh?

A. Not right at that instant, no.

Q. . . . Now, in Finocchio's, have you ever heard the word "cocksucker" used from the stage?

A. No, sir, I never have.

Q. . . . Now, at the Moulin Rouge, Officer, they do have a comedian as well as a strip show, isn't that right?

A. That's right.

Q. Have you ever heard the comedian at the Moulin Rouge use the term, "cocksucker"?

A. No, sir, never.

Q. Did you have a conversation with the defendant Bruce after his performance?

A. Yes, I did.

Q. And where was that?

A. In front of the Jazz Workshop.

Q. . . . Was that in relation to any of the terms used?

A. Yes, it was.

Q. And what was that?

A. I asked the defendant at that time, "Didn't I hear you use the word 'cocksucker' in your performance? And he says, 'Yes, I did.' "

Later, Mr. Wollenberg examined the other police officer, Sergeant James Solden.

Q. . . . And did you have occasion while in that area (the Jazz Workshop) to see the defendant Bruce? . . . Did you have a conversation with him?

A. I had a conversation with Mr. Bruce as we led—took him from the Jazz Workshop to the patrol wagon . . . I spoke to Mr. Bruce and said, "Why do you feel that you have to use the word 'cocksucker' to entertain people in a public night spot?" And Mr. Bruce's reply to me, was, "Well there are a lot of cocksuckers around, aren't there? What's wrong with talking about them?"

Mr. Bendich made his opening statement to the jury, "to tell you what it is that I am going to attempt to prove to you in the course of the presentation of the defense case. . . . I am going to prove through the testimony of several witnesses who will take the stand before you, ladies and gentlemen of the jury, that Mr. Bruce gave a performance in the Jazz Workshop on the night of October fourth last year which was a show based on the themes of social criticism, based upon an analysis of various forms of conventional hypocrisy, based upon the technique of satire which is common in the heritage of English letters and, as a matter of fact, in the heritage of world literature. We are going to prove, ladies and gentlemen of the jury, that the nature of Mr. Bruce's performance on the night of October the fourth was in the great tradition of social satire, related intimately to the kind of social satire to be found in the works of such great authors at Aristophanes, Jonathan Swift . . ."

MR. WOLLENBERG: I'm going to object. Aristophanes is not testifying here, your Honor, or any other authors, and I'm going to object to that at this time as improper argument.

MR. BENDICH: Your Honor, I didn't say I would call Mr. Aristophanes.

THE COURT: I don't think you could, very well . . .

Chapter Nineteen

It seems fitting that the first witness for the defense was Ralph J. Gleason, a brilliant jazz critic and columnist for the *San Francisco Chronicle*. Gleason was my first real supporter, the first one who really went out on a limb for me, to help my career.

Mr. Bendich examined him.

Q. . . . Mr. Gleason, will you describe for us, if you will, please, what the themes of Mr. Bruce's work were during the appearance in the Workshop for which he was arrested?

MR. WOLLENBERG: I will object to just the themes, your Honor. He can give the performance or recite what was said, but the "themes" is ambiguous.

THE COURT: Overruled.

THE WITNESS: The theme of the performance on the night in question was a social criticism of stereotypes and of the hypocrisy of contemporary society. . . . He attempted to demonstrate to the audience a proposition that's familiar to students of semantics, which is that words have been given, in our society, almost a magic meaning that has no relation to the facts, and I think that he tried in the course of this show that evening to demonstrate that there is no harm inherent in words themselves.

Q. . . . How important, if at all, was the theme of semantics with reference to the entire show given on the evening in question?

A. In my opinion, it was very important—vital to it.

Q. And what dominance or predominance, if any, did the theme of semantics occupy with respect to the content of the entire show on the night in question?

A. Well, it occupied an important part in the entire performance, not only in the individual routines, but in the totality of the program.

Q. Yes. Now, with respect to the rest of the program, Mr. Gleason, would you tell us about some of the other themes, and perhaps illustrate something about them if you can, in addition to the theme of semantics which Mr. Bruce worked with?

A. Well, to the best of my recollection there was a portion of the show in which he attempted to show satirically the hypocrisy inherent in the licensing

112

of a ticket taker who had a criminal record for particularly abhorrent criminal acts and demanding a bond for him . . .

Mr. Gleason was asked to read to the jury an excerpt from an article in *Commonweal*, a Catholic magazine. The article was by Nat Hentoff, who's Jewish, so it doesn't really count. Gleason read:

"It is in Lenny Bruce—and only in him—that there has emerged a cohesively 'new' comedy of nakedly honest moral rage at the deceptions all down the line in our society. Bruce thinks of himself as an ethical relativist and shares Pirandello's preoccupation with the elusiveness of any absolute, including absolute truth.

"His comedy ranges through religion-in-practice ('What would happen if Christ and Moses appeared one Sunday at Saint Patrick's?'); the ultimate limitations of the white liberal; the night life of the hooker and her view of the day; and his own often scarifying attempts to make sense of his life in a society where the quicksand may lie just underneath the sign that says: TAKE SHELTER WHEN THE CIVILIAN DEFENSE ALARM SOUNDS.

"Bruce, however, does not turn a night club into Savonarola's church. More than any others of the 'new wave,' Bruce is a thoroughly experienced performer, and his relentless challenges to his audience and to himself are intertwined with explosive pantomime, hilarious 'bits,' and an evocative spray of Yiddishisms, Negro and show-business argot, and his own operational semantics. Coursing through everything he does, however, is a serious search for values that are more than security blankets. In discussing the film *The Story of Esther Costello*, Bruce tells of the climactic rape scene: 'It's obvious the girl has been violated. . . . She's been deaf and dumb throughout the whole picture. . . . All of a sudden she can hear again . . . and she can speak again. So what's the moral?' "

Later—after the judge had pointed something out to the Deputy District Attorney ("Mr. Wollenberg," he said, ". . . your shirttail is out.")—Mr. Gleason was asked to read to the jury a portion of an article by Arthur Gelb in *The New York Times*.

"The controversial Mr. Bruce, whose third visit to Manhattan this is, is the prize exhibit of the menagerie, and his act is billed 'for adults only.'

"Presumably the management wishes to safeguard the dubious innocence of underage New Yorkers against Mr. Bruce's vocabulary, which runs to four-letter words, of which the most printable is Y.M.C.A. But there are probably a good many adults who will find him offensive, less perhaps for his Anglo-Saxon phrases than for his vitriolic attacks on such subjects as facile religion, the medical profession, the law, pseudo-liberalism and Jack Paar. ('Paar has a God complex. He thinks he can create performers in six days,' Mr. Bruce is apt to confide.)

"Although he seems at times to be doing his utmost to antagonize his audience, Mr. Bruce displays such a patent air of morality beneath the brashness that his lapses in taste are often forgivable.

"The question, though, is whether the kind of derisive shock therapy he administers and the introspective free-form patter in which he indulges are legitimate night-club fare, as far as the typical customer is concerned.

"It is necessary, before lauding Mr. Bruce for his virtues, to warn the sensitive and the easily shocked that no holds are barred at Basin Street East. Mr. Bruce regards the night-club stage as the 'last frontier' of uninhibited entertainment. He often carries his theories to their naked and personal conclusions and has earned for his pains the sobriquet 'sick.' He is a ferocious man who does not believe in the sanctity of motherhood or the American Medical Association. He even has an unkind word to say for Smokey the Bear. True, Smokey doesn't set forest fires, Mr. Bruce concedes. But he eats boy scouts for their hats.

"Mr. Bruce expresses relief at what he sees as a trend of 'people leaving the church and going back to God,' and he has nothing but sneers for what he considers the sanctimonious liberal who preaches but cannot practice genuine integration.

"Being on cozy terms with history and psychology, he can illustrate his point with the example of the early Romans, who thought there was 'something dirty' about Christians. 'Could you want your sister to marry one?'—he has one Roman ask another—and so on, down to the logical conclusion in present-day prejudice.

"At times Mr. Bruce's act, devoid of the running series of staccato jokes that are traditional to the night-club comic, seems like a salvationist lecture; it is biting, sardonic, certainly stimulating and quite often funny—but never in a jovial way. His mocking diatribe rarely elicits a comfortable belly laugh. It requires concentration. But there is much in it to wring a rueful smile and appreciative chuckle. There is even more to evoke a fighting gleam in the eye. There are also spells of total confusion.

"Since Mr. Bruce operates in a spontaneous, stream-of-consciousness fashion a good deal of the time, he is likely to tell you what he's thinking about telling you before he gets around to telling you anything at all . . ."

Mr. Bendich resumed his line of questioning.

Q. Mr. Gleason, would you tell us, please, what in your judgment the *predominant* theme of the evening's performance for which Mr. Bruce was arrested was?

A. Well, in a very real sense it's semantics—the search for the ultimate truth that lies beneath the social hypocrisy in which we live. All his performances relate to this.

Q. Mr. Gleason, as an expert in this field, would you characterize the performance in question as serious in intent and socially significant?

MR. WOLLENBERG: I will object to this as irrelevant and immaterial.

THE COURT: Overruled.

THE WITNESS: Yes, I would characterize it as serious.

MR. BENDICH: And how would you characterize the social significance, if any, of that performance?

A. Well, I would characterize this performance as being of high social significance, in line with the rest of his performances.

Q. Mr. Gleason, what in your opinion, based upon your professional activity and experience in the field of popular culture, and particularly with reference to humor, what in your opinion is the relation between the humor of Lenny Bruce and that of other contemporary humorists, such as Mort Sahl, Shelley Berman, Mike and Elaine?

MR. WOLLENBERG: That's immaterial, your Honor, what the comparison is between him and any other comedian.

THE COURT: Objection overruled.

THE WITNESS: Mr. Bruce attacks the fundamental structure of society and these other comedians deal with it superficially.

MR. BENDICH: Mr. Gleason, you have already testified that you have seen personally a great many Lenny Bruce performances, and you are also intimately familiar with his recorded works and other comic productions. Has your prurient interest ever been stimulated by any of Mr. Bruce's work?

A. Not in the slightest.

MR. WOLLENBERG: I will object to that as calling for the ultimate issue before this jury.

THE COURT: The objection will be overruled. . . . You may answer the question.

THE WITNESS: I have not been excited, my prurient or sexual interest has not been aroused by any of Mr. Bruce's performances.

The complete transcript of my San Francisco trail runs 350 pages. The witnesses—not one of whose sexual interest had ever been aroused by any of my night-club performances—described one after another, what they remembered of my performance on the night in question at the Jazz Workshop, and interpreted its social significance according to his or her own subjectivity.

For example, during the cross-examination, the following dialog ensued between Mr. Wollenberg and Lou Gottlieb, a Ph.D. who's with the Limeliters:

Q. Doctor, you say you have heard Mr. Bruce in Los Angeles?

A. Yes.

Q. And what was the last remark he makes on leaving the stage in his show in Los Angeles?

A. I must say that Mr. Bruce's last remarks have varied at every perform-ance that I have ever witnessed.

Q. Did he make any reference to eating something in his last remarks in Los Angeles when you heard him perform?

A. No.

Q. . . . Now, Doctor, you say the main theme of Mr. Bruce is to get laughter?

A. That's the professional comedian's duty.

Q. I see. And do you see anything funny in the word "cocksucker"?

A. . . . To answer that question with "Yes" or "No" is impossible, your Honor.

MR. WOLLENBERG: I asked you if you saw anything funny in that word.

THE COURT: You may answer it "Yes" or "No" and then explain your answer.

THE WITNESS: I found it extremely unfunny as presented by Mr. Wollen-berg, I must say, but I can also——

THE COURT: All right, wait a minute, wait a minute. I have tolerated a certain amount of activity from the audience because I knew that it is difficult not to react at times, but this is not a show, you are not here to be entertained. Now, if there's any more of this sustained levity, the courtroom will be cleared. And the witness is instructed not to argue with counsel but to answer the questions . . .

THE WITNESS: I do not (see anything funny in that word), but as Mr. Bruce presents his performances he creates a world in which normal dimensions . . . become—how shall I say? Well, they are transmuted into a grotesque panorama of contemporary society, into which he places slices of life, phonographically accurate statements that come out of the show-business world . . . and sometimes the juxtaposition of the generally fantastic frame of reference that he is able to create and the startling intrusion of slices of life in terms of language that is used in these kinds of areas, has extremely comic effect.

Q. . . . Doctor, because an agent uses that term when he talks to his talent, you find nothing wrong with using it in a public place because you're relating a conversation between yourself and your agent? This excuses the use of that term?

A. What excuses the use of that term, Mr. Wollenberg, in my opinion, is its unexpectedness in the fantastic world that is the frame of reference, the world which includes many grotesqueries that Mr. Bruce is able to establish. Then when you get a phonographic reproduction of a snatch of a conversation, I find that this has comic effect very frequently.

Q. Do you mean "phonographic" or "photographic"?

A. "Phonographic." I mean reproducing the actual speech verbatim with the same intonation and same attitudes and everything else that would be characteristic of, let's say, a talent agent of some kind.

Q. I see. In other words, the changing of the words to more—well, we might use genteel—terms, would take everything away from that, is that right?

A. It wouldn't be phonographically accurate. It would lose its real feel; there would be almost no point.

Q. . . . And taking out that word and putting in the word "homosexual" or "fairy," that would take away completely, in your opinion, from this story and make it just completely another one?

A. I must say it would.

Similarly, Mr. Wollenberg cross-examined **Dr. Don Geiger**, associate professor and chairman of the department of speech at the University of California in Berkeley; also author of a few books, including *Sound, Sense and Performance of Literature,* as well as several scholarly articles in professional journals.

Q. . . . And what does the expression "I won't appear there because it's overrun with cocksuckers" infer to you?

A. "I won't go there because it's filled with homosexuals."

Q. I see. And does the word "cocksucker" denote any beauty as distinguished from the word homosexual?

A. I couldn't possibly answer that, I think. That is, you would have to provide a context for it, and then one could answer that. I would say this about it . . . that "homosexual" is a kind of neutral, scientific term which might in a given context itself have a freight of significance or beauty or artistic merit. But it's less likely to than the word "cocksucker," which is closer to colloquial, idiomatic expression.

Later, Kenneth Brown, a high school English teacher, testified as to his reaction to the "to come" part of my performance:

THE WITNESS: The impression is, he was trying to get over a point about society, the inability to love, the inability to perform sexual love in a creative way. The routine then would enter a dialog between a man and a woman and they were having their sexual difficulties at orgasm in bed; at least, one of them was. And one said, "Why can't you come?" And, "Is it because you don't love me? Is it because you can't love me?" And the other one said,

"Why, you know me, this is where I'm hung up. I have problems here." And that was enough to give me the impression that—with the other things in context that were going on before and after—that he was talking, dissecting our problems of relating to each other, man and woman. . . . Great comics throughout literature have always disguised by comedy, through laughter, through jokes, an underlying theme which is very serious, and perhaps needs laughter because it is also painful . . .

MR. BENDICH: May I ask you this question, Mr. Brown: On the basis of your professional training and experience, do you think that the work of Mr. Bruce as you know it, and in particular the content of Mr. Bruce's performance on the night of October fourth, for which he was arrested, for which he is presently here in this courtroom on trial, bears a relation to the themes and the fashion in which those themes are in the works which we have listed here [*Lysistrata* by Aristophanes; *Gargantua and Pantagruel* by Rabelais; *Gulliver's Travels* by Jonathan Swift]?

A. I see a definite relationship, certainly.

Q. Would you state, please, what relationship you see and how you see it?

MR. WOLLENBERG: I think he hasn't qualified as an expert on this, your Honor.

THE COURT: Well, he may state what the relationship is that he sees.

THE WITNESS: These works use often repulsive techniques and vocabulary to make—to insist—that people will look at the whole of things and not just one side. These artists wish not to divide the world in half and say one is good and one is bad and avoid the bad and accept the good, but you must, to be a real and whole person, you must see all of life and see it in a balanced, honest way. I would include Mr. Bruce, certainly, in his intent, and he has success in doing this, as did Rabelais and Swift.

At one point during the trial, a couple of 19-year-old college students were admonished by the judge; they had been distributing the following leaflet outside the courtroom:

WELCOME TO THE FARCE!

Lenny Bruce, one of America's foremost comedians and social critics, is at this moment playing an unwilling part as a straight man in a social comedy put on by the City and County of San Francisco.

Incongruously, in our urbane city, this is a poor provincial farce, insensitively played by some of the city's most shallow actors.

Bruce may be imaginative, but the dull-witted, prudish lines of the police department are not, neither are the old-maidish lyrics of section 311.6 of the California Penal Code, which in genteel, puritan prose condemns the users of — — — — — — and — — — — — — and other common expressions to play a part in the dreary melodrama of "San Francisco Law Enforcement."

Really, we are grown up now. With overpopulation, human misery and the threat of war increasing, we need rather more adult performances from society.

You know, and I know, all about the hero's impure thoughts. We've probably had them ourselves. Making such a fuss isn't convincing at all —it lacks psychological realism—as do most attempts to find a scapegoat for sexual guilt feelings.

Forgive Lenny's language. Most of us use it at times; most of us even use the things and perform the acts considered unprintable and unspeakable by the authors of (Section 311.6 of the Penal Code of the State of California), though most of us are not nearly frank enough to say so.

Lenny has better things to do than play in this farce; the taxpayers have better uses for their money; and the little old ladies of both sexes who produce it *should* have better amusements.

With a nostalgic sigh, let's pull down the curtain on *People vs. Bruce* and its genre; and present a far more interesting and fruitful play called *Freedom of Speech*. It would do our jaded ears good.

The writer and distributor of the leaflet were properly chastised by the judge.

And so the trial continued.

One of the witnesses for the defense was Clarence Knight, who had been an assistant district attorney for a couple of years in Tulare County, California, and was deputy district attorney for four years in San Mateo, where he evaluated all pornography cases that were referred to the district attorney's office. He had passed on "probably between 200 and 250 separate items of material in regard to the pornographic or nonpornographic content thereof."

As with the others, his prurient interests were not aroused by my performance at the Jazz Workshop. In fact, he said, while being cross-examined about the "cocksucker" reference: "In my opinion, Mr. Wollenberg, it was the funniest thing Mr. Bruce said that night."

Chapter
Twenty

Finally, I was called as a witness in my own behalf. I took the stand, and Mr. Bendich examined me.

Q. Mr. Bruce, Mr. Wollenberg yesterday said (to Dr. Gottlieb) specifically that you had said, "Eat it." Did you say that?

A. No, I never said that.

Q. What did you say, Mr. Bruce?

A. What did I say when?

Q. On the night of October fourth.

MR. WOLLENBERG: There's no testimony that Mr. Wollenberg said that Mr. Bruce said, "Eat it," the night of October fourth, if your Honor please.

THE COURT: The question is: What did he say?

THE WITNESS: I don't mean to be facetious. Mr. Wollenberg said, "Eat it." I said, "Kiss it."

MR. BENDICH: Do you apprehend there is a significant difference between the two phrases, Mr. Bruce?

A. "Kissing it" and "eating it," yes, sir. Kissing my mother goodbye and eating my mother goodbye, there is a quantity of difference.

Q. Mr. Wollenberg also quoted you as saying, "I'm coming, I'm coming, I'm coming." Did you say that?

A. I never said that.

MR. BENDICH: . . . Mr. Bruce, do you recall using the term "cocksucker"?

A. Yes.

Q. Can you recall accurately now how you used that term?

A. You mean accuracy right on the head—total recall?

Q. Yes, Mr. Bruce.

A. If a "the" and an "an" are changed around, no. I don't have that exact, on-the-head recall. That's impossible; it's impossible. I defy anyone to do it. That's impossible.

Q. Mr. Bruce, if a "the" and an "an" were turned around, as you have put it, would that imply a significant difference in the characterization of what was said that evening?

120

A. Yes, yes.

Q. Are you saying, Mr. Bruce, that unless your words can be given in exact, accurate, verbatim reproduction, that your meaning cannot be made clear?

THE WITNESS: Yes, that is true. I would like to explain that. The "I am coming, I am coming" reference, which I never said—if we change——

THE COURT: Wait a minute, wait a minute. If you never said it, there's nothing to explain.

THE WITNESS: Whether that is a coming in the Second Coming or a different coming——

THE COURT: Well, you wait until your counsel's next question, now.

MR. BENDICH: Mr. Bruce, in giving your performance on the night of October fourth in the Jazz Workshop, as a consequence of which you suffered an arrest and as a result of which you are presently on trial on the charge of obscenity, did you intend to arouse anybody's prurient interest?

A. No.

There had been a tape recording made of that particular show. I listened to it, and when I came to the first word that San Francisco felt was taboo or a derogatory phrase, I stopped; then I went back about ten minutes before I even started to relate to that word, letting it resolve itself; I did this with the three specific things I was charged with, put them together and the resulting tape was played in court . . . this tape I made to question a father's concept of God who made the child's body but qualified the creativity by stopping it above the kneecaps and resuming it above the Adam's apple, thereby giving lewd connotations to mother's breast that fed us and father's groin that bred us.

Before the tape was played, Mr. Bendich pointed out to the judge that "there are portions of this tape which are going to evoke laughter in the audience."

THE COURT: I anticipated you; I was going to give that admonition.

MR. BENDICH: Well, what I was going to ask, your Honor, is whether the audience might not be allowed to respond naturally, given the circumstances that this is an accurate reproduction of a performance which is given at a night club; it's going to evoke comic response, and I believe that it would be asking more than is humanly possible of the persons in this courtroom not to respond humanly, which is to say, by way of laughter.

THE COURT: Well, as I previously remarked, this is not a theater and it is not a show, and I am not going to allow any such thing. I anticipated you this morning, and I was going to and I am now going to admonish the spectators that you are not to treat this as a performance. This is not for your entertainment. There's a very serious question involved here, the right of the People and the right of the defendant. And I admonish you that you are to

121

control yourselves with regard to any emotions that you may feel during the hearing this morning or by the taping and reproduction of this tape. All right, you may proceed.

And the tape was played:

. . . The hungry i. The hungry i has a Grayline Tour and American Legion convention. They took all the bricks out and put in Saran Wrap. That's it. And Ferlinghetti is going to the Fairmont.

You know, this was a little snobby for me to work. I just wanted to go back to Ann's. You don't know about that, do you? Do you share that recall with me? It's the first gig I ever worked up here, a place called Ann's 440, which was across the street. And I got a call, and I was working a burlesque gig with Paul Moore in the Valley. That's the cat on the piano here, which is really strange, seeing him after all these years, and working together.

And the guy says, "There's a place in San Francisco but they've changed the policy."

"Well, what's the policy?"

"Well, I'm not there anymore, that's the main thing."

"Well, what kind of a show is it, man?"

"A bunch of cocksuckers, that's all. A damned fag show."

"Oh. Well, that is a pretty bizarre show. I don't know what I can do in that kind of a show."

"Well, no. It's—we want you to change all that."

"Well—I don't—that's a big gig. I can't just tell them to stop doing it."

Oh, I like you, and if sometimes I take poetic license with you and you are offended—now this is just with semantics, dirty words. Believe me, I'm not profound, this is something that I assume someone must have laid on me, because I do not have an original thought. I am screwed—I speak English—that's it. I was not born in a vacuum. Every thought I have belongs to somebody else. Then I must just take—ding-ding-ding—somewhere.

So I am not placating you by making the following statement. I want to help you if you have a dirty-word problem. There are none, and I'll spell it out logically to you.

Here is a toilet. Specifically—that's all we're concerned with, specifics—if I can tell you a dirty toilet joke, we must have a dirty toilet. That's what we're talking about, a toilet. If we take this toilet and boil it and it's clean, I can never tell you specifically a dirty toilet joke about this toilet. I can tell you a dirty toilet joke in the Milner Hotel, or something like that, but this toilet is a clean toilet now. Obscenity is a human manifestation. This toilet has no central nervous system, no level of consciousness. It is not aware; it is a dumb toilet; it cannot be obscene; it's impossible. If it could be obscene, it could be cranky, it could be a Communist toilet, a traitorous toilet. It can do none of these things. This is a dirty toilet here.

Nobody can offend you by telling you a dirty toilet story. They can offend you because it's trite; you have heard it many, many times.

Now, all of us have had a bad early toilet training—that's why we are hung up with it. All of us at the same time got two zingers—one for the police department and one for the toilet.

"All right, he made a kahkah, call a policeman. All right, OK, all right. Are you going to do that anymore? OK, tell the policeman he doesn't have to come up now."

All right, now we all got "Policeman, policeman, policeman," and we had a few psychotic parents who took it and rubbed it in our face, and those people for the most, if you search it out, are censors. Oh, true, they hate toilets with a passion, man. Do you realize if you got that wrapped around with a toilet, you'd hate it, and anyone who refers to it? It is dirty and uncomfortable to you.

Now, if the bedroom is dirty to you, then you are a true atheist, because if you have any of the mores, superstitions, if anyone in this audience believes that God made his body, and your body is dirty, the fault lies with the manufacturer. It's that cold, Jim, yeah.

You can do anything with the body that God made, and then you want to get definitive and tell me of the parts He made; I don't see that anywhere in any reference to any Bible. Yeah. He made it all; it's all clean or all dirty.

But the ambivalence comes from the religious leaders, who are celibates. The religious leaders are "what *should* be." They say they do not involve themselves with the physical. If we are good, we will be like our rabbi, or our nun, or our priests, and absolve, and finally put down the carnal and stop the race.

Now, dig, this is stranger. Everybody today in the hotel was bugged with Knight and Nixon. Let me tell you the truth. The truth is "what *is.*" If "what is" is, you have to sleep eight, ten hours a day, that is the truth. A lie will be: People need no sleep at all. Truth is "what *is.*" If every politician from the beginning is crooked, there is no crooked. But if you are concerned with a lie, "what should be"—and "what should be" is a fantasy, a terrible, terrible lie that someone gave the people long ago: This is what *should* be—and no one ever saw what should be, that you don't need any sleep and you can go seven years without sleep, so that all the people were made to measure up to that dirty lie. You know there's no crooked politicians. There's never a lie because there is never a truth.

I sent this agency a letter—they are bonded and you know what that means: anybody who is bonded never steals from you, nor could Earl Long. Ha! If the governor can, then the bond is really—yeah, that's some bond.

Very good. Write the letter. Blah, blah, blah, "I want this," blah, blah, blah, "ticket taker."

Get a letter back, get an answer back, Macon, Georgia:

"Dear Mr. Bruce: Received your letter," blah, blah, blah. "We have ticket sellers, bonded. We charge two-and-a-half dollars per ticket seller, per hour. We would have to have some more details," blah, blah, blah, "Sincerely yours, Dean R. Moxie."

Dean R. Moxie . . . Dean R. Moxie . . . Moxie, buddy. Dean R. Moxie, from the Florida criminal correctional institution for the criminally insane, and beat up a spade-fed junkie before he was thrown off the police force, and then was arrested for *schtupping* his stepdaughter. Dean R. Moxie. Hmmm.

All right, now, because I have a sense of the ludicrous, I sent him back an answer, Mr. Moxie. Dig, because I mean this is some of the really goodies I had in the letter, you know. He wants to know details.

"Dear Mr. Moxie: It would be useless to go into the definitive, a breakdown of what the duties will be, unless I can be sure that the incidents that have happened in the past will not be reiterated, such as ticket takers I have hired, who claimed they were harassed by customers who wanted their money back, such as the fop in San Jose who is suing me for being stabbed. Claims he was stabbed by an irate customer, and it was a lie—it was just a manicure scissors, and you couldn't see it because it was below the eyebrow, and when his eye was open, you couldn't see it anyway. (So I tell him a lot of problems like that.) And —oh yes, oh yeah—my father . . . has been in three mental institutions, and detests the fact that I am in the industry, and really abhors the fact that I have been successful economically and has harassed some ticket sellers, like in Sacramento he stood in line posing as a customer and, lightning flash, grabbed a handful of human feces and crammed it in the ticket taker's face. And once in Detroit he posed as a customer and he leaned against the booth so the ticket seller could not see him, and he was exposing himself, and had a sign hanging from it, saying: WHEN WE HIT $1500, THE GUY INSIDE THE BOOTH IS GOING TO KISS IT."

Now, you'd assume Dean R. Moxie, reading the letter, would just reject that and have enough validity to grab it in again.

"Dear Mr. Moxie: You know, of course, that if these facts were to fall into the hands of some yellow journalists, this would prove a deterrent to my career. So I'm giving you, you know, my confessor, you know," blah, blah, blah. "Also, this is not a requisite of a ticket seller, but I was wondering if I could have a ticket seller who could be more than a ticket seller—a companion."

Really light now. This is really subtle.

"A companion, someone who I could have coffee with, someone who is not narrow-minded like the—I had a stunning Danish seaman type in Oregon, who misinterpreted me and stole my watch."

Ha! Ha, is that heavy?

"Stole my watch. Am hoping to hear from you," blah, blah, blah, "Lenny Bruce."

OK. Now I send him a booster letter.

"Dear Mr. Moxie: My attorney said I was mad for ever confessing what has happened to me, you know, so I know that I can trust you, and I have sent you some cologne."

Ha!

"Sent you some cologne, and I don't know what's happened . . ."

Isn't this beautiful?

"And I don't know what's happened to that naughty postman, naughtiest . . ."

Get this phraseology. I hadn't heard, you know. Now I get an answer from him:

"We cannot insure the incidents that have happened in the past will not reoccur. A ticket seller that would socialize is out of the question."

I think this is beautiful.

"And I did not receive any cologne nor do we care for any. Dean R. Moxie . . ."

(*With drum and cymbal accompaniment.*)
To is a preposition.
    To is a preposition
    Come is a verb.
    To is a preposition.
    Come is a verb.
    To is a preposition.
    Come is a verb, the verb intransitive.
    To come.
    To come.
I've heard these two words my whole adult life, and as a kid when I thought I was sleeping.
    To come.
    To come.
    It's been like a big drum solo.
    Did you come?
    Did you come?

Good.
Did you come good?
Did you come good?
Did you come good?
Did you come good?
Did you come good?
Did you come good?
Did you come good?
I come better with you, sweetheart, than anyone in the whole god-
damned world.
I really came so good.
I really came so good 'cause I love you.
I really came so good.
I come better with you, sweetheart, than anyone in the whole world.
I really came so good.
So good.
But don't come in me.
Don't come in me.
Don't come in me, me, me, me, me.
Don't come in me, me, me, me.
Don't come in me.
Don't come in me, me, me.
Don't come in me, me, me.
I can't come.
'Cause you don't love me, that's why you can't come.
I love you, I just can't come; that's my hang-up, I can't come when
I'm loaded, all right?
'Cause you don't love me. Just what the hell is the matter with you?
What has that got to do with loving? I just can't come.

Now, if anyone in this room or the world finds those two words decadent, obscene, immoral, amoral, asexual, the words "to come" really
make you feel uncomfortable, if you think I'm rank for saying it to you,
you the beholder think it's rank for listening to it, you probably can't
come. And then you're of no use, because that's the purpose of life, to
re-create it.

Mr. Wollenberg called me to the witness stand for cross-examination:
Q. Mr. Bruce, had you a written script when you gave this perform-
ance?
A. No.
MR. BENDICH: Objected to as irrelevant, your Honor.
THE COURT: The answer is "No"; it may stand.
MR. WOLLENBERG: I have no further questions.

THE COURT: All right, you may step down.
THE WITNESS: Thank you.
MR. BENDICH: The defense rests, your Honor.

The time had come for the judge to instruct the jury:
"The defendant is charged with violating Section 311.6 of the Penal Code
of the State of California, which provides:

> Every person who knowingly sings or speaks any obscene song, bal-
> lad, or other words in any public place is guilty of a misdemeanor.

" 'Obscene' means to the average person, applying contemporary standards, the predominant appeal of the matter, taken as a whole, is to prurient
interest; that is, a shameful or morbid interest in nudity, sex or excretion
which goes substantially beyond the customary limits of candor in description
or representation of such matters and is matter which is utterly without
redeeming social importance.

"The words 'average person' mean the average adult person and have no
relation to minors. This is not a question of what you would or would not
have children see, hear or read, because that is beyond the scope of the law in
this case and is not to be discussed or considered by you.

" 'Sex' and 'obscenity' are not synonymous. In order to make the portrayal of sex obscene, it is necessary that such portrayal come within the
definition given to you, and the portrayal must be such that its dominant
tendency is to deprave or corrupt the average adult by tending to create a
clear and present danger of antisocial behavior.

"The law does not prohibit the realistic portrayal by an artist of his subject
matter, and the law may not require the author to put refined language into
the mouths of primitive people. The speech of the performer must be
considered in relation to its setting and the theme or themes of his production. The use of blasphemy, foul or coarse language, and vulgar behavior
does not in and of itself constitute obscenity, although the use of such words
may be considered in arriving at a decision concerning the whole of the
production.

"To determine whether the performance of the defendant falls within the
condemnation of the statute, an evaluation must be made as to whether the
performance as a whole had as its dominant theme an appeal to prurient
interest. Various factors should be borne in mind when applying this yard-
stick. These factors include the theme or themes of the performance, the
degree of sincerity of purpose evident in it, whether it has artistic merit. If
the performance is merely disgusting or revolting, it cannot be obscene,
because obscenity contemplates the arousal of sexual desires.

"A performance cannot be considered utterly without redeeming social importance if it has literary, artistic or aesthetic merit, or if it contains ideas, regardless of whether they are unorthodox, controversial, or hateful, of redeeming social importance.

"In the case of certain crimes, it is necessary that in addition to the intended act which characterizes the offense, the act must be accompanied by a specific or particular intent without which such a crime may not be committed. Thus, in the crime charged here, a necessary element is the existence in the mind of the defendant of knowing that the material used in his production on October 4, 1961, was obscene, and that, knowing it to be obscene, he presented such material in a public place.

"The intent with which an act is done is manifested by the circumstances attending the act, the manner in which it is done, the means used, and the discretion of the defendant. In determining whether the defendant had such knowledge, you may consider reviews of his work which were available to him, stating that his performance had artistic merit and contained socially important ideas, or, on the contrary, that his performance did not have any artistic merit and did not contain socially important ideas."

The court clerk read the verdict:

"In the Municipal Court of the City and County of San Francisco, State of California; the People of the State of California, Plaintiff, *vs.* Lenny Bruce, Defendant; Verdict . . ."

I really started to sweat it out there.

"We, the jury in the above-entitled case, find the defendant not guilty of the offense charged, misdemeanor, to wit: violating Section 311.6 of the Penal Code of the State of California . . ."

"Ladies and gentlemen of the jury, is this your verdict?"

THE JURY: Yes.

THE COURT: All right. Do you desire the jury polled?

MR. WOLLENBERG: No, your Honor.

THE COURT: Would you ask the jury once again if that is their verdict?

THE CLERK: Ladies and gentlemen of the jury, is this your verdict?

THE JURY: Yes.

Isn't that weird! It's like saying, "Are you *sure?*"

Chapter
Twenty-One

Marijuana will be legal some day, because the many law students who now smoke pot will some day become Congressmen and legalize it in order to protect themselves.

You wouldn't *believe* how many people smoke pot. If anybody reading this would like to become mayor, believe me, there is a vast, untapped vote. Of course, you wouldn't want to be the Marijuana Mayor, so you'd have to make it a trick statute, like; "The Crippled Catholic Jewish War Children in Memory of Ward Bond Who Died for Your Bill to Make Marijuana Legal."

Just like the gynecologist who pretends "It doesn't mean anything to me—I see that all the time," there are untold numbers of men and women and college students all over the country who play the "I know and you know but we'll both make believe we're asleep" game with the Zig-Zag cigarette paper people.

And yet at this very moment there are American citizens in jail for *smoking flowers*. (Marijuana is the dried flowering top of the hemp plant.)

I don't smoke pot, and I'm glad because then I can champion it without special pleading. The reason I don't smoke it is because it facilitates ideas and heightens sensations—and I've got enough shit flying through my head without smoking pot.

At this time, ladies and gentlemen of the jury, the State will present its closing argument in the case against marijuana: It leads to the use of heroin and other dangerous, addictive drugs.

If this syllogism holds true, the bust-out junkie will say to his cellmate: "I am a heroin addict. I started smoking marijuana and then naturally I graduated to heroin. By the way, my cellmate, what happened to you? How did you come to murder three guys in a crap game? You've got blood on your hands. How did you first get obsessed with this terrible disease of gambling? Where did it all start?"

"Oh, I started gambling with Bingo in the Catholic Church. . . ."

The newspapers said that the late Pope John was being fed intravenously.

"We don't like to do this, Pope, but we've got to take you downtown. Those marks on your arm there . . . now don't give us any of that horseshit about intravenous feeding—we hear it all the time."

I'm neither anti-Catholic nor pro-Catholic, but if I were Catholic myself I'd be quite hostile toward the press. To quote from the *Los Angeles Herald-Examiner:* "Short of a miracle, he [Pope John] could be expected to die at any moment."

Superstitious people all over the world waited and waited for that miracle, but it never came.

Yes, brothers, anyone who does anything for pleasure to indulge his selfish soul will surely burn in hell. The only medicine that's good for you is iodine, because it burns. That stone is lodged in your urinary tract because Nature *meant* it to be there. So retie that umbilical cord, snap your foreskin back on, and drown in the amniotic fluid, 'cause we're havin' a party and the people are nice . . .

The religious factor enters (as opposed to the scientific) because the scientists ask for prima-facie evidence and the religionists ask for circumstantial evidence. The argument that medicine is not an exact science and is therefore circumstantial, is merely a wish-fulfillment posed by those who know that "When all else fails, prayer will be answered."

QUERY: "Doctor, I'm sorry to wake you in the middle of the night like this, but I have a serious question about opinion versus fact. In your opinion, can my wife and I use the same hypodermic syringe to inject insulin for our diabetic conditions? Because I'm almost in shock. Oooops, here I go. Take it, Sadie."

"Hello, Doctor, this is Tim's wife. Listen, it's serious. Should we share the syringe? I've got Staphylococcus septicemia and he's got infectious hepatitis. You do remember me, don't you? You told me it was all right to marry my first husband, the one who died of syphilis. I never regretted it. We have a lovely son who, incidentally, would like your address—he wants to send you some things he's making at The Lighthouse, a broom and a pot holder."

Actually, I sympathize with doctors, because they perform a devilish job, and I certainly admire anyone with the stick-to-itiveness to spend that much time in school. They are actually underpaid in relation to the amount of time invested in training, no matter how much they make. A specialist may have nearly 20 years of no income at all to make up for. But people evaluate *their* time with *his,* and then they figure his fees are exorbitant.

That's why they have no moral compunction about hanging the doctor up with his bills while they'll pay the TV repairman right off. Besides, they rationalize, the doctor is in it because of his desire to serve humanity. But they also say: "If you haven't got your health, money isn't worth anything." Oh, yeah? If you're deathly ill, money means a hell of a lot. Especially to the doctor.

One illness I had, started out with a rash on my face. I received all the sage advice of my friends:

"Don't pick it."

"That's the worst thing you can do, is pick it."

"If you pick it, it will take twice as long to heal."

I heeded them. I didn't pick it—and there were times I could have. Times when I was alone and had the door locked. I could have just picked it to my heart's content. And I even schemed that if anyone were to ask me later, "Have you been picking your face?" I would look very hurt and say, "Do I look like a moron? What am I, deaf or something? I'm not going to do the worst thing in the world!"

I didn't pick it, though. And it got worse.

Finally I decided to see a skin specialist. He laid me down on a cold leather couch and the first thing he did was pick it.

He didn't even use tweezers. He *picked* it—with his fingers.

That's the secret. The doctors are the ones who start the "Don't pick it" campaigns, because they want to have exclusive pickings.

"What is it?" I asked, as he washed his hands and smeared gook on my face.

"It's going around," he said, intently.

"What do you mean, 'It's going around'?" I demanded. *"You* haven't got it."

"It'll go away," he assured me.

Those are the two things all doctors must learn, just before they graduate. After they've spent years and years learning all the scientific knowledge accumulated by the medical profession, just as they are handed their diplomas, the Surgeon General whispers in their ears: "It's going around, and it'll go away."

It did go away. Just the way colds "go away" and headaches "go away." Did you ever wonder where all the colds and headaches and rashes *go* when they go away? Back to some central clearing area, I suppose, to wait their turn to "go around" again.

As a result of a severe case of hepatitis in the Navy, and a subsequent recurrence after the War, I have been plagued for many years with spells of lethargy. Some of the spells could even be described as attacks. The lethargy was more than just a drowsiness. I would find myself simultaneously dictating and sleeping—and since I speak in a stream-of-conscious, apparently unrelated pattern, secretaries would be typing into eight-ten minutes of mumbling and abstraction, such as one might expect from a half-awake, half-asleep reporter.

Once, while driving a disc-jockey friend of mine into town about one o'clock in the afternoon, I fell asleep at the wheel.

I woke up in a rut.

The name of a good doctor was suggested to me. He asked me if I had any history of narcolepsy—that's a condition characterized by sharp attacks of deep sleep. I said no. And he prescribed an amphetamine, which I believe is the generic term for Dexedrine, Benzedrine, Byphetamine, and the base for most diet pills, mood elevators, pep pills, thrill pills, etc.

This was in Philadelphia. I was working at a night club in Pennsauken—which is really Philadelphia, only it's in New Jersey geographically—just as Newark, New Jersey is really New York City. The Red Hill Inn is a 600-seater with a five-dollars-per-person cover and minimum.

It was Thursday and I had a terrible seizure of uncontrollable, teeth-chattering chills. When I have the chills, I always like to talk while my teeth clack together and go, "Ja-ja-ja-ja-ja-Jeezus, I'm freezing ma-ma-ma-ma-ma-myassoff."

My doctor came and said not to get out of bed. I had a fever of 102 degrees. Next day it was 103. He came to my hotel twice that day.

Friday night was six hours away. That's the one correct thing about show business. The nighttime is specifically defined. "I'll see you tonight" means 10:30. Evening is 9:30.

In six hours either I would be on the stage or the boss would be guaranteed a loss of $6000. Now, what would you do if you had a 103-degree fever, knowing that if you didn't get on the stage, you wouldn't be paid the $1800 that was yours from the gross? Having a conscience and realizing that $1800 is a lot of friggin' money—I naturally felt the show must go on; a trouper to the end—I worked, and came home with a fever of 105 degrees.

My doctor called in a consultant. The consultant called a nurse to try to bring my fever down. The fever subsided and the Staph bug lay dormant. It woke up six months later nice and strong, and almost killed me for a month and a half; for a week I was on the critical list at Mount Sinai Hospital in Miami Beach.

A year later, in September, 1961, I was arrested for the first time on a charge of following my doctor's orders. I was playing Pennsauken again. I was staying at the John Bartram Hotel in Philadelphia, across the street from Evans' Pharmacy, six blocks away from my doctor's office, several miles away from the Red Hill Inn, and twenty-four hours away from my second visit to the hospital.

I started to get chills and, fearing a recurrence of Staph, I telephoned my doctor. He was away for the weekend. But his consultant put me into Haverford Hospital. I stayed four days before going back to the hotel.

At ten minutes after twelve noon on September 29th I heard a knock on my door at the hotel. Which was indeed disturbing, because I had left an adamant request that I not be disturbed.

"It's the manager." *Bam! Bam! Bam!*

"Can you manage to refrain from knocking at my door?"

"You better open up—it's for your own good." *Bam! Bam! Bam!*

"Hello, desk? There's some kind of a nut outside my door who says he's the manager. I'd like the police."

Crunch! Crack! Plaster fell, and the door walked in wearing size-12 shoes.

"It's the police."

"Christ, what service. I just called for you guys."

"Never mind the shit, where's the shit?"

Now is that weird—these guys say "Where's the shit?" knowing that I'll do a bit. If I copped out to it—that is, if there were any shit—"The shit, sir, if you're referring to the products of Parke Davis, is scattered on my dresser. And if you will kindly remove that DO NOT DISTURB sign from my arm . . . I cannot do so with your handcuffs restraining me."

Incidentally, I use the word "shit" in context. It's not obscene as far as narcotics is concerned—that's the Supreme Court ruling on the picture *The Connection*. In other words, if you shit in your pants and smoke it, you're cool.

Officer Perry of the Philadelphia Narcotics Unit testified at a hearing the next day: "Armed with a search and seizure warrant signed by Magistrate Keiser, we went to the John Bartram Hotel, room 616. Upon gaining entrance to the room, we did conduct a search of the defendant's room and found in a bureau drawer the following paraphernalia: One green box containing thirty-six ampules labeled Methedrine, and also one plastic vial containing eleven white tablets, not labeled, one glass bottle containing——"

And the court interposed in the person of Der Keiser himself (the magistrate who had issued the warrant and was now passing on the validity of his procedures): "Identified then as what?"

"We don't know, sir. It hasn't been analyzed yet."

THE DISTRICT ATTORNEY: "Does it contain liquids, or powder or pills?"

OFFICER PERRY: "I stated eleven tablets in plastic vial, not labeled; one plastic bottle containing a clear liquid with George Evans Pharmacy label, narcotic No. 4102, No. 98–351; one plastic vial containing thirteen white tablets, labeled antihistamine; five glass syringes; twenty plastic syringes; four needles.

"We interrogated the defendant pertaining to the paraphernalia, sir. The defendant stated to me, in company with the other officers, that he had gotten these legitimately.

"I then told the defendant to dress himself, he would come down to Narcotics Headquarters.

"The defendant stated he was too ill to be moved. The procedure was to call the police surgeon. . . . Lenny Bruce refused to let this doctor examine him."

I had said, "He's your doctor, *schmuck*. I want my doctor."

The transcript, by the way, is incorrectly punctuated on this point. It comes out reading, "He's your Doctor Schmuck . . ."

My doctor's consultant's name was on my prescription, and the officer contacted him because, as he explained to the court, he had wanted to check with the doctor to see whether I could be moved. The consultant supposedly told him I could be.

I was just out of the hospital and he gave this diagnosis over the phone!

The officer continued his testimony: "At that time Lenny still refused to be moved. I called for a police wagon and a stretcher. The defendant was taken out of the John Bartram Hotel on a stretcher——"

They got me on the stretcher, and everybody was sullen and quiet, including Dr. Schmuck, until we got to the elevator. Now, stretchers are made for *hospital* elevators. They are seven feet long, and most elevators fall several feet short of that. The dialog ran as follows:

STRETCHER-BEARER NUMBER ONE: "How the hell are we gonna get this thing in the elevator? [*To patient*] Hey, Bruce, why don't you cooperate and get out of this thing till we get to the street, then you can get back in it."

"I'd like to oblige you, Mr. Ayres, but as noble as your intentions are, some old *cum laude* district attorney will pervert your words on cross-examination: 'So he said he was too ill to be moved, but he got out of the stretcher before getting into the elevator . . .'"

How they resolved the problem was to put the stretcher in the way it fit: up and down. Feet up, head down.

Because I didn't cooperate, a slant-board position was my reward. People getting into the elevator—"Hello, Mr. Bruce." I was looking up everybody's bloomers.

And where do you think they brought me, boys and girls? Where would you bring *anyone* who is on your stretcher? Why, to police headquarters, of course.

Yes, I got the whole police treatment which, I go on record to state before any committee, is like being dealt with by the monitors that we used to have in school. Police brutality is a myth, no doubt propagated by felons ashamed of having finked out eagerly at their first sight of bars. Anticipating continual sly references by mother and brother, they grasp for a method of self-serving.

Oh, how they beat me
Rubber hosed and Sam Levened me
And Brian Donlevy'd me
In their back rooms.
"Give us names, Bruce,
Give us the names and you
Can walk out a free man.
Give us the names of a
Few of your friends."
But I, Spartan-sired,
Would do ten years in prison
Before I would give
The name of one friend—
Or is that a little bullshit?
I would give names upon names
Of those yet unborn
Rather than do a 50th birthday
In some maximum security.
The halls of justice.
The only place
You see the justice,
Is in the halls.

"The rotten D.A., how about that son of a bitch wantinta send those two poor babies to the gas chamber, two poor kids barely out of their teens, who just shot and killed their way across the country—48 gas-station attendants who just missed supper and their lives. And the kids only got 18 cents and a couple of packs of cigarettes and a blown-out tire. Ladies and gentlemen of the jury, the District Attorney wants to send those two poor kids to the gas chamber for a pack of smokes and 18 cents and a no-good tire."

The halls of justice.
The only place
You see the justice,
Is in the halls
Where the felon hears
A judge at recess talking
To that guy from the Capitol:
"You sure it's all right?"
"Would I tell you it was
All right if it wasn't
All right? You just tell her
You're a friend of the judge's."

135

Call Crestview 4, Franklin 7,
Michigan 8, Circle 5, Republic 3,
They're all her answering services,
Those unseen pimps who
Work for Madam Bell.

"I'm sorry, but Miss Kim Pat doesn't answer her telephone. And I *did* try one ring and hang up, then three rings."

"Well, operator, I'll be truthful with you, I wanna get laid, and if she's busy, how about you? I'm blind, you see, no one will ever know unless you should identify me at some line-up that you might be participating in."

Police brutality. Think about it. Think about the time it happened to you. If your frame of reference is the South, that's not police brutality, it's Southern revolution. That's a separate *country* down there.

"They beat the crap out of me, but I proved I was a man. They kept beating me, but I didn't give them no names."

"What names, *schmuck?* You were arrested for exposing yourself."

As I look at the transcript of my Philadelphia hearing, I see a crystallization of the argument that the Judicial and the Executive are one, lessening the checks-and-balances effect that was intended by Ben Franklin and those other revolutionaries who got together in Philadelphia.

Cross-examination by my attorney, Malcolm Berkowitz, elicited the following from the cop who made the arrest:

Q. Do you have your search and seizure warrant?

A. Yes, sir.

Q. May we see it?

A. Positively. (*Search and seizure warrant is examined by Mr. Berkowitz.*)

THE COURT: I'll attest to the fact it's my signature thereon.

Q. Now, in this search and seizure warrant the signature of the person requesting the warrant is Policeman Albert T. Perry, a member of the Narcotics Unit. Person to be searched, Lenny Bruce, white male, John Bartram Hotel, Broad and Locust, room 616. Property to be seized: opium, heroin, Demerol, morphine, codeine, Dilaudid, cocaine, marijuana, and any and all other tablets, powders or liquids. Now of those articles to be seized, Officer Perry, did you seize any opium?

A. No, sir.

Q. Did you seize any heroin?

A. No, sir.

Q. Did you seize any Demerol?

A. No, sir.

Q. Did you seize any morphine?

A. No, sir.

Q. Did you seize any cocaine?

A. No, sir.

THE COURT (*Interposing*): Wait; are you saying no to generalize?

A. Your Honor, they are derivatives, sir, of opium. It contains the opium base. (*Officer Perry should brush up on his pharmacology: cocaine is not a derivative of opium.*)

THE COURT: You can't say no.

MR. BERKOWITZ: I object to this conversation, for the record.

THE COURT: I asked the question of the police officer to be more alert as to his answer in relationship to this situation when——

DISTRICT ATTORNEY HARRIS (*Interposing*): He was being truthful, sir. He said he did not confiscate heroin, or morphine, or opium. They haven't been mentioned in the warrant.

MR. BERKOWITZ: Of five of the things to be seized in this search and seizure warrant, he said he took none of them. (*Addressing witness*) Now . . . do you know if you confiscated any Dilaudid?

A. I do not know.

Q. Codeine?

A. I do not know.

Q. Marijuana?

A. I know there's no marijuana there.

Q. In other words, you found nothing in this man's apartment that's listed on this search and seizure warrant, did you?

MR. HARRIS: Objection, sir. That's not true. The warrant calls for any other tablets, powders or liquids.

THE COURT: Sustain your objection.

MR. BERKOWITZ: Your Honor, the question I've asked——If you have sustained the objection, he can't answer——but the question I've asked is a question relating to a material matter of fact in this case. I asked the officer who made an affidavit that he was going there to seize those listed articles and others of like kind whether he had found any marijuana, as was on that list, or anything like it, and his answer to that question should be made. There's nothing improper about that question. It is material.

THE COURT: You're asking this man, this police officer, to make a statement on certain things that were found in that room that have not been analyzed as of yet.

MR. BERKOWITZ: Your Honor, he made an affidavit that he was going there to pick things of that nature up.

THE COURT: He eventually will be able to prove or disprove that.

MR. HARRIS: I think Mr. Berkowitz is overlooking the entire section——the line "Any other tablets, powders or liquids"——and they were confiscated.

MR. BERKOWITZ: Your Honor, if he had aspirin in his apartment or any other powders or liquids of that type, there would be no violation of the law involved. It's only if he possesses something which he has no right to possess under any of our laws that this man could be guilty of crime, and Detective Perry, who made the affidavit and who signed an oath that he was going to this man's apartment to find those things named in that warrant, that search and seizure warrant——

THE COURT (*Interposing*): That's what he expected to find.

MR. BERKOWITZ: But I have to ask him, because he's the one placing the charge and we have a hearing this morning.

THE COURT: He did answer those questions.

MR. BERKOWITZ: He said "No."

THE COURT: Where he was specifically certain—for instance, in marijuana, sir, he found no marijuana. There are certain prescriptions here, certain bottles and vials that have not been analyzed as yet.

MR. BERKOWITZ: Your Honor, he went further than that. He said: "No, I found no opium." "No, I found no heroin . . ."

THE COURT (*Interposing*): Right.

MR. BERKOWITZ (*Continuing*): "No, I found no Demerol." "No, I found no codeine." "No, I found no Dilaudid." "No, I found no cocaine." "No, I found no marijuana."

DISTRICT ATTORNEY HARRIS: As far as he knows.

MR. BERKOWITZ: Well, who else knows if he doesn't?

MR. HARRIS: The police chemist.

MR. BERKOWITZ: Where is the police chemist?

MR. HARRIS: He's home sleeping. You know that, Mr. Berkowitz.

MR. BERKOWITZ: Didn't he know he had a hearing this morning?

THE COURT: The hearing would not make any difference. He has not had the opportunity of analyzing it. If you're raising a request for analysis, I'll have to give a further hearing for that analysis, if you're pressing for the analysis.

MR. BERKOWITZ: I'm pressing for an analysis. I want an analysis now, this morning of our hearing. What are the police doing making arrests without being interested in finding out if they have a case; and take a man never arrested before and stand him up before the bar of the court and hold him in custody. If they have evidence, let them produce it. Give us a hearing this afternoon. Let them tell us if there is anything——

THE COURT (*Interposing*): This court, nor the District Attorney's office, nor the police department, are they in control of the city chemist to force him to give an immediate analysis at the convenience of the defendant.

MR. BERKOWITZ: I'm not asking for convenience.

THE COURT: That's what you're asking for. You're asking for an analysis. I'll be glad to order an analysis and hold this defendant in proper or appropriate bail pending that analysis.

MR. BERKOWITZ: On what charge, your Honor?

THE COURT: On the charge of violation of the narcotics laws and the illegal use of drugs as so stipulated as of this warrant.

MR. BERKOWITZ: Where is there any evidence to entitle you to hold him on a further hearing on any charge?

THE COURT: We will produce it . . .

MR. BERKOWITZ (*Continuing cross-examination*): Now, let me ask you this: Was the city chemist off duty between the time you confiscated it in that apartment at ten minutes after noon yesterday and the end of the normal business day yesterday?

A. No, sir.

THE COURT: I don't think the witness has to answer this, because he described earlier that this defendant was the one who probably deprived the police department of getting this to a chemist at an appropriate time by his own actions and refusal to be apprehended, to be checked, to be examined, and to have this sent to the city chemist in sufficient time to have an analysis for this day.

MR. BERKOWITZ: How many officers went with you to the hotel room where Lenny Bruce was staying?

A. Three; Officers Miller and Zawackis.

Q. How many of you had to carry him on the stretcher . . . ?

A. We called a wagon.

Q. You didn't carry him?

A. I helped carry him, yes, sir.

Q. Did the other two officers with you help carry him?

A. I think Officer Zawackis assisted the other policemen at that time.

Q. How many officers carried him down on the stretcher?

A. Four.

Q. How many officers were present?

A. Five.

Q. Now, who had control of the various things that are displayed before his Honor?

A. I had that in my custody.

Q. What prevented you from taking it to the city chemist that afternoon for analysis?

THE COURT (*Interposing*): Let me answer for the police officer. The police officer could not get anything there to the chemist until he had been apprehended properly and an arrest report made, and these reports that must accompany this to the city chemist.

MR. BERKOWITZ: Is that your answer, Officer Perry, under oath?

A. That's my answer. That's the correct answer . . .

Q. Because you were the one who didn't go to the chemist?

A. My answer is by the time we got done with the defendant—he wanted to be looked at by a medical doctor, and we made a call to the surgeon, and by the time I contacted the doctor to see if he could be moved, it was late. I got into my office and prepared the paperwork and it was too late to deliver to the chemist. The chemist is closed at five o'clock . . .

Q. What made you go look up Lenny Bruce, other than the fact he was a big-name headliner?

MR. HARRIS: Objection, sir. They don't have to reveal the source of their information.

THE COURT: I sustain the objection.

MR. BERKOWITZ: You ever see him use any drugs yourself?

A. No, sir.

Q. Did you ever see him buying anything that he shouldn't have bought?

A. I didn't even know the defendant, sir.

Q. You never heard of him, either?

A. Never heard of him.

Q. Never knew he was a headliner?

A. Never heard of him. And he's supposed to be topnotch? I never heard of him.

Q. How about Mort Sahl, do you know who he is?

A. Yes, he reads a book or something.

Since I was scheduled to open in San Francisco the next week—where, you may recall, I was to be arrested for obscenity—I was let go on $1500 bail. In the end, the Philadelphia grand jury refused to accept the bill, and they stamped across it: BILL IGNORED.

Chapter
Twenty-two

For self-protection, I now carry with me at all times a small bound booklet consisting of photostats of statements made by physicians, and prescriptions and bottle labels. For example, here is a letter written December 29, 1961 by a Beverly Hills doctor:

To Whom It May Concern:

Mr. Lenny Bruce has been under my professional care for the past two years for various minor orthopedic conditions. In addition, Mr. Bruce suffers from episodes of severe depression and lethargy.

His response to oral amphetamine has not been particularly satisfactory, so he has been instructed in the proper use of intravenous injections of Methedrine (methamphetamine hydrochloride). This has given a satisfactory response.

Methedrine in ampules of 10cc(20mg), together with disposable syringes, has been prescribed for intravenous use as needed.

Mr. Bruce has asked that I write this letter in order that any peace officer observing fresh needle marks on Mr. Bruce's arm may be assured that they are the result of Methedrine injections for therapeutic reasons.

Norman P. Rotenberg, M.D.

I might add that historically there was quite a problem in England where the king's men were stopping people on the street to see if they were fit for burning—i.e., if they had rejected the Anglican church. So these malcontents, later known as the Pilgrim Fathers, cowards that they were, fled to escape persecution.

Upon arriving here, they entered into their illegal beliefs, these Protestants, and formed their sinister doctrine that is at this late date still interfering with law-enforcement agencies, still obstructing justice throughout our land, because of technicalities such as the 13th Amendment to the Constitution, which guarantees that persons will be safe in their homes against unreasonable searches and seizures.

I guess what happens is, if you get arrested in Town A (Philadelphia) and then Town B (San Francisco)—with a lot of publicity—then when you get to

Town C they *have* to arrest you or what kind of a shithouse town are *they* running?

It's a pattern of unintentional harassment.

Town C: Chicago. In December 1962 I was working at the Gate of Horn. During one of my performances, I was arrested for obscenity.

The police report starts out with some incestuous data.

Victim's Name: Arresting Officers.

Person Reporting Crime to Police: Officer Cavanaugh.

Person Who Discovered Crime: Arresting Officers.

Witnesses' Names: Reporting Officers.

Victim's Occupation: Police Officers.

Coincidentally, PLAYBOY was tape-recording some of my shows, and what follows is a study in contrast: quotes from the police report on my arrest, as opposed to excerpts from the transcript of what I actually said onstage that night.

POLICE REPORT: "Mr. Bruce held up a colored photograph showing the naked breast of a woman and said 'God, your Jesus Christ, made these tits.' "

THE TAPE: A Chicago newspaper columnist who is sort of, to the out-of-towners, is sort of a Christ in Concrete, and he's got a thing going: what's decent, indecent; what is good, and good is God, is Danny Thomas, and so I said I'll show you pictures of tramps, these are bums . . ." (*Holding up a page from a calendar which was for sale at several newsstands and stores on the arresting officer's beat.*) "Let's see, here's an indecent woman—you're kidding! Indecent? How can that pretty lady be indecent? Whew! Ah, what kind of flower is that? Those are, they're lilacs, yeah, they're pretty. Lilies-of-the-valley and lilacs are my favorite flowers, I really dig them. That is a *shiksa*, there's a pink-nippled lady: that's one thing about the *goyim,* boy, they've got winner chicks. The real bums you can spot. They usually have babies in their bellies—that's the real tramps—and no rings on their fingers. And they get their just deserts by bleeding to death in the back of taxicabs. . . . 'You don't love me, you just want to ball me'—that's the usual cry. How about *doing it,* how do you feel about that, you people, is that about the dirtiest thing we could do to each other? Priests don't do it, nuns don't do it, Patamonza Yoganunda doesn't do it, rabbis are close to celibacy—it's really not very nice, is it, *doing it . . . ?*" (*Couple walks out.*) "They were very nice people, they could have been very ugly about it, they could have been. No, they were cool, gentle—they didn't like it and they split. Before all of you escape, let me explain something to you. You see, you defeat your purpose. It's God, your filthy Jesus Christ, made these tits, that's all. Now you've got to make up your mind, you've got to stand up to Jesus, and you've got to say, 'Look, I admit that *doing it* is filthy, I will stop doing it.' And, believe me, if you'll just set the rules, I will obey them.

But . . . stop living the paradox. Tell me that it's filthy, that fags are the best people; I will live up to the misogynist, I will be the woman-hater, I will be the nice guy that takes your daughter out. 'He's a nice guy, he didn't try to fool around with me, he was a nice faggot.' "

POLICE REPORT: "They say we fuck our mothers for Hershey bars."

THE TAPE: "I realize that my mother's body is dirty; I realize that I'm a second-rate power; I realize that you have sold out my country. Do you know why they hate Americans anywhere, everywhere? I think I did a little more traveling than anyone in this audience. I think I've been in more invasions than anyone in this audience. I made six. I made some real daddies. I was on a cruiser called the *U.S.S. Brooklyn*. I was second-best gunner's mate. I was mating it from 1942 to 1945, July—that's when Germany fell, in July. *Doing it* is dirty. They hate Americans everywhere. You know why? Because we fucked all of their mothers for chocolate bars, and don't you forget that, Jim."

POLICE REPORT: "I want to fuck your mothers. Oh, thank you, thank you, thank you."

THE TAPE: "You don't think those kids who have heard it since 1942—'You know what those Americans did to your poor mother, they lined her up, those bastards, your poor father had to throw his guts up in the kitchen; while he waited out there, that Master Sergeant *schtupped* your mother for their stinking coffee and their eggs and their frigging cigarettes, those Americans!' That's it, Jim, that's all they've heard, those kids. Those kids now, at 23–25 years old: 'The Americans, there's the guy that did it to my mother!' Would you assume that this is sizably correct . . . ? 'There's the fellow who fucked my mother—oh, thank you, thank you, thank you. Thank you for that, and for giving us candy.' "

POLICE REPORT: Then talking about the War he stated, "If we would have lost the War, they would have strung Truman up by the balls . . ."

THE TAPE: "Priests and rabbis walk with guys in death row. There's a clergyman, he's willing to be the hangman in Australia. No one else will do it. He couldn't get a brown suit, though. It's amazing. Priest or rabbi: 'Yes, my son, you must be brave.' 'Sure, *schmuck,* you're splitting, he's sitting.' . . . (*Into German accent.*) 'And people say Adolf Eichmann should have been hung. *Nein.* Do you recognize the whore in the middle of you—that you would have done the same if you were there yourselves? My defense: I was a soldier. I saw the end of a conscientious day's effort. I saw all of the work that I did. I watched through the portholes. I saw every Jew burned and turned into soap. Do you people think yourselves better because you burned your enemies at long distance with missiles without ever seeing what you had done to them? Hiroshima *auf Wiedersehen.*' (*German accent ends.*) If we would have lost the War, they would have strung Truman up by the balls, Jim. Are you kidding with that? Not what kid told kid told kid.

They would just *schlep* out all those Japanese mutants. 'Here they did; there they are.' And Truman said they'd do it again."

POLICE REPORT: Then referring to the good sisters of the Church, he stated, "The sisters cannot like to do it to sisters, fuck, good, good."

THE TAPE: "All right, now—'How to Relax the Colored People at Parties.' The party is in motion." (*In this bit I do a dialog between a Caucasian and a Negro, taking both parts myself; the white man is speaking.*):

". . . Anyway, you know, I'd like to have you over to the house, you know that?"

"Thank you."

"Be dark soon. Tell you what, I'd like to have you over to the house—I tell you this, you know, because I know you people get offensive—but I got a sister, you know what I mean?"

"Yes."

"What the hell is it with you guys? What do you want to hump everybody's sister for?"

"Well, that's—we're born that way. You see, it's natural—that's where the rhythm comes in, see, we have this natural sense of rhythm control, the Margaret Sanger clinic, and we never knock them up, that's the thing about it."

"And you really like to do it to everybody's sister?"

"Well, no, you missed the vernacular; it's not everybody's sister— we like to do it to *sisters*."

"What do you mean, sisters?"

"Just that—sisters."

"Oh, you don't mean *sister* sisters?"

"Yeah."

"Ah, that's impossible—I never knew that—oh, that's a lot of horseshit, you can't do that to the sisters! No kidding, do they put out, those sisters?"

"Well, I mean, if you're built the way we are—you know, we're built abnormally large. You know that, don't you?"

"I heard you guys got a wang on, you son-of-a-gun."

"Yes. To use the vernacular, it is sort of like a baby's arm with an apple in its fist—I think that's what Tennessee Williams said."

"Well, you mind if I see it?"

"No, I couldn't do that. I'm just playing guitar at this party."

"What the hell, just whip it out there; let's see that roll of tar paper you got there, Chonga . . ."

POLICE REPORT: "Sure, who does it; nothing wrong. Everybody's barring somebody. I bug three married women. All you people out there have at some time or another bugged someone's wife."

THE TAPE: "Now I am not particularly proud of this, but in my life I have been intimate with maybe three married ladies that are still happily married, and they convinced me that they never made it with anybody else but their husband and me. . . . Now if I did—and, Christ, I'm not that unique— I bet probably every guy in this audience has made it with one married chick or two that's still married. And both of us, we didn't pull out. No offense, mind you. So when I see brothers and sisters that don't look alike, that's it Jim. I wouldn't swear for *nobody*. Uh-uh. It just takes that one . . ."

POLICE REPORT: Then talking about God and Jesus Christ, he led into a mockery of the Catholic Church and other religious organizations by using the Pope's name and Cardinal Spellman and Bishop Sheen's name . . .

THE TAPE (*This bit is based on a visit to earth by Christ and Moses.*): "Come on down to the West Coast and visit the *schuls*. There are no *schuls*. Yes, there is a reform temple where the rabbi—no, it's a doctor, he is a doctor of law. His beard is gone. . . . 'You know, someone had the *chutzpah* to ask me the other day—they said, "Tell me something, Doctor of Law, is there a God or not?" What cheek to ask this in a temple! We're not here to talk of God—we're here to sell bonds for Israel. Remember that. A pox upon you, Christ and Moses . . .'

"Christ and Moses are confused. They go to New York . . . Saint Patrick's Cathedral. There is Bishop Sheen, played by Ed Begley. Cardinal Spellman, played by Hugh Herbert—'Woooo, woooo, terrible, terrible, terrible.' Christ and Moses standing in the back of Saint Pat's. Confused, Christ is, at the grandeur of the interior, the baroque interior, the rococo baroque interior. His route took him through Spanish Harlem. He would wonder what fifty Puerto Ricans were doing living in one room. That stained glass window is worth nine grand! Hmmmmm. . . . (*Spellman and Sheen decide to call the Pope long distance.*) 'Will you get me Rome? Hello. Hey, woppo, what's happening? You were sick, weren't you, fatso? If you'd stop *fressing* so much. . . .' Now, dig—we're in Chicago—fifty miles away from here I got punched in the face for doing that. Milwaukee . . ."

POLICE REPORT: "He used a Jewish word, 'smuck', numerous times."

I had already been arrested on the West Coast for saying *schmuck*—by a Yiddish undercover agent who had been placed in the club several nights running to determine if my use of Yiddish terms was a cover for profanity. The officer said it was. I asked the judge if I could bring my Aunt Mema to court to cross-examine him.

It's interesting, though, that the Chicago police report did *not* make any mention of the following excerpt from my performance that night:

There's an article here in *Chicago's American* about these transvestites that are posing as policemen, and how they're thwarting the

145

rapists. . . . According to Sergeant Dolan, one of the original members of the gang, the rough and ready policemen go to great lengths to appear as fascinating females—only, you've got to really go through all of it, right? "Well, I'll put it between my legs once and that's all; I'll try it and—now frig that method acting." (*Reading.*) "The most hazardous part of the preparation for duty, said Dolan, is learning how to walk on high-heeled shoes. Attackers have a sharp eye, Dolan said, and will shy away from an amateur, wobbly ankle. . . ." Now dig, the beautiful part about this is that they don't know that some of these rapists are that dedicated—they find out they're cops, they don't care, they'll *schtup* anyway, man. "I'm a peace officer." "I don't care, you got a cute ass, that's all I know." And that's it. Would you assume that there is the slightest bit of *entrapment* involved in this thing? That's not very nice, to incite. . . .

I was released on bail and continued working at the Gate of Horn. Meanwhile a police official, who had originally ordered the arrest, came into the Gate of Horn and with two waitresses witnessing, he conducted the following conversation with the manager:

POLICE OFFICIAL: I want to tell you that if this man ever uses a four-letter word in this club again, I'm going to pinch you and everyone in here. If he ever speaks against religion, I'm going to pinch you and everyone in here. Do you understand?

MANAGER: I don't have anything against any religion.

POLICE OFFICIAL: Maybe I'm not talking to the right person. Are you the man who hired Lenny Bruce?

MANAGER: Yes, I am. I'm Alan Ribback.

POLICE OFFICIAL: Well, I don't know why you ever hired him. You've had good people here. But he mocks the Pope—and I'm speaking as a Catholic—I'm here to tell you your license is in danger. We're going to have someone here watching every show. Do you understand?

MANAGER: Yes.

True, I *had* been taking advantage of something we used to be famous for. It's known as the right to worship as you please—and criticize as you please.

Chicago (population, 3,550,404) has the largest membership in the Roman Catholic Church—2,163,380—of any archdiocese in the country. Even so, that the panel of 50 persons from which the jury for my trial was to be selected should include 47 Catholics, was an interesting coincidence. Moreover, their names were not drawn out of a drum, as is the customary procedure, but rather, jurors were chosen according to where they were *seated.* And they kept *changing* seats.

The eventual jury consisted entirely of Catholics.

The judge was Catholic.

The prosecutor and his assistant were Catholic.

On Ash Wednesday, the judge removed the spot of ash from his forehead and told the bailiff to instruct the others to go and do likewise. I could never conjure up a more bizarre satire than the reality of a judge, two prosecutors and twelve jurors, each with a spot of ash on his forehead.

When the late Brendan Behan heard about this, he said: "That scares *me*—and I'm Catholic!"

At the very beginning of the trial, Judge Daniel J. Ryan ordered all children to be escorted from the courtroom. And, on the fourth day, thirty girls from Holy Rosary, a Catholic college, dropped in on a tour of the court, and Judge Ryan asked *them* to leave because of the nature of the testimony. This was the sort of thing that really did me in with the jury.

Not to mention the Sixth Amendment of the Constitution, which provides for a public trial. Of course, only gangsters and Communists make reference to that document.

The Assistant State's Attorney, in his opening statement to the jury, declared: "Truthfully, I am not permitted to say what I feel [but] I am sure that you have noticed the perspiration on my nose and my upper lip."

Thus was the tone of the trial set.

In San Francisco, where I was acquitted on the same charge, the arresting officers admitted that my material didn't arouse their prurient interest. In Chicago, Judge Ryan refused to permit that line of cross-examination by the defense.

An officer testified that I had said: "Cardinal Spellman, Fulton Sheen, and the Pope, they must do it to the sisters."

And that I held up the *Chicago's American,* and said: "These are police officers dressed up in women's clothes. You have to be a fag to be a police officer."

And that I said, "The sisters like to do it to sisters. Umm, umm, fuck, good, good."

In his summation, the Prosecutor stated: "During the course of his performance the defendant . . . made various references to different acts which all people, I assume—I know—consider sacred, a sacred part of marriage. . . . He also made reference to a photograph . . . as you recall, of a woman, a nude woman's body . . . He pointed to a portion of this picture, which is part of a woman which is beautiful, useful, but not something that I, Mr. Bruce, or anyone else should comment on in a manner in which he did. . . . Mr. Bruce, at another time, made certain statements in which he gave a story about Germany, I believe soldiers in Germany. During this story, certain terms—he used a particular term in a particular way. I don't think I have to tell you the term, I think that you recall it. Basically it was a term that was aptly put . . . as a word that started with an 'F' and ended with a 'K' and sounded like 'truck.' Basically you heard the word, you know it, and heard the way it was used."

At one point the trial had been adjourned, and with the judge's knowledge I left for a booking in Los Angeles. My intention was to return to Chicago for the rest of the trial, but not long after I landed in Los Angeles (Town D), I was arrested on a narcotics charge. It was my fifth arrest in that city alone. The international grand total of arrests is nineteen. At this writing.

(Incidentally, shortly after I'd left Chicago, the Gate of Horn lost its liquor license and the owner had to sell out.)

While out on bail in Los Angeles, I received the following communication from Celes Bail Bond, the local company which was standing my surety:

> Sir: It has come to our attention through news media that you are to be in court in Chicago today. May I suggest to you that you are not to violate the conditions of your bail. You are not to leave the jurisdiction of Los Angeles County, considering all the other court appearances that you are to make here in Los Angeles.

So, if I left California, I would be arrested for jumping bond. I remained there. And in Chicago I was found guilty of obscenity—*in absentia*—and sentenced to the maximum penalty of one year in the county jail and a fine of $1000.

The case, on appeal, bypassed the appellate court and went directly to the Illinois State Supreme Court. On June 18, 1964—the same day they declared Henry Miller's *Tropic of Cancer* obscene—my verdict of guilty was unanimously upheld.

Ordinarily, my next court of appeal would have been the United States Supreme Court, but a case was already in their hands that would have an effect on the outcome of my hearing, *Jacobellis v. State of Ohio,* involving a movie, *The Lovers.* On June 22, 1964, the U.S. Supreme Court ruled that the film was *not* obscene on the grounds it was of social importance. Because of their ruling, the Illinois Supreme Court dropped its affirmation of my guilt and ordered a reargument which was held July 7, 1964, and concluded:

> "Our original opinion recognized defendant's right to satirize society's attitudes on contemporary social problems and to express his ideas, however bizarre, as long as the method used in doing so was not so objectionable as to render the entire performance obscene. Affirmance of the conviction was predicated upon the rule originally laid down in *American Civil Liberties Union v. City of Chicago* . . . that the obscene portions of the material must be balanced against its affirmative values to determine which predominates. We rejected defendant's argument that *Roth v. United States* . . . struck down this balancing test

and held that material, no matter how objectionable the method of its presentation, was constitutionally privileged unless it was utterly without redeeming social importance. It is apparent from the opinions of a majority of the court in *Jacobellis* that the 'balancing test' rule of *American Civil Liberties Union* is no longer a constitutionally acceptable method of determining whether material is obscene, and it is there made clear that material having *any* social importance is constitutionally protected.

"While we would not have thought that constitutional guarantees necessitate the subjection of society to the gradual deterioration of its moral fabric which this type of presentation promotes, we must concede that some of the topics commented on by defendant are of social importance. Under *Jacobellis* the entire performance is thereby immunized, and we are constrained to hold that the judgment of the circuit court of Cook County must be reversed and defendant discharged.

"Judgment reversed."

They're really saying that they're only sorry the crummy Constitution won't permit them to convict me, but if they had *their* choice . . .

Chapter
Twenty-Three

The most impressive letter I've ever received came from the vicar of St. Clement's Church in New York:

Dear Mr. Bruce:

I came to see you the other night because I had read about you and was curious to see if you were really as penetrating a critic of our common hypocrisies as I had heard. I found that you are an honest man, and I wrote you a note to say so. It is never popular to be so scathingly honest, whether it is from a night-club stage or from a pulpit, and I was not surprised to hear you were having some "trouble." This letter is written to express my personal concern and to say what I saw and heard on Thursday night.

First, I emphatically do *not* believe your act is obscene in intent. The method you use has a lot in common with most serious critics (the prophet or the artist, not the professor) of society. Pages of Jonathan Swift and Martin Luther are quite unprintable even now because they were forced to shatter the easy, lying language of the day into the basic, earthy, vulgar idiom of ordinary people in order to show up the emptiness and insanity of their time. (It has been said, humorously but with some truth, that a great deal of the Bible is not fit to read in church for the same reason.)

Clearly your intent is not to excite sexual feelings or to demean but to shock us awake to the realities of racial hatred and invested absurdities about sex and birth and death . . . to move toward sanity and compassion. It is clear that you are intensely angry at our hypocrisies (yours as well as mine) and at the highly subsidized mealymouthism that passes as wisdom. But so should be any self-respecting man. Your comments are aimed at adults and reveal to me a man who cares deeply about dishonesty and injustice and all the accepted psychoses of our time. They are aimed at adults and adults don't need, or shouldn't have, anyone to protect them from hearing truth in whatever form it appears no matter how noble the motive for suppression . . .

> May God bless you,
> The Rev. Sidney Lanier

Reverend Lanier says that my comments "are aimed at adults." Often I am billed at night clubs with a sign saying FOR ADULTS ONLY. I am very interested in the motivation for such billing. I must assume that "for adults only" means that my point of view, or perhaps the semantics involved with my point of view, would be a deterrent to the development of a well-adjusted member of the community.

The argument is that a child will ape the actions of an actor. What he sees now in his formative years, he may do as an adult, so we must be very careful what we let the child see.

So, then, I would rather my child see a stag film than *The Ten Commandments* or *King of Kings*—because I don't want my kids to kill Christ when he comes back. That's what they see in those films—that violence.

Well, let me just take your kids to a dirty movie:

"All right, kids, sit down now, this picture's gonna start. It's not like *Psycho,* with a lot of four-letter words, like 'kill' and 'maim' and 'hurt'—but you're gonna see this film now and what you see will probably impress you for the rest of your lives, so we have to be very careful what we show you. . . . Oh, it's a dirty movie. A couple is coming in now. I don't know if it's gonna be as good as *Psycho* where we have the stabbing in the shower and the blood down the drain. . . . Oh, the guy's picking up the pillow. Now, he'll probably smother her with it, and that'll be a good opening. Ah, the degenerate, he's putting it under her ass. Jesus, tsk tsk, I hate to show this crap to you kids. All right, now he's lifting up his hand, and he'll probably strike her. No, he's caressing her, and kissing her—ah, this is disgusting! All right, he's kissing her some more, and she's saying something. She'll probably scream at him, 'Get out of here!' No, she's saying, 'I love you, I'm coming.' Kids, I'm sorry I showed you anything like this. God knows this will be on my conscience the rest of my life—there's a chance that you may do this when *you* grow up. Well, just try to forget what you've seen. Just remember, what this couple did belongs written on the walls of a men's room. And, in fact, if you ever want to do it, do it in the men's room."

I never did see one stag film where anybody got killed in the end. Or even slapped in the mouth. Or where it had any Communist propaganda.

But doing it is pretty rank. I understand intellectually that a woman who sleeps with a different guy every night is more of a Christian than a nun, because she has that capacity for love—but emotionally I'm only the 365th guy . . . because I learned my lesson early, and you can't unlearn it.

I know intellectually there's nothing wrong with going to the toilet, but I can't go to the toilet in front of you. The worst sound in the world is when the toilet-flush noise finishes before I do.

If I'm at your house, I can never say to you, "Excuse me, where's the toilet?" I have to get hung up with that corrupt façade of "Excuse me, where's the little boys' room?"

"Oh, you mean the tinkle-dinkle ha-ha room, where they have sachets and cough drops and pastels?"

"That's right, I wanna shit in the cough-drop box."

One of the things I got arrested for in Chicago was showing a picture of a girl that was really pretty. I wanted to point out the God-made-the-body paradox of the decent people who would object to that groovy-looking chick.

Christ, I could never sit on a jury and put anybody away for *looking*. If I'm dressing and there's that chick across the way—that blue-eyed, pink-nippled, sweet high-ass from Oklahoma—I am going to look, and I am going to call my *friends* to look.

But, in our society, it's "Pull down the shade"—and charge two bucks to get in.

That's what repression does.

I'd really like to fight the Chicago obscenity rap on a whole different issue. The obscenity law, when everything else boils away, is: Does it appeal to the prurient interest?

I must get you horny—that's what it means.

If I do a *disgusting* show—a show about eating pork—that's not obscene. Although you Jews and vegetarians and Moslems will bitch your asses off, that's my right as an American, to talk about pork, to extol its virtues, to run in front of a synagogue, yelling: "Here's pork! Look at it, rabbi!"

"Get him out of here, he should be arrested—that's disgusting!"

It doesn't matter. Again, that's why the Pilgrims left England, man. If a guy wants to wail with pork, that's his *schtick*.

Or, if I do a vulgar show—if I sing rock and roll tunes, wear platform shoes, Kitty Kellys with ankle straps—it's not obscene.

No, obscenity has only one meaning: to appeal to the prurient interest.

Well, I want to know what's *wrong* with appealing to prurient interest.

I really want the Supreme Court to stand up and tell me that fucking is dirty and no good.

The lowest of the low—from both the policeman's and the felon's point of view—is the child molester. But his most heinous crime is simply that he is bereft of the proper dialog, for if he spake his lines thusly, he would never be busted:

"C'mere, Ruthie, c'mere to your Uncle Willie . . . look at those little apples on you, lemme lift you up, she's gonna have to get a bra-*zeer* soon . . . let your Uncle Willie tickle-ickle-ickle you, rump-bump-bump on the floor . . . she's getting some hair on her booger, tickle-ickle-ickle, watch her wriggle-wiggle-giggle in Uncle Willie's ruddy palm . . . don't tell Mommy or you'll break the magic charm."

And Uncle Willie's Mason signet ring snags little Ruthie's nylon under-things . . . children don't wear *panties.*

Town E: New York, I'd been playing New York, concerts and night-club engagements, for eight years, but in 1964 I got busted for obscenity at the Café Au Go Go. I continued performing and got busted there again that same week.

Then I got pleurisy. My lung was filled with fluid. I couldn't breathe. I went to a doctor, but he wouldn't see me because he didn't want "to get involved." I finally did get a doctor—who, coincidentally, was a fan—and I ended up in a hospital, on the receiving end of a five-hour operation.

When *Newsweek* called up a friend of mine to find out how I was, he told them the surgeon cut all that *filth* out of my system, too.

The trial in New York was postponed while I recuperated in Los Angeles.

When I returned to New York, it turned out that the police didn't have complete tapes of the shows I was arrested for, so they actually had a guy in court *imitating my act*—a License Department Inspector who was formerly a CIA agent in Vietnam—and in his courtroom impersonation of me, he was saying things that I had never said in my *life,* on stage or off.

Witnesses for the prosecution included *New York Daily News* columnist Robert Sylvester, Marya Mannes from *The Reporter,* John Fischer, editor of *Harper's* magazine, and a minister.

Witnesses for the defense included Jules Feiffer, Nat Hentoff, Dorothy Kilgallen, and *two* ministers.

"Sitting in on Lenny Bruce's current New York 'obscenity' trial," Stephanie Gervis Harrington wrote in the *Village Voice,* "one gets the feeling of being present at an historical event—the birth of the courtroom of the absurd. Of course, if you sit through it long enough, you gradually adjust to the fact that eight grown men are actually spending weeks of their time and an unreckoned amount of the taxpayers' money in deliberation—passionate deliberation on the prosecutor's good days—over whether another grown man should be able to use four-letter words in public without going to jail."

The ludicrousness of it all was inadvertently summed up by my attorney, Ephraim London, when he asked a witness who had been at my performance at the Café Au Go Go: "Did you see Mr. Crotch touch his Bruce?"

On reporting the incident, *The Realist* predicted, "Henceforth and forever-more, we shall have had at that precise moment a meaningful new synonym added to our language." And the magazine's editorial proceeded to demonstrate its use:

"Mommy, look, there's a man sitting over there with his bruce hanging out."

"Beverly Schmidlap is a real bruceteaser, y'know?"

"Kiss my bruce, baby."

And a cartoon by Ed Fisher had a judge saying, "Before I pass sentence on you, Lenny Bruce, is there anything you wish to say—anything printable, that is?"

Meanwhile, back in real life, a three-judge Criminal Court, in a 2–1 split vote, sentenced me to three four-month terms in the workhouse, to be served concurrently. But the State Supreme Court has granted me a certificate of reasonable doubt and—at this writing—the case is on appeal.

What does it mean for a man to be found obscene in New York? This is the most sophisticated city in the country. This is where they play Genet's *The Balcony*. If anyone is the first person to be found obscene in New York, he must feel utterly depraved.

I was so sure I could reach those judges if they'd just let me tell them what I try to do. It was like I was on trial for rape and there I was crying, "But, Judge, I can't rape anybody, I haven't got the wherewithal," but nobody was listening, and my lawyers were saying, "Don't worry, Lenny, you got a right to rape anyone you please, we'll beat 'em in the appellate court."

The *New York Law Journal* pleaded guilty to not publishing the lower court's statement, with an explanation: "The majority opinion, of necessity, cited in detail the language used by Bruce in his night-club act, and also described gestures and routines which the majority found to be obscene and indecent. The *Law Journal* decided against publication, even edited, on the grounds that deletions would destroy the opinion, and without the deletions publication was impossible within the *Law Journal* standards."

Among the examples of my "obscene references" that the court had quoted in its opinion, the very first was this: "Eleanor Roosevelt and her display of 'tits.'"

Now, in the course of my research I obtained the legislative history from Albany of the statute under which I had been arrested, and I discovered back in 1931 there was added to that statute an amendment which *excludes from arrest* stagehands, spectators, musicians and *actors*. The amendment was finally signed into law by Governor Roosevelt. The court refused to be influenced by this information.

Well, I believe that ignoring the mandate of Franklin D. Roosevelt is a great deal more offensive than saying that Eleanor had lovely nay-nays.

June 1964—graduation time—honorary degrees were being handed out all over the place. The TV show, *That Was The Week That Was,* bestowed on me—or rather upon a photograph of me with a graduation cap superimposed on my head—an honorary Doctor of Letters: "To the man who won fame using them four at a time."

I'm really so fed up with the "dirty word" thing. People think, Christ, I'm *obsessed* with that. But I just *have* to defend myself because you don't know how much I'm attacked on it. Every new time I go on the road, the papers are filled with it.

Now I'll say "a Jew" and just the word *Jew* sounds like a dirty word, and people don't know whether to laugh or not. They'll seem so brazen. So there's just silence until they know I'm kidding, and then they'll break through.

A Jew.

In the dictionary, a Jew is one who is descended from the ancient tribe of Judea, but—I'll say to an audience—you and I know what a Jew is: one who killed our Lord. Now there's dead silence there after that.

When I did this in England, I said, "I don't know if you know that over here, but it got a lot of press in the States." Now the laughs start to break through. "We did it about two thousand years ago, and there should be a statute of limitations with that crime." Now they know—the laughter's all there—but I'm *not* kidding, because there *should* be a statute of limitations for that crime, and those who pose as Christians—paraphrasing Shakespeare —neither having the gait of Christians nor the actions of Christians—still make the Jews pay their dues.

I go from a pedantry (Shakespeare) to the hip argot (pay their dues) for another deuce.

Then I ask, why should Jews pay these dues? Granted that we killed him and he was a nice guy; although there was even some talk that we didn't kill Christ, we killed Gesmas, the one on the left. (There were, you recall, three who got done in that day.) But I confess that we killed him, despite those who said that Roman soldiers did it.

Yes, we did it. I did it. My family. I found a note in my basement: "We killed him—signed, Morty."

"Why did you kill Christ, Jew?"

"We killed him because he didn't want to become a doctor, that's why."

Now sometimes I'll get sort of philosophical with it and maybe a little maudlin: "We killed him at his own request, because he was sad—he knew that people would use him."

Or sometimes I will tag it with, "Not only did we kill him, but we're gonna kill him again when he comes back."

I suppose that if *I* were Christlike, I would turn the other cheek and keep letting you punch me out and even kill me, because what the hell, I'm God's son, and it's not so bad dying when you know that you've got a pass to come back indefinitely. All right, so you have to take a little crap when you come home and you have to "get it" from your Father . . .

"Oh, you started again, you can't get along. Who was it this time? The Jews, eh? Why can't you stop preaching? Look, this is the last time I'm telling you, the next time you get killed, you're *staying* there. I've had enough aggravation with your mother."

Of all the comedians I have ever met, Steve Allen is not only the most literate, but also the most moral. He not only talks about society's problems, but he *does* things about them. He's a good person, without being all sugar and showbiz, and I really dig him for that.

I was on the *Steve Allen Show* twice. Now, if I work for an hour in a night club, out of that hour I will ad-lib perhaps four minutes; sometimes, if I'm really fertile, ten minutes. But for me ever to have to come out and open with the same word and finish with the same word and do the same bits in the same order in each show, then I wouldn't feel like a comic at all. But you have to do this for television. And it bugs me.

They sat me down there, and I'm doing the bit for 15 guys. And I got into material that they wouldn't let me do on the *Allen Show*. I have a tattoo on my arm, and because of this tattoo, I can never be buried in a Jewish cemetery. That's the Orthodox law. You have to go out of the world the same way you came in—no marks, no changes.

Anyway, I told how, when I got back from Malta and went home to Long Island, I was in the kitchen, washing with soap, and my Aunt Mema saw the tattoo. So she flips. A real Jewish yell.

"Look what you did! You ruined your arm! You're no better than a gypsy!"

So the producer says that I can't do this on the show because it would definitely be offensive to the Jewish people.

"You're out of your *nut*," I responded.

No, he said, every time we get into a satire of any ethnic group, we get a lot of mail. You can't talk about that.

I argued with them. I said if they wouldn't let me do that, I wouldn't do the show. Now, I'll never use four-letter words for shock value—it has to fit and swing with the character whom I want to say it—but I know I can't use four-letter words on television in *any* case. But here, I wasn't making any such references, I was just doing a true bit.

They had a meeting about it. They argued for about an hour while I was kept waiting in a corner, like a leper with a bell on my neck.

"We talked it over, Lenny. You know, it's not only offensive to the Jewish people, but it's definitely offensive to the Gentile people too."

"Oh, yeah—how do you figure that?"

"Well, what you're saying in essence is that the Gentiles don't *care* what they bury."

The funny thing is, friends of mine are always showing me anti-Semitic articles. "Look at what this bigoted bastard wrote!" And then I dug something. Liberals will buy anything a bigot writes.

In fact, they really *support* hatemongers.

George Lincoln Rockwell, head of the American Nazi Party, is probably a very knowledgeable businessman with no political convictions whatsoever. He gets three bucks a head and works the mass rallies consisting of nothing but angry Jews, shaking their fists and wondering why there are so many Jews there.

And Rockwell probably has only two *real* followers—and they're deaf. They think the swastika is merely an Aztec symbol.

Chapter
Twenty-four

It was *Time* magazine that originally labeled me "the sickest of them all." The reason: In connection with the Leopold-Loeb case, I had said: "Bobby Franks was snotty."

Of course, if Nathan Leopold had any sense of humor, the day he got out he would have grabbed another kid!

When I hear someone say, "I love the human race," I get a little wary. But when the Associated Press interviewed me on—of all things—sick comedy, the dialog went something like this:

INTERVIEWER: I know you must really hate someone or something to have your point of view on humor.

LENNY: Actually, when you hate someone or something, it makes you a little uncomfortable to *see* it or *hear* it.

INTERVIEWER: Boy, Lenny, you hate so many things you can't even make a choice, can you?

LENNY: I hate to shave . . . I hate to be alone . . . I hate liver.

INTERVIEWER: Come on, stop kidding, that'll never do. What are you, a saint? Give me some guy you really hate.

LENNY: Oh, a *guy* . . . George Bernard Shaw!

INTERVIEWER: George Bernard Shaw? What the hell have you got *against* him?

Now, the truth is, I had never even *read* anything by Shaw. My reading matter ran the gamut from a technical book on intercontinental ballistic missiles to Jean-Paul Sartre's study of anti-Semitism, but all I knew about Shaw was that he wrote *Pygmalion*. And what he looked like. And that he was dead and unable to defend himself. I'm not *proud* that I was completely ignorant of George Bernard Shaw. It's just a fact. I blurted the name out of the blue. Now the AP interviewer wanted to know what I had against him.

LENNY: What have I got against *Shaw*? Didn't you ever hear about the Whorten Incident?

INTERVIEWER: Well, uh, yeah, but what the hell, you can't expect . . . George Bernard Shaw, that's wild . . . I mean it's OK but— you're too much . . . another question I want to ask——"

I had him by the balls. There wasn't any "Whorten Incident." I was improvising as I went along, and I just threw that in. I figured he was too insecure to admit that there was a subject he wasn't hip to. I sensed I had him up against the pseudo-intellectual rope.

LENNY: Well, do you feel Shaw was *right* in the Whorten Incident?

INTERVIEWER: Lenny, you know better than anyone that you—well, I have to see something before I believe it.

LENNY: See it? Jesus, it was in all the papers. His heirs had *proof*.

INTERVIEWER: Yeah, Lenny, but you know yourself that people are only interested in what they can get out of a person.

LENNY: Well, getting all you can and sleeping with a guy's wife, is two different things. And you wouldn't believe it, but you talk to the majority of people—and I mean people that are supposed to be bright, erudite, literary-oriented people—and you mention the Whorten Incident, and they look at you as if you've been smoking the weed or giving away the secrets of the Rosicrucians.

INTERVIEWER: Lenny, when are you going to learn that everyone else isn't as honest as you?

LENNY: What the hell has honesty got to do with a guy getting another guy's wife started on dope and hanging around Lesbians? What was that Lesbian's name, anyway? . . . They had her picture plastered all over at the time. . . . Is that something, I forgot her name. . . . I think it was Helen. Yeah, that's it, Helen. I almost forgot her name.

INTERVIEWER: Yeah, that was it, Helen. Boy, people are characters. You've got a great memory, Lenny.

The reporter left, saying that the story would probably break the next week.

The next week, I searched and searched, and there was no AP story. And then I finally found it, in John J. Miller's column in the *National Enquirer*. There it was, right between Fidel Castro doing one of his unnatural acts and Elvis Presley sticking a *Fraülein's* bosom in his paratrooper boots.

THE PIG THAT WROTE PYGMALION

Lenny Bruce is a comedian who is currently appearing at the hungry i in San Francisco. The owner, Enrico Banducci, gave Lenny the go-ahead to expose the infamous "Whorten Incident" thrill-slaying, dope and abortion-ring case involving George Bernard Shaw . . .

The news media have done me in—from Walter Winchell's lies ("Lenny Bruce was being heckled and he handed the mike to a patron, walked over and slugged the heckler, who was a New York judge . . .") to the TV newscaster's lies ("Lenny Bruce, the sick comedian, was really sick today. Bruce, who's had more than his share of brushes with the law, charted a new course with a narcotics arrest. He has admitted to using heroin since he was eighteen years old. Bruce, shown here with his attorney, stops and mugs for the cameraman and promises to stir a little commotion at tomorrow's hearing . . . ") dignified by his balding crown resting in shadowed bas-relief Himalayas.

I could never expect to get a jury that didn't read the papers and watch television, and to make sure they were prejudiced and that The People had their side of the story in first, they saw to it that I glommed the first handicap: the stigma of being arrested. That in itself puts one in an unsavory light. "Bruce Arrested for Dope."

Who gave them the item that was on the street even before I was out on bail?

Look at the bottom of my arrest report—all of them—and you'll find: "LAPD (Los Angeles Police Department) Press Room was notified and City Newsroom was called."

A press notice on an arrest report. But don't get me wrong, brother, I love Hollywood.

In Van Nuys court the photographers were taking pictures and I really got tired of them. I asked them to stop. They continued. I put my coat up over my ears. Their cameras still clicked away. I walked behind the state flag, but a guy jerked it away. I walked out of the court. They followed me. When I walked, they walked. When I ran, they ran. See Lenny run. See the photographers run. See Lenny stop. See the photographers stop. See Lenny wave his arm. All fall down.

I had stopped short, only to be charged with assaulting a photographer.

The newspaper is the most dramatic medium of the written word, whether it's Dr. Alvarez with his arthritic pen pals or Prudence Penny's 12 ways to make leftovers attractive. It is because of newspapers—their disregard for the truth when it comes to reporting—that my reputation has been hurt.

Walter Winchell wrote: "The comic, Lenny Bruce, was booed offstage in England." All right, now that's another lie, I was never booed offstage, and the owner sent me a letter to the contrary.

The truth is, I was received with great aplomb in England. Kenneth Tynan, Britain's leading drama critic, wrote about me: "We are dealing with an impromptu prose poet, who trusts his audience so completely that he talks in public no less outrageously than he would talk in private. . . . Hate him or not, he is unique, and must be seen."

The best write-up I ever got in my whole life was by George Miller in the *New Statesman*. I'm not concerned with whether he was pro— or anti—Lenny Bruce—I don't care about that—but his beautiful *style* . . . he described me as "lemurlike."

I know all about British people from the movies.

England is a country in India. The men have two jobs—they're either in the R.A.F. or they're accountants. They reject IBM machines and do everything in scroll. They wear scarfs and caps all the time and they have bad teeth. They governed everybody to death. The Queen has two outfits. She has the riding outfit and a long satin thing with a tiara. The Windsors are about 200 years old by now. But the kids never grow up; the kids have been kids forever and ever. And there's not many farms in England. Those who live in farm areas are lewd, lascivious people that are always strangling children and saying, "There's a little bit of Hyde in all of us."

I had a lot of fun in England—although I didn't get laid once. I had heard that, gee, in England you really get a lot of girls, but I was there a month and I never got laid.

The one time I almost scored was in this hotel. The chick came up to my room after she fell for what I call my innocuous come-on: "Hey, I gotta go upstairs for a minute, why don't you come up, I've gotta——" And the rest is said on the car-door slam, and mumbled into the carpeting on the stairs.

"What'd you say?" is answered by, "We'll just be a minute," leaving the door open, keeping your topcoat on, and dashing for a bureau drawer as if to get something, throwing open the closet and grabbing a briefcase, rumbling through it while muttering, "Siddown, I'll be just a second."

All this is done very rapidly, with a feeling of urgency.

"Christ, where the hell did I put that? Make yourself a drink. What time is it? We gotta get the hell outta here. Now where the hell did I put that damn—remind me to get a new maid. Hey, are you warm? Christ, it's hot in here . . ."

Well, I didn't even get to the second paragraph, when a knock came at the door, synchronized with the key turning in the lock.

"Mr. Bruce, I'm afraid we don't have any of that here."

(What a temptation to finish the joke: "And I'm not, either.")

To my amazement, the manager smirked knowingly as the girl looked up apprehensively, and I sat down gingerly as his thin lip curled snarlingly.

"Out, the both of you—out!"

Ask anyone who has been to England. They do not allow persons who come into hotels to bring members of the opposite sex with them, because they know what it's liable to lead to. It's a wonder the *maids* ever get into the rooms. That's a thought, though. Maybe it's the maids who instituted that action. God, what if all the maids in England were whores?

I think that the Profumo scandal was a beautiful commentary on the British image of an asexual people, puritanically moral.

The reason most men could indict those people, when they themselves were probably guilty of the same crime which is not a crime, is that most men won't admit that *they* have ever been with whores. Not for the morality of it; the reason they don't cop out is because of the *ego* aspect. "What kind of guy has to pay for pussy, man? I get it for nothing—the girls give *me* money!"

It was right before the Profumo scandal that they wouldn't permit me even to *enter* England again for what was to have been my second engagement at The Establishment. I actually flew to London and was rejected without anyone thinking any more about it than if I were to fly from Los Angeles to San Francisco. They kept me overnight in the same cell they had used for Dr. Soblen—the international-espionage agent who committed suicide.

Then I got back to Idlewild—and for the first time in my life, after coming in and out of this country maybe 20 times—my luggage was thoroughly searched. I was taken into a private room where I was stripped and internally searched—and, goddamn, that is humiliating.

It sure bugs you to stand naked in front of five guys with suits and shoelaces and pens in their pockets.

What if you got a hard-on?

"All right, take your shoes off now and—what the hell's the matter with you?"

"I beg your pardon?"

"Why don't you put that away?"

"In my shoes, sir?"

"I mean make it go down. A damn weirdo—getting a hard-on at Customs. All right, put your clothes on."

"I'd like to, sir, but I don't know if you noticed my pants—they're rather tight. I'll have to wait till this goes away."

"Come on, now, cut the silliness and get your pants on and get the hell out of here."

"I'll try, sir, but . . . it's never done this before. I guess it's nerves."

"Well, try to pee."

"Where, sir?"

"Out there in the hall in the men's room."

"But I can't get my whatchamacallit, my oh-my, into my pants. Do you know anyone who could make it go away? Or could you gentlemen go out while *I* make it go away, up and down . . . Oh, here, I know what I'll do, I'll put it in the wine basket and I'll carry it."

By the way, I've figured out a sure way that you'll score every time. You meet a chick and you tell her, "Look, I'd like very much to take you out, but I've got a bit of a problem. I know you aren't familiar with my problem but I'll just go out with you and I'll be very happy—but I don't make it with anybody. I'm a celibate and that's the way it's got to be. So you know in front there can be no sexual rapport between us. I just wanted to tell you that now because a couple of times I've gone with girls and they said, "Why didn't you tell me, you've ruined the night and everything."

And sure enough, driving along, she'll ask: "How come you don't make it with anybody?"

"I don't like to talk about it."

"I never heard of not making it with anybody."

"I have, but not for years."

"Why not?"

"I told you, I can't talk about it."

"You can tell me. I like to hear other people's problems."

"All right. It's the way I'm built. I'm abnormally large."

"You're that big?"

"Yeah."

"Oh, are you kidding me?"

"Haven't had an affair with a woman since 1947."

"And what was *her* reaction?"

"She's been in the hospital all these years."

"Are you really serious? I mean, didn't you ever go to visit her?"

"They would have me killed. Her brother is still looking for me. I can't wear walking shorts in public."

"Really? Well, how big *is* it?"

"Makes me sick. I've tried to forget about it."

"Could I see it?"

"No, not a chance. It's all locked up anyway. I don't even have the key. My father has one key; the mayor has the other."

Chapter
Twenty-five

It's quite possible that one of the reasons I've gotten busted so often goes back to an unsuccessful extortion attempt on me right after that first arrest in Philadelphia. I was approached by an attorney who has since died—he was one of the biggest lawyers in the state—he could have gotten Ray Charles a driver's license.

"How do you do, son, could I talk to you? I don't know if you've heard of me, but I understand you had a little beef today . . ."

And he promised to quash the whole thing for $10,000.

Now there was a witness to that scene, a young attorney from a prominent Philadelphia family. He couldn't believe what he saw. He said to me, "I figured maybe his secretary gets a pen, but to be that blatant . . ."

After the hearing, outside the court, reporters asked me if I had any statement.

"Yes, I'd like to say that so-and-so's a crook!"

"What?"

I gave the details. Then I spotted the witness standing in the crowd. I grabbed him, identified him and asked: "Is this true?"

"Yes, and the whole idea was thoroughly repugnant to me . . ."

The headline in the *Philadelphia Daily News* read, "COMIC BRUCE CLAIMS TRY AT SHAKEDOWN IN NARCOTICS CASE." They were going to have an investigation, with me as material witness.

Are they kidding? Let them *schlep* in Sonny Liston instead. Believe it or not, I have a dread of being a martyr.

Medication in any form proves to be a deterrent to me now. When I was very ill, coming down with pneumonia—in San Francisco, and then again in Miami—I got turned down by doctors.

I said, "I'm *sick,* are you *kidding?*"

"Look, there's a lot of heat on . . ."

The peace officers' explanation, continually, for the medication I use intravenously is this: they say that I just take the non-narcotic to cover up the narcotic that I take.

The Red Hill Inn . . . Philadelphia . . . over a thousand Methedrine prescriptions later . . . *muy*-multimiligrams self-injected with disposable syringes that bring memos from irate managers . . . "In all the years that I have been the custodian of the Selkirk Hotel Circuit, we have never had a toilet stopped up with needles before . . ."

There is a well-known hobby shop in the Sherman Oaks section of Los Angeles. It is one of the most unique stores in all of California. They had a $10,000 remote-control sports-car track. One afternoon I went to look at the sports cars.

I wound up being booked on a narcotics possession charge.

Sergeant John L. White testified in court that he saw me drop a matchbook containing a packet of heroin and run into a bicycle shop, that he followed me in, frisked me for weapons, and arrested me.

"Mr. Bruce," the District Attorney asked me, "do you think that these officers have to frame people? That's what you're saying when you deny dropping this pack of matches."

The judge interceded: "I think instead of 'framing,' you can say 'tell an untruth.' I'd like that better. 'Take the stand and tell an untruth under oath' rather than the word 'frame.'"

You'd assume that legions of perjurers would ask with feigned innocence: "Well, how come a peace officer swore to God and then lied?"

Yes, why would peace officers lie to the Lord or whatever deity that our hellish Constitution thwarts? They said they had a hobby shop under surveillance. They did not have any persons under surveillance besides the owner of the hobby shop. But they had no warrant to enter the hobby shop, so in order to keep within the margin of the law, they had to wait until a person left the shop who was a criminal.

If they could catch a criminal coming out—namely, Lenny Bruce allegedly drops a packet of matches, which they can construe as a furtive action—then they'd have a *probable cause* and could go into the hobby shop without a warrant.

Which they did.

The owner was charged with possession of heroin, pleaded guilty and was committed to the Department of Correction as a narcotics addict.

When it was my turn to take the stand, I had refused to swear on the Bible. "It seems like sort of a mockery to do this," I explained. "I don't really care to but I will. I don't mean to be contemptuous of the court, but——"

The judge interrupted: "I don't understand your thinking in this matter. That is the custom here and the rule is that you have to take an oath to get on the stand."

(Actually, you have the legal alternative of simply "affirming" to tell the truth.)

The judge continued: "Do you have any objection to it? If it's a mockery, that is your personal opinion. You have a right to your opinion, but that is the way we do it here."

"Yes, sir."

"All right, swear the witness."

THE CLERK: You do solemnly swear to tell the truth, the whole truth, and nothing but the truth in the matter now pending before this court, so help you God?

THE WITNESS: I will tell the truth.

The bicycle-shop man and his assistant both substantiated my testimony that the arrest never took place. The assistant, incidentally, was a 15-year-old kid with a harelip who went to parochial school.

The jury found me guilty of possession of heroin.

I had private detectives interview individuals of the jury—a perfectly legal procedure—and the following is an excerpt from a report of their findings:

Briefly, the . . . jury membership, generally speaking, made various incredible statements; to wit, Mr. Bruce's manner of dress and his way of taking the oath, both contributed to a number of jurors' decision that he was guilty as charged. Further, more than one juror expressed knowledge of Mr. Bruce's activities, which knowledge . . . they denied they had prior to taking an oath in order to serve on his jury. A juror alleged that the jury had knowledge of "other evidence" not "brought out" in the trial, which did influence them in their final verdict. A juror stated that a young boy who was employed in a bike shop, which bike shop was the locale around which there was conflicting testimony, "was obviously tutored"; the juror went on to state that this "tutored" boy witness contributed to the guilty verdict because he had been "tutored."

One juror had been asked, during the selection of the jury, "Have you read or heard anything about [Lenny Bruce], either through magazine articles, newspapers, or otherwise?" She answered: "No, I have not."

But private investigator Seymour Wayne's post-trial taped interview with her elicited the following:

Q. Well, for example, when you, uh, does, er, the newspaper there, the radio, there, the TV——

A. I saw [Lenny Bruce] on TV even before he was on trial.

Q. Before [he was on] trial, er, you saw him on TV. Where did you see him on TV?

A. When he was picked up on the news.

Q. Oh, I see. I did not know they had a movie of it.

A. Are you kidding? It's been on there since then a couple of times.

Q. Meaning tha——

A. Picked up again! After he was convicted he was picked up again.

Q. . . . Wait a minute, before the trial started there [was] news of his being arrested or picked up?

A. Why, sure. And didn't you know about this?

The interview with another juror included this dialog:

Q. What about when Bruce got up to be sworn in? What was your feeling about what happened there?

A. Well, it certainly was confusing, uh——

Q. How did you feel about it?

A. Well, it—I don't think it did him any good, frankly. He almost refused to take the oath. I forget the exact words, but he turned to the judge and said something about isn't this a farce, or something, that you should take an oath before testifying.

Q. How do you feel about it?

A. Confused, I mean, what I—I don't know what his back—what his reasoning would be, but they certainly expect people to come up and raise their hand and swear to tell the truth. Now, when he doesn't, what do you think? I don't know—I was thoroughly confused at why.

Q. Did you dislike him for it?

A. Not necessarily dislike him. I certainly didn't understand it. It is a customary thing in court—you testify—or you swear to tell the truth.

Q. How—did some of the other jurors make comments about the incident?

A. Yes, they certainly did.

Possession of heroin is a felony for which I could be given two years in prison. The court, however, adjourned criminal proceedings so that my fate could be decided by "Department 95," pursuant to the terms of Senate Bill 81. California's legislative branch was responsible for this bill, the purpose of which is theoretically to halt the cruel punishment that was being forced upon sick persons, i.e., narcotics addicts.

It is the function of a Department 95 hearing "to determine whether the defendant is addicted to the use of narcotic drugs or by reason of repeated use of narcotics is in imminent danger of becoming so addicted."

Thus, the judge was making it possible for me to have, instead of two years in prison, ten years of rehabilitation—if I'm eligible—based on the recommendation of two physicians appointed by the court.

"Mr. Bruce, you're lucky, we're going to give you ten years of help."

"I don't deserve it, really, I'm a rotten bastard . . ."

My Department 95 hearing was held: "The People of the State of California, for the best interest and protection of society and Lenny Bruce, an Alleged Narcotic Drug Addict."

167

Dr. Thomas L. Gore, Chief Psychiatrist in Los Angeles Superior Court, stated: "[Lenny Bruce] is a narcotic drug addict." Dr. Berliner, who "examined" me with Dr. Gore, concurred: "I believe that Mr. Bruce is a narcotic drug addict."

My attorney cross-examined Dr. Gore:

Q. When did you sign this certificate [stating that Lenny Bruce is a narcotic addict]?

A. I signed it shortly after the examination was made.

Q. You signed the certificate before you came to court today to hear any other testimony, isn't that correct, Doctor?

A. I made a statement which was very plain English. I signed the certificate in the room immediately above this within ten minutes after you and your client had walked out of the room.

Q. Are you familiar, Doctor, with the provision in the law that enables you to hear all the testimony that comes before the court before offering your certificate to have someone placed in the Narcotic Drug Rehabilitation Center? . . .

A. I haven't submitted this thing yet. I have it right here in front of me.

Q. Is the copy you have in front of you signed?

A. Yes . . .

THE COURT: It is signed, and Doctor, if you care to, take the court's pen and strike your signature . . . [The doctors] could easily add or subtract to their testimony if they found pertinent information or evidence adduced which may tend to cause them to alter, or change their testimony.

Q. If the Judge had not directed you to take the pencil and strike out your name, Doctor, would you have changed that signature based on any testimony that you may have heard here today?

A. I haven't heard any.

Q. If you had heard testimony to the contrary of your own opinion, would you have crossed out your signature and submitted the certificate?

A. If I had heard a dozen witnesses testify, I would still sign the certificate.

There were a few doctors who testified in my defense.

First, Dr. Keith Dittman stated that the best way a doctor could determine conclusively whether or not a man is a narcotic addict would be to hospitalize him and see him develop withdrawal symptoms and then counteract those symptoms of withdrawal with the drug to which he is believed to be addicted. This would be done within the period of a week or possibly two weeks.

Q. Doctor, now can you tell me whether or not you feel any qualified physician could conclusively conclude [as did Gore and Berliner] . . .

that any person was a narcotic addict after a 15, 20, or 30-minute interview and visual examination of the veins?

A. I don't know of any way that it can be done.

Q. Is it an accepted method to merely visually observe the veins of a person and in the absence of observation under clinical conditions to make a conclusion [as did Gore and Berliner] that a person is a narcotic addict?

A. You mean only to confine it to that? No.

Q. Doctor, could the injection into the vein of a non-narcotic over a period of time under some circumstances produce discoloration or certain visual conditions that are similar to conditions that might be occasioned over a period of time from the injection of a narcotic?

A. Yes.

Q. During the course of your examination of Mr. Bruce, was it brought to your attention . . . that he had received over a period of time any Methedrine?

A. He told me who was prescribing it. I asked him if it was all right that I call that doctor to talk with him about it, and I did, and the doctor confirmed that he was by prescription giving Methedrine and the hypodermic syringes.

Next Dr. Norman Rotenberg, whose patient I have been since 1959, was called to the stand. My attorney examined him.

Q. . . . Now, Doctor, in your opinion, are you able to distinguish between marks that exist on a person's arm that might have been occasioned by an injection of narcotics or may have been occasioned by an injection of a non-narcotic?

A. No, in my opinion there is no method of distinguishing between marks, sir.

Q. . . . Dr. Rotenberg, over the years . . . how many times would you say you saw Mr. Bruce?

A. . . . Perhaps I have seen him a dozen times in the office.

Q. With regard to these 12 visits over approximately a three-and-a-half-year period of time—or let's say, four visits, approximately quarterly, every three months—let's talk about those. On any of these visits, did Mr. Bruce appear to you to be undergoing withdrawal from narcotic drugs?

A. No, he did not.

Q. Are you familiar with the traditional symptoms that are occasioned by someone who has a reliance upon a narcotic drug when he is going through the withdrawal or needs that narcotic drug?

A. Yes.

Q. And none of these symptoms appeared, is that correct?

A. They did not.

Cross-examination followed:

Q. Now, Doctor, if a person takes Methedrine, would that stave off going through the withdrawals [of heroin]?

A. No, I don't think it would. No, sir, it would not.

Q. In other words, he would go through the withdrawals even with taking Methedrine?

A. Yes, if he was a narcotic addict.

Q. . . . Now, Doctor, Mr. Bruce told you that he suffered from a lethargic condition; is that right?

A. Lethargy?

Q. Yes, that is sleepiness and this and that.

A. Yes.

Q. Are you familiar with the conditions of a person who is under the influence of heroin?

A. Some of the conditions.

Q. Would that be one of the conditions that would be produced in the person who is taking heroin? Would he be lethargic?

A. He could be, yes, sir.

Q. Also, Doctor, you gave him a letter stating that, in substance, that if the police see fresh puncture marks on his arm, that could be from Methedrine?

A. Yes.

Q. Also, it could also be from heroin, could it not?

A. It could be from anything, yes, sir.

Q. . . . A person reading the letter would see the fresh marks and couldn't know if that was from heroin or from Methedrine?

A. I feel there is no way of determining what it was from. He could merely state that I had prescribed a drug for him and that he had been using it intravenously.

Q. . . . Could you say at this time with your experience that he is not an addict?

A. I say definitely that Mr. Bruce is not a narcotic at this time.

Q. . . . But you don't know if he is within the last two weeks and few months ago, you don't know whether or not he has taken an injection of heroin?

A. I don't know, no, sir.

Redirect examination by my attorney:

Q. Doctor . . . in your opinion, is Mr. Bruce a narcotic addict?

A. No, my opinion is that Mr. Bruce is not a narcotic addict.

Q. In your opinion, is Mr. Bruce in imminent danger of becoming a narcotic addict?

A. No, my opinion is that this man is not in imminent danger of becoming a narcotic addict.

Then came Dr. David Neimetz, who had administered a Nalline test [the accepted means of determining drug addiction] which, he testified, indicated that "there was no narcotic in Mr. Bruce's system." A week later, another Nalline test also proved negative. On the day he testified, during a court recess, he administered still another Nalline test. Result: negative.

Q. Doctor, in your opinion, is Lenny Bruce a narcotic addict?

A. No.

At one point, the judge asked him: "Supposing, now, the individual is a narcotic addict on a given day and he is unable to either obtain the narcotic due to unavailability of the drug or he is incarcerated for one reason or another, and he is unable to obtain the drug until the physical need for the drug has disappeared. Would you consider that individual to be addicted at that time?

THE WITNESS: Oh, yes, certainly, because at this particular time the person would probably be having withdrawal symptoms due to his inability to get the drug.

THE COURT: In other words, after the physical need for the drug has ceased—say, after three weeks there is no withdrawal evidence—would you consider that individual to be a narcotic addict?

THE WITNESS: Medically, you couldn't consider him to be an addict. You'd have no basis, nothing to base it on.

THE COURT: Supposing the psychological need continued, Doctor, for the drug?

THE WITNESS: Well, this is getting into the realm of what is an addict, the basis and theories.

Hmmmm, could Lenny Bruce be a psychological addict?

"Are you thinking about it now, Lenny?"

"Yeah, I'm thinking about jerking off and taking dope . . ."

The final witness for the defense was Dr. Joel Fort, a specialist in public health and criminology, with particular interest in narcotic addiction, dangerous drugs and alcoholism. He is director of the Center on Alcoholism in Oakland and lecturer in the School of Criminology at the University of California in Berkeley, where he teaches a course dealing with narcotic addiction, dangerous drugs and alcoholism.

He is Court Examiner in Alameda County and Chairman of the Alameda-Contra Costa Medical Association Committee on Alcoholism and Dangerous Drugs. He was formerly consultant to the Alameda County Probation Department. For two years he was on the staff of the U.S. Public Health Service Narcotics Hospital in Lexington, Kentucky, and he also worked at an addiction research center there.

He was an invited delegate to the White House Conference on Narcotic Drug Use. In connection with his appearance before Congress with regard to narcotic addiction, the Chairman of the Subcommittee stated in the *Congres-*

sional Record that his was the most outstanding testimony presented on narcotics before the committee.

His articles on narcotic addiction have appeared in a number of publications, including the *California Law Review*. Over the years, he has worked with, diagnosed, treated and administered to narcotic or would-be narcotic addicts numbering in the thousands. He serves on the Advisory Committee of the California Narcotics Rehabilitation Center Program.

So much for his credits.

Dr. Fort testified: "I would say that [Lenny Bruce] is not a narcotic addict . . . It is absolutely impossible."

Q. . . . Is there such a thing as a psychological or psychic drug addict?

A. I have never heard that term used by an experienced person.

Q. . . . Would Lenny Bruce, would this man here who you have examined, benefit by being sent to the State Narcotic Rehabilitation Center if he were sent there today by the Court?

A. I do not think that he would. I think that he would be harmed by being sent there.

Q. Would the community benefit, Doctor, in your opinion?

A. I feel that the community would be harmed also.

Nevertheless, the judge decided that I am a narcotic addict and would be committed to ten years of rehabilitation.

On June 26, 1963, my attorney moved for a stay of the commitment, pending a final disposition of the appeal. The notice of the appeal automatically stayed the proceedings.

The matter is still pending. My hands tremble as I write this. Soon it will be dark and my veins will begin to palpitate and I must have the stuff. Judge Munnell's use of power has let a drug addict loose upon the citizenry of Los Angeles—a crazed man who will surely steal in order to have his next fix. The blood of pleading storekeepers will be upon the judge's hands . . .

Chapter
Twenty-six

Between the time I was acquitted of obscenity charges for the second time in Los Angeles and the start of my New York obscenity trial, some 80-odd prominent figures—including many nonfans—signed a public protest on my behalf.

The signators included theologian Reinhold Neibuhr; psychoanalyst Theodor Reik; Arnold Beichman, chairman of the American Committee for Cultural Freedom; entertainers Woody Allen, Theodore Bikel, Richard Burton, Godfrey Cambridge, Bob Dylan, Herb Gardner, Ben Gazzara, Dick Gregory, Tommy Leonetti, Paul Newman, Elizabeth Taylor, Rip Torn, Rudy Vallee; novelists and playwrights Nelson Algren, James Baldwin, Saul Bellow, Kay Boyle, Jack Gelber, Joseph Heller, Lillian Helman, James Jones, Norman Mailer, Arthur Miller, Henry Miller, John Rechy, Jack Richardson, Susan Sontag, Terry Southern, William Styron, John Updike, Gore Vidal, Arnold Weinstein; artists Jules Feiffer, Walt Kelly and Ben Shahn; poets Gregory Corso, Lawrence Ferlinghetti, Allen Ginsberg, Leroi Jones, Peter Orlovsky, Louis Untermeyer; critics Eric Bentley, Robert Brustein, Malcom Cowley, Les Crane, Harry Golden, Michael Harrington, Nat Hentoff, Granville Hicks, Alfred Kazin, Alexander King, Max Lerner, Dwight Macdonald, Jonathan Miller, Philip Rahv, Mark Schorer, Harvey Swados, Jerry Tallmer, Lionel Trilling, Dan Wakefield, Richard Gilman; editors and publishers Ira Gitler (*Down Beat*), Robert Gottlieb (Simon & Schuster), Irving Howe (*Dissent*), Peter Israel (Putnam's), William Phillips (*Partisan Review*), George Plimpton (*Paris Review*), Norman Podhoretz (*Commentary*), Barney Rossett (Grove Press).

The petition reads as follows:

We the undersigned are agreed that the recent arrests of night-club entertainer Lenny Bruce by the New York police department on charges of indecent performance constitutes a violation of civil liberties as guaranteed by the First and Fourteenth amendments to the United States Constitution.

Lenny Bruce is a popular and controversial performer in the field of social satire in the tradition of Swift, Rabelais, and Twain. Although

173

Bruce makes use of the vernacular in his night-club performances, he does so within the context of his satirical intent and not to arouse the prurient interests of his listeners. It is up to the audience to determine what is offensive to them; it is not a function of the police department of New York or any other city to decide what adult private citizens may or may not hear.

Whether we regard Bruce as a moral spokesman or simply as an entertainer, we believe he should be allowed to perform free from censorship or harassment.

Harassment is a leprous label that draws bully taunts: "Oh, are they picking on you, little boy? They're always picking on you. It's funny, that doesn't happen to your brother."

People ask, why don't they leave you alone?

I say there's nobody picking on me. Except the ones that don't piss in the sink. But we *all* do! That's the one common denominator to seize upon. Every man reading this has at one time pissed in the sink. I have, and I am part every guy in the world. We're all included. I *know* you've pissed in the sink. You may have pretended to be washing your hands, but you were definitely pissing in the sink.

Recently there was a news item about a cat burglar who broke into the fourth floor of the Hotel America in New York at 12:05 A.M.

I used to stay at the Hotel America when I was in New York. A suite there was available for $36 a month, and was rented by the year by the Wallace Brothers Circus in case a trained bear was pregnant—you know, if an animal gets knocked up while working Madison Square Garden, the Hotel America is the only one that will take a pregnant bear, because the maid only goes in once a year.

Now, my theory is that it wasn't a cat burglar, it was actually a tenant. Somebody in the Flanders Hotel across the street had spotted the prowler. "I was looking at the stars through my binoculars," said R. Lendowski, Grand Central Station maintenance porter. "I just happened to be looking and I saw this guy."

When questioned, the suspect said that there was no toilet in his room, that he had recent surgery done on his little toe and so walking to the bathroom in the hall was terribly painful, and that his roommate caught him pissing in the sink. Actually, he wasn't *caught* by his roommate, he was just about to *start*, and he got out of it by saying that he was taking a sponge bath and had to continue bathing from the waist up, while his roommate kept interjecting: "For a minute I thought that you were trying to piss in the sink . . . I once caught a guy doing that at Paris Island . . . Can you imagine someone pissing in the sink? . . . The same type of dirty guy that pisses in the ocean . . ."

So he waited until his friend fell asleep, still mumbling about those guys sneak-pissing in the sink.

Then he decided to piss out the window, but he felt guilty about it in case some guy that might be an even bigger nut on ocean-pissers who happened to be passing by. What if you pissed on a guy like *that?*

Then the police arrived.

"Don't move—I see which window that spray is coming from. You! With your hand on the sill, shaking it on the screen—stop in the name of the law! Okay, we've got you surrounded! Don't drop anything!"

Later, at police headquarters, the suspect is confessing:

". . . So I searched out all the possibilities, and I went out on the ledge to make sure I wouldn't get it on anyone. It was 12:05 A.M., and I saw a whole bunch of binoculars from different windows watching me. Before I knew it, this priest was on the ledge with me. He said, 'Son, is this the only way?'

"I said, 'It's either this or pissing in the sink, Father. The fire engines are here now and I have a choice of confessing as a cat burglar or a Peeping Tom, but to tell the truth, my roommate won't let me piss in the sink . . .'"

It's virtually unanimous that we've all pissed in the sink, including President Johnson and myself, and Mickey Cohen and Billy Graham. Of course, I've also done a few things in my life that I am so ashamed of I would never tell *anybody*, ever. I'll take those secrets to my grave. Naturally I won't tell them to you, but I will reveal a *minor* skeleton hanging around in my confessional booth.

A friend of mine, who shall remain nameless, was an m.c. in a night club that had strippers. He came over to my pad about five o'clock one morning, woke me up and showed me a big diamond ring. He said that there was this drunk he had helped out to a cab. While shaking hands and saying "Good night, sir," he had managed to slip the ring off the drunk's finger.

Now my friend wanted to know how much I thought it was worth.

I said, "Leave it with me, I know a bartender who's also a jeweler, and I'll be seeing him later today."

He left it with me. I stayed up till 8:30 and then drove downtown. The ring had a three-carat stone in it and a baguette on each side. I took it to a jeweler and asked for an appraisal. He said it was worth about $1500 or $2000. I then went three stores down and asked how much it would cost to have a zircon made that would match this diamond centerstone exactly.

"About twenty dollars."

"Do it."

He did it while I waited.

And I split. Two hours later it dawned on my friend: "What the hell am I leaving that ring with *him* for—he might steal it." An hour later he came by. "I just thought of it," he said, "my cousin's got a friend who's a jeweler and I'm going by there later." So I gave the ring back to him.

Again he asked me, "What do you think it's worth?"

"I don't know, probably a couple of thousand dollars."

That was the last I heard of the ring for six months. Then he started talking of going into the dry-cleaning business with his father.

"Where you gonna get the bread?"

"I'm going to dig up the ring," he said. "I've had it buried in the back yard." And for the next three months, he spent that buried ring fifty times. "I'm not gonna dig it up till I'm sure, because then I'll just piss the money away."

A miniature golf course, that would be it. He even had the real-estate guy draw up the papers. He asked me to drive him downtown. We were going to sell the ring. Oh, God. As we walked into the first pawnshop, I waited for the cruncher.

"How much will you give me for this diamond?"

"C'mon, it's too hot today for jokes."

"I'm not kidding, I wanna sell it."

"It's a coke bottle. Take it back and get three cents deposit on it. It's glass."

"Why don't you put that thing up to your eye?"

But before the pawnshop owner could answer, my friend grabbed the ring back in desperation. We hit three We-Buy-Old-Gold jewelry stores and got the same answer.

Finally, a less jaded merchant, who hadn't sold a graduation watch for 50 cents down all day, said: "Son, the platinum is worth about twelve dollars, and the little chips on each side about six dollars apiece, and the zircon in the middle, five dollars, including labor. I'll give you three dollars for it."

"How do you like that phony bastard, wearing a three-dollar ring, and I had it buried in the back yard."

About a year later—I still had the stone—I was very busted, and a successful comedian, a good friend of mine, gave me $700 for it because he wanted to help me. He wrote out the check for "Special Material." A few months later, I was making some money, and since the back-yard diamond planter was a very good friend I couldn't resist telling him how it came about that he buried that piece of glass. And then I gave him half the bread.

There's another minor skeleton in my confessional booth. It would be my undoing if I were ever to run for public office. "Mr. Bruce," my opponent would sneer, "is it not the truth that when you were twelve years old, you jerked off a dog? In fact, you've jerked off *several* dogs. And isn't it true that when a certain cocker spaniel used to come to your house, he would push his hind end toward his front paws?"

"I didn't know what I was doing. I was crazy with fear. They bite. He was vicious. Friends of mine had told me, 'Jerk him off and he won't bite you.'"

"Ladies and gentlemen, is that the kind of man you want for United States Senator? No! We're looking for a religious man—one who'd see to it that anyone that had sinned would be made to suffer forever . . ."

Someone goes to jail, and after 15 years of incarceration, you make sure you get him back in as soon as you can by shaming anyone who would forgive him, accept him, give him employment; by shaming them on television—"The unions knowingly hired ex-convicts." Driving in New Jersey once, I would occasionally pass signs stating: CRIMINALS MUST REGISTER.

Does this mean that in the middle of the hold-up, you have to go to the County Courthouse and register? Or does it mean that you must register if you *once* committed a criminal act?

Do you know there are guys in jail for doing it to *chickens?*
Bestiality.

Hey, lady, wouldn't you get bugged if *your* husband balled a chicken?

"I was the last one to know!"

"But she was only sitting on my *lap.* I was *feeding* her."

"Oh, sure, you were feeding her. Everybody *told* me what you were doing to her. And on *our* bed!"

"It wasn't on the bed, it was over there——"

"What's happened to your chicken? Have you seen your chicken lately? Tell your *chicken* to fix dinner . . ."

Once I was talking to a horse trainer and a jockey. I'm not hip to track people and their life, but this trainer told me how he really loved animals, and to have a horse that's a winner, you've got to lock him up all the time. Just keep him a prisoner and boxcar him from town to town and never let them have any fun with lady horses. It's the lowest. Just keep them so when that race comes, he's a real nut! And then, *whoosh* . . .

"You know, Lenny," the jockey said, "sometimes in the morning when the light just starts to break through, some of those fillies are so beautiful, they look like pretty women. When they've got those fly-sheets on, it looks like negligees flying in the wind."

"Oh, yeah? Uh—did you ever——?"

"No."

"Because that's a very interesting transference you just had there. I can't see any girlie thing in horses. Now tell me the truth—because I know *I'd* deny it too if I made it with a filly—but I mean, you know, did you ever?"

He said no, he never did, but then he told me a story that really flipped me, about this horse called I Salute out of Isaacson Stables. This horse was a big winner—purse after purse—she really had it made, and the season was almost over.

Then, five o'clock one morning, they caught a 50-year-old exercise man with the horse. Naturally, they busted him. The charge: sodomy. They arraigned him, convicted him, and he got a year in the joint.

Now I started thinking . . . what a hell of a thing to do *time* for, you know?

"Hey, what are you in for?"

"Never mind."

The most ludicrous thing would be making the arrest, I assume. You'd be so embarrassed.

"I, uh, you're under arrest—uh, ahem, come out of there!"

Or the judge. How could he really get serious with that? "All right, where's the complaining witness?"

Anyway, the exercise man went to prison, and the horse must have missed him a lot, because she just didn't want to run anymore. And she never did race again.

Chapter
Twenty-Seven

After this autobiography had been serialized in PLAYBOY magazine, there were many letters to the editor. I think it would be pertinent at this point to quote two particular letters from that group.

The first is from John E. Dolan, President of the Dolan-Whitney Detective Service:

> Having investigated numerous aspects of, and the peculiarities surrounding, Lenny Bruce's Los Angeles arrest for the alleged "possession of narcotics" and the subsequent trials, I am conversant with numerous facts and other valid data concerning the case.
>
> You might be interested to know, for instance, that John L. White, the officer who arrested Lenny Bruce for "possession of narcotics," has himself since been arraigned in Federal Court. White is now serving a five-year sentence in Federal Prison after being found guilty of "illegal importation of narcotics."

The other letter to PLAYBOY was from Dr. Joel Fort:

> In addition to commending you for your publication of Lenny Bruce's valuable and interesting social document, I would like to elaborate briefly on the section of his autobiography describing my testimony during his trial for narcotic addiction . . .
>
> I brought out in my testimony the criteria that should be used in making a diagnosis of drug addiction which would include both the detailed history of drug use by a particular individual and the physical signs of such use. Mr. Bruce at the time of my examination and during the weeks immediately prior to his trial, showed no such evidence of being an addict, and in fact had numerous negative tests for the presence of narcotics in his body.
>
> The doctors certifying him as an addict had had little experience with narcotic addiction and seemed to use as their main criterion the fact that he had been arrested for possession of heroin, which should not be a crucial factor in reaching a medical diagnosis. In these addiction proceedings, as in his numerous obscenity charges, Mr. Bruce was and is

bearing the brunt of unjust and irrational reaction to his outspoken criticism of a society pervaded by hypocrisy and deceit.

If such dissent is successfully shut off by various official and unofficial policing bodies, freedom of speech will have suffered a further crippling blow and robotization of our society will have moved one step closer.

A private investigator I hired dug into the background of Dr. Thomas L. Gore, who was so anxious to give me ten years of help. And, on October 3, 1963, Dr. I. W. J. Core, Medical Examiner for the Metropolitan Government of Nashville, Davidson County, in Tennessee, signed an affidavit which stated:

During the years 1947 and 1948, I was Chief of Staff at Davidson County Hospital, a mental institution situated in Nashville, Tennessee . . . for the entire fifteen (15) months of Thomas L. Gore's administration as superintendent of the Davidson County Hospital . . . during which time the following incidents occurred . . . which eventually culminated and led to Thomas L. Gore's dismissal:

(1) Thomas Gore was constantly engaged, during the majority of the time he presided as superintendent, in disputes with the personnel of the Davidson County Hospital, as well as with employees and members of the County Court, and members of the Board of Hospital Commissioners.

(2) In complete violation of the law of the State of Tennessee, which law does not provide for such procedures, Thomas Gore castrated a patient from Joelton, Tennessee, which surgery was performed by Thomas Gore without consent of the patient, the guardian of said patient, or the Board of Hospital Commissioners. Upon being informed of such illicit activity, as Chief of Staff and a member of the Board, I personally investigated this matter and determined beyond all doubt this operation to have been performed by Gore. This activity on the part of Gore caused the County considerable trouble, and while, at the time, there was some discussion on the part of the parents of this patient upon whom Gore had performed an illegal operation, relative [to] pursuing their legal remedies, no further action was ever taken by the parents. Under the Law of the State of Tennessee, castration of this patient was, of course, definitely illegal.

(3) For reasons undetermined, and at tremendous expense to the County, Thomas Gore caused to be excavated on County property, adjacent [to] the dairy of the Davidson County Hospital, a huge hole, which excavation was never utilized, and which was then in my opinion, a matter of extremely poor judgment. My opinion on that matter to the present day has remained unchanged.

(4) In complete violation of the law, Gore purchased a herd of cattle at public auction, again without County consent, and again without the consent or knowledge of the Board.

(5) Thomas Gore caused to be built during his administration a corn crib, and which under his direction was constructed so as to be airtight, thereby destroying any value for which it may have been constructed.

(6) On one occasion during his administration, Thomas Gore informed me that while a member of the Armed Forces, he was a money lender. Subsequent to his discharge from the Army and while the Superintendent of the Davidson County Hospital, he attempted to borrow money from me to lend to Army personnel. I refused to become involved and in turn refused to lend Gore monies for such purposes.

(7) During Gore's administration, grates were removed from the first floor windows and, as a result, a number of patients were lost from the institution causing the County great anxiety and expense in returning them to said institution. Following Gore's release, I was then appointed temporary Superintendent and immediately rectified the situation, replacing the grating, whereby the number of escapees were reduced immensely. Again, at the time of the removal of the grating in this mental institution, I considered Gore's judgment faulty.

In conclusion, your deponent says that Thomas Lee Gore's administration was totally and completely unsatisfactory. He was released for his inability to manage employees and for mismanagement in general. Gore was completely unsuited for and totally unfitted for the job of Superintendent, and after our experience with Thomas Gore, the Board decided that we never again would have a retired service man as head of the institution. The Board knew and realized they had made a mistake in engaging Gore. He was arrogant and bullheaded and unable to get along with civilian personnel. In my opinion the man was indeed paranoiac, and I consider him a very sick man. I do not consider Gore's judgment was trustworthy, and I cannot nor would not give full faith and credit to any oath of his in a court of justice.

Incidentally, back in June 1955, Dr. Gore the castrator wrote an article in *Federal Probation* entitled "The Antidote for Delinquency: God-Inspired Love."

I have really become *possessed* with winning—vindicating myself rather than being vindictive—and my room is always cluttered with reels of tape and photostats of transcripts.

Recently, when I pretended to doubt the word of my eight-year-old daughter, Kitty, she said: "Daddy, you'd believe me if it was on *tape*."

Recently I was offered a writing gig on a TV series for $3500 a week. And

I really was happy about that. But after two days, negotiations went right into the can. The company's legal department had killed it.

Because of the morality clause.

When Rod Amateau had come backstage and offered me the writing assignment, I had just given my last two possessions—my record player and my camera—to a secretary in lieu of payment.

Moral turpitude.

They said the decision related to my arrests for obscenity and narcotics, and the sponsor. The thing I really felt bad about was that Rod Amateau had worked so hard to get me the gig, and I'm sure he felt ashamed. He shouldn't have been subjected to that.

When I had been a writer for 20th Century-Fox several years prior to this, I lost the job for a reason that I could relate to perhaps more objectively than the morality clause.

My boss there was a producer. He had a stable of writers, made a lot of money and went out with a pretty starlet. He had his own private dining room at the studio that looked like a ship. He'd say: "Stay in your office, write twenty pages a day, and if you get bored, look out my office window at the green lawn with the hard-working gardeners, and be happy you can write."

One day I looked out the window, only to see him dying of a heart attack that had started in his dining room and lasted all the way down Darryl F. Zanuck's stairs.

He died on the lawn.

And I knew that I was finished there because I didn't get invited to the funeral.

Actually, everybody he'd hired got fired upon his death.

He had introduced me to a big star who became even bigger by playing Las Vegas in a peekaboo dress, and she asked me to write a piece of special material for her for $500. I did, and she sent me a wire from her show, thrilled—"The material was great." She was never home after that, though, and I wanted to get my money. Her mother gave me the brush: "Look, you—we found out you work in burlesque, and if you bother us once more, we're going to black-list you with the Writers' Guild."

Since all the moralists and purists support Las Vegas as the entertainment capital of the world, one would assume that the attraction at The Star Dust is *The Passion Play* or a Monet exhibit or the New York City Ballet with Eugene Ormandy conducting. But, no; what *is* the big attraction?

"Tits and ass."

I beg your pardon?

"Tits and ass, that's what the attraction is."

Just tits and ass?

"No, an apache team in between for rationalization."

Well, that must be just one hotel—what's the second bit attraction?

"More tits and ass."

And the third?

"That's it, tits and ass, and more tits and ass."

Do you mean to tell me that *Life* magazine would devote three full pages to tits and ass?

"Yes, right next to the articles by Billy Graham and Norman Vincent Peale."

Well, that may be the truth, but you just can't put "Tits and Ass" up on a marquee.

"Why not?"

Because it's dirty and vulgar, that's why.

"Titties are dirty and vulgar?"

No, you're not gonna bait me, it's not the titties, it's the words, it's the way you relate them. You can't have those words where kids can see them.

"Didn't your kid ever see a titty?"

I'm telling you, it's the words.

"I don't believe you. I believe, to you, it's the titty that's dirty, because I'll change the words to '*Tuchuses* and *Nay-nays* Nightly!' "

That's a little better.

"Well, that's interesting. You're not anti-Semitic idiomatic, you're anti-Anglo-Saxon idiomatic. Then why don't we get really austere? Latin: '*Gluteus maximus* and *Pectorales majores* Nightly!' "

Now, that's clean.

"To *you, schmuck*—but it's dirty to the Latins!"

Well, you just can't put tits and ass up there, that's all.

"*La Parisiene*—The Follies—class with ass—French tits and ass—that's art! And if we don't make any more money with that you can have a *Japanese* nude show that absolves us both politically and spiritually, because who but a dirty Jap would show their kiester? And we'll get the Norman Luboff choir to sing *Remember Pearl Harbor*. And then, if we don't make any more money with that, we'll combine the contemporary and the patriotic: American tits and ass. Grandma Moses' tits and Norman Rockwell's ass . . ."

(Draw my ass. If you can draw my ass, you can draw. My ass, you can draw.)

Soon they will have just a big nipple up on the marquee, and maybe that's why you want to have FOR ADULTS ONLY, because you're ashamed to tell your kids that you're selling and exploiting and making an erotic thing out of your mother's breast that gave you life.

The morality clause.

And I had really wanted that job, because I got really busted out financially as the number of arrests had begun to mount up, and my income was more and more cut off. For the first time in my life I had checks bouncing, and I ruined an eight-year credit rating. Right down the drain.

I've played Detroit for almost eight years, and was due to open at The Alamo in March 1964, but when the Detroit Board of Censors learned of this, they wouldn't permit my appearance—depriving me of my rights without even so much as a judicial proceeding.

I have been calling up night-club owners all over the country, but they're all afraid to book me.

Variety, the Bible of Show Business, refuses to accept an ad from me that simply states I'm *available.*

And I can't get into England.

Fighting my "persecution" seems as futile as asking Barry Goldwater to speak at a memorial to send the Rosenberg kids to college, or asking attorney James Donavan, "On your way back from trading the prisoners in Cuba, stop off and see if you can get just one more pardon for Morton Sobell."

I mean, when I think of all the crap that's been happening to me, the thing that keeps me from getting really outraged or hostile at the people involved is—and I'm sure that Caryl Chessman, or perhaps his next-cell murderer who sits waiting to be murdered, felt this, too—that in the end, the injustice anyone is subjected to is really quite an *in* matter.

Sure, *other* people *do* care, but how long does it ever last . . .

The police visit me occasionally.

One night recently I was in the bathroom shaving when four peace officers showed up on my property. I knew two of them; one, in fact, had testified in court against me—the Trojan that Horse built—the others were loud and out of line. I asked them to leave if they didn't have a search warrant, whereupon one of them took out his gun, saying: "Here's my search warrant."

If I am paranoid, then I have reached the acute point of stress in my life. It's this bad:

Recently, while walking to work at the Off-Broadway, a night club in San Francisco (*Variety* deemed it newsworthy enough to report that I *wasn't* arrested during that engagement), I observed a young couple in front of me. They were walking several feet ahead of me. They turned the corner that I was going to turn. And just before I got to the club, they turned into a hotel and went up the stairs.

My fear: I was afraid that they were afraid that I was following them.

Chapter
Twenty-Eight

I don't get involved with politics as much as Mort Sahl does, because I know that to be a correct politician and a successful one, you must be what all politicians have always been: chameleonlike.

I voted in the 1960 Presidential election, but I didn't get too emotionally involved and vehement with the attitude that "My man is the best man"—because I didn't *know* the man I voted for. I think the cliché is that you don't know a man till you live with him, and since I never slept with Nixon or Kennedy I can only tell you if they were good in retrospect.

I voted for Kennedy because I thought I'd be able to see the reflection of a human being with dimension. I've seen a child born in the White House. Up till now, Presidents have never seemed like real people to me.

I could never visualize Eisenhower even kissing his wife. Not on the mouth, anyway. He didn't even go to the toilet either, he just stood there. He didn't even go to bed, he just sat up all night with his clothes on, worrying.

And even Nixon—well, he kissed his wife, but on the forehead, and only on Thanksgiving, in front of his in-laws.

One particular facet of the election—the Great Debate—convinced me more than ever that my "ear of the beholder" philosophy is correct; that the listener hears only what he wants to hear. I would be with a bunch of Kennedy fans watching the debate and their comment would be, "He's really slaughtering Nixon." Then we would all go to another apartment, and the Nixon fans would say, "How do you like the shellacking he gave Kennedy?"

And then I realized that each group loved their candidate so that a guy would have to be this blatant—he would have to look into the camera and say: "I am a thief, a crook, do you hear me, I am the worst choice you could ever make for the Presidency!"

And even then his following would say, "Now there's an honest man for you. It takes a big guy to admit that. There's the kind of guy we need for President."

And now Lyndon Johnson is President.

We forgave the Japanese once, the Germans twice, but the White Southerner we've kicked in the ass since Fort Sumter. We pour millions into propagandizing Europe, but never a penny for Radio Free South. Lyndon Johnson could cut Schopenhauer mind-wise but his sound chills it for him. The White Southerner gets kicked in the ass every time for his sound.

"Folks, Ah think nuclear fission——"

"Get outa here, *schmuck,* you don't think nothin'."

The bomb, the bomb—oh, thank God for the bomb. The final threat is: "I'll get my brother—the bomb." Out of all the teaching and bullshitting, that's the only answer we have.

Well, it's a little embarrassing. You see, 17,000 students marched on the White House and Lyndon Johnson was left holding the bag.

"Mr. Johnson, we're 17,000 students who have marched from Annapolis, and we demand to see the bomb."

"Ah'd like to see if mahself, son."

"Aw, c'mon, now, let's see the bomb, we're not gonna hurt anybody, we just wanna take a few pictures, then we'll protest, and that's it."

"Son, you gonna think this is a lot of horseshit, but there never was a bomb. Them Hebe Hollywood writers made up the idea and they spread it around, and everybody got afraid of this damn bomb story. But there is no bomb. Just something we keep in the White House garage. We spent three million dollars on it, and once we got it started, it just made a lot of noise and smelled up the whole house, so we haven't fooled with it since."

"Now, wait a minute. You see, I led the March, and I've got 17,000 students that are protesting the bomb. So don't tell me there's no bomb."

"Son, Ah'd like to help you if Ah could. If Ah had a bomb——"

"But what am I gonna tell all those poor kids out there? That there's no bomb?"

"The only thing that did work out was the button."

"What button?"

"The button that the madmen are always gonna push."

"That's what the bomb is—a button?"

"Yes—it's a button."

"Well, goddamnit, give me the *button,* then."

"Cain't do that, son. It's on a boy scout's fly. And sometime, somewhere, a fag scoutmaster is gonna blow up the world."

If the bomb *is* going to go off, I can't stop it because I'm not in charge yet. Maybe I'll be working again that night—a New Year's Eve show. It'll be around 11:30 and everybody's waiting with their hats and their horns. I've got my scene and they've got theirs.

Now it's about three minutes to go, and I'm the only one who knows about the bomb.

"Ha, ha, a lot of you people didn't get noisemakers, but I've got a beaut coming up, and it's really going to gas everybody. The people who haven't had the two-drink minimum, you don't have to have it, all right? And listen, you guys in the band, why don't you go back to the dressing room and lay on the floor for a while? Don't ask questions, just do it. Folks, you know, a lot of you have seen me work before, but I've got a new bit, we're really going to bring in the new year right"—and then, *Boooooom!*

One guy will probably be heckling me on his way out through the roof. And I can just see the owner. "Look, don't do that bit anymore, we're getting a lot of complaints. Put back Religions, Inc., if you have to, and Christ visiting earth—the whole bit . . ."

If the Messiah were indeed to return and wipe out all diseases, physical and mental, and do away with all man's inhumanity to man, then, I, Lenny Bruce—a comedian who has thrived both economically and egotistically upon the corruption and cruelty he condemns with humor, who spouted impassioned pleas to spare the life of Caryl Chessman and Adolf Eichmann alike, who professed the desire to propagate assimilation and thereby evolve integration—would in truth know that I had been a parasite whose whole structure of success depended on despair: like J. Edgar Hoover and Jonas Salk; like the trustees, wardens, death-house maintenance men, millions of policemen, uniform makers, court recorders, criminal-court judges, probation officers and district attorneys whose children joyously unwrap Christmas presents under the tree bought with money earned by keeping other men from seeing *their* child's face beam at a cotton angel, who would have been without jobs if no one in the world had ever violated the law; like the Owl-Rexall-Thrifty Drugstores, crutch makers, neurological surgeons and Parke-Lilly employees on the roof of the Squibb pharmaceutical house, ready to jump because the blind can see, the deaf can hear, the lame can walk; like the ban-the-bomb people who find out there really is no bomb to ban and they don't know what to do with their pamphlets. The dust would gather on all the people who hold that superior moral position of serving humanity, for they will have become aware that their very existence, creative ability and symbolic status had depended wholly upon intellectual dishonesty. For there is no anonymous giver, except perhaps the guy who knocks up your daughter.

In the movies, Porter Hall and Gene Lockhart were always successful businessmen, but Everett Sloane was a *tycoon*. He would get his gun off disillusioning Joel McCrea, who wanted to publish a newspaper that would make a statement, and telling him: "M'boy, you'll see when you get old that it's all a game." And I used to think "No, it's not that way, this cynical old bastard is bullshitting, there *are* the Good Guys and the Bad Guys, the liars and truth-tellers."

But Everett Sloane was right.

There is only what *is*. The what-*should*-be never did exist, but people keep trying to live *up* to it. There is only what *is.*

A bronze honor roll, black wreaths, and those dopey green sticks with dye running that support them.

My uncle always used to lie and say that he just bought a poppy.

There is only what *is*.

And so the figures will never be in, relating to the unspoken confessions of all those criminals who purchase contraceptives unlawfully, and willfully use them for purposes other than the prevention of disease.

There is only what *is*.

My friend Paul Krassner once asked me what I've been influenced by in my work.

I have been influenced by my father telling me that my back would become crooked because of my maniacal desire to masturbate . . . by reading "Gloriosky, Zero!" in *Little Annie Rooney* . . . by listening to Uncle Don and Clifford Brown . . . by smelling the burnt shell powder at Anzio and Salerno . . . torching for my ex-wife . . . giving money to Moondog as he played the upturned pails around the corner from Hanson's at 51st and Broadway . . . getting hot looking at *Popeye* and *Toots and Casper* and *Chris Crustie* years ago . . . hearing stories about a pill they can put in the gas tank with water but the "big companies" won't let it out—the same big companies that have the tire that lasts forever—and the Viper's favorite fantasy: "Marijuana could be legal, but the big liquor companies won't let it happen" . . . Irving Berlin didn't write all those songs, he's got a guy locked in the closet . . . colored people have a special odor . . . James Dean is really alive in a sanatorium . . . and Hitler is waiting to book me for six weeks in Argentina . . .

It was an absurd question.

I am influenced by every second of my waking hour.